The Loving Room

The Loving Room

Richard J. Toner

Authors Choice Press
San Jose New York Lincoln Shanghai

The Loving Room

Authors Choice Press
an imprint of iUniverse.com, Inc.

For information address:
iUniverse.com, Inc.
5220 S 16th, Ste. 200
Lincoln, NE 68512
www.iuniverse.com

ISBN: 0-595-17757-3

Printed in the United States of America

Dedication

To Dan, who generously gave me back all the years that we had missed together when he was a youngster, and to Joan, my loving wife, my best friend, my most valued critic and faithful editor.

Foreword

When we decided to buy the Birchwood Inn, we thought that it might be important to have a written record of our experiences as innkeepers, if for no other reason than to be able to look back in our dotage at the high times and the low. It seemed relatively unproductive merely to keep a journal whose pages might never see the light of day again. We had the foresight to realize that time would be our most precious commodity and we did not wish to waste it. We had already decided to maintain a log book to keep track of phone calls, reservations and other important day-to-day events, but that wouldn't be sufficient to chronicle the high—and low-lights of the journey which we were beginning.

So that we might record the details of the more significant events—and the nuances that seem deeply embedded when they occur but have a way of fading with time—we opted for writing periodic letters. And who better to write to than our old Air Force friends, Chris and Tom House, who were living in California. Not only were they one of our principal benefactors whose investment made our venture possible, they were also as excited and interested in what we were doing as if they had become innkeepers themselves.

"The Loving Room" is a compilation of many of the letters that were written during the eight years that we owned the inn, giving the Houses a play by play account of the humorous events and the roller coaster ride of emotions that we often encountered. As we look back it is also a first-hand insight into the life we were living. The letters have been patched together with additional elaboration and explanations that are necessary to put our experiences into context. We hope the readers will be able to gain some appreciation of the joys and trials, laughs and tears that we experienced during our eight years as hands-on, fully involved innkeepers.

Prologue

It really wasn't cool enough that first October to begin using the guest room fireplaces, but we decided that nothing would add to the ambiance better for our newly engaged couple than to make an exception and begin laying the fires that weekend. From what was written in the memory book in their room, we were exactly correct.

According to their very graphic entries, they decided that first night to start the fire, open bottle of wine and get naked on the carpet in front of the fireplace. Every kiss and caress from thence forward was described in convincing detail. Every action and countermove was detailed. What went through each of their minds as this happened or that response took place was meticulously recorded. And as the fondling and embracing progressed, and as the inevitable outcome resulted, the climax was described by each in what can only be termed as lurid clarity.

But that wasn't the end of it. They paused to enjoy a few sips of wine and then the whole process began again, accompanied by the same eloquent enumeration of the experience. And so it went the next day and evening. They must have each used ten pages of the book recording the most intimate aspects of their experiences, in a style that seemed to suggest that this was their private diary and no one else would ever gain access to it.

Joan was clearly shocked to read some of the passages but even more stunned that someone would be inclined to share these most intimate details with not just anyone, but with everyone. Subsequent guests didn't have the same reaction. To many of them, it became a game of "Can You

Top This?" Guest after guest began to follow the same pattern of sharing their most deep-rooted passions and intimate behavior with they knew not whom. But everyone clearly had read what previous occupants of the room had written in the memory book and they were determined, through fact or fantasy, to outdo the chronicle that had been laid down before them. This was the only room in the Inn in which this phenomenon of public passion was so consistently repeated, and we began to wonder whether there was some aphrodisiacal quality about the decor or if it was simply the power of suggestion and a very active sense of imagination.

Within the innkeeping community, there seems to be a tendency for innkeepers to name their rooms rather than use such a mundane designation as Room 1 or Room 3. Some of the Lenox innkeepers had named their rooms after great classical composers, an apt tribute that fits in very nicely with the Tanglewood Festival. Others saw fit to name their rooms after members of their own family, and provide a short biography in each room explaining why their relatives were worthy of this honor.

We considered giving names to our rooms on a number of occasions, and probably had a variety of bases on which to dream up interesting and appropriate names for each room. Joan has always been a great collector of stuffed animals, especially teddy bears, and there was a wonderful assortment of names that we could have appropriated. We could have had a Winnie the Pooh room and a Paddington Bear room and any number of other names—including Teddy, of course. But for reasons that probably can't be explained to this day, we decided just to make it simple and leave our rooms numbered.

But now the exception had arisen. There was no way that Room 5 could any longer be Room 5 after the months and years of torrid lovemaking scenes that had allegedly taken place there. From that time forward, the brass number on the door continued to read "5", just as every other room had a brass number of its own. No guest who ever stayed there ever knew of or heard that their room had a name. But to Joan, Dan and me, that room was known forever after as "The Loving Room".

          *   *   *

Part I

Getting Started

The Town of Lenox is a picture postcard lovely little village and unlike many places in the Berkshire Mountains of western Massachusetts, it remains that way to this day. But it was only the foresight of some of the earlier town leaders that preserved its beauty when, twenty years before our arrival, they weathered a very acrimonious debate to provide for a bypass around the town center. For as long as anyone could remember, U.S. Routes 7 and 20 had gone directly through the center of town and were further intersected right in front of the Town Hall by State Route 183.

As the Berkshires became a more popular destination, especially during the Tanglewood Festival season, it became obvious to a few far-sighted folks in Lenox that vehicles would eventually strangle the downtown area. Traffic signals and trailer trucks would soon make the idyllic setting a place to be avoided, an unsightly bottleneck not unlike the centers of the neighboring towns of Lee and Stockbridge were fast becoming. So in spite of dire predictions that businesses would be destroyed and the outside world would turn Lenox into a ghost town, a beautifully scenic, four-lane divided road was built about a half-mile to the east that routed all the through traffic around the town center. And thus, Lenox is the only town of any size in the Berkshires, which today retains its colonial heritage and picturesque grace.

The epicenter of the town is the crossroads of Main and Walker Streets, marked by the Egleston-Patterson Revolutionary War Memorial, a 20-foot granite obelisk at the center of the intersection. Both Walker Street, which approaches from the east, and Main Street, which extends to the north, officially end at the monument. But continuing straight across from Walker to the opposite side of the monument, West Street, to no one's surprise, wends its way westward toward the Tanglewood grounds through roughly a mile of elegant old mansions partially hidden in tree shaded groves of stately old oaks and maples. To the south from the monument, Old Stockbridge Road, the former main route to that other historic Berkshire town, is likewise a shaded, lightly traveled road of century old mansions in a rustic setting. The intersection itself is anchored on the southeast corner by the turn-of-the-century Georgian brick Town Hall, with the main fire station attached to one side and the police station in the rear. On the opposite side of Walker Street, the old four-story brick Curtis Hotel, long since converted to a low-income residence for senior citizens, stands guard against time and change to this enchanting historic village.

Proceeding north from the monument on Main Street, many of the old estates have been converted into banks, inns and business offices, but their original beauty and grace have been faithfully preserved. Nestled among them is the old county court house, now the privately funded Lenox Library, and on the opposite side of the street is the Academy Building, the home of the first school built in Lenox in the early 19th century. A little farther along is a small parking area, adjacent to a picturesque little building in which a few quaint shops share space with the Post Office. It is a common meeting place for friends and neighbors whose somewhat pastoral life is neither hurried nor hectic.

A quarter of a mile or so up Main Street, the road rises sharply as it heads north toward Pittsfield. Old-timers tell stories of the days when the hill used to be so steep that under-powered tractor trailer truck drivers had to couple up their tractors in order to breast the hill and continue on their route. There are even those who claim to recall when the local folks could make a little money by hitching their team of horses to smaller trucks and helping them up the steep grade. But all that has changed, and not just because the truck engines are more powerful or that through traffic now uses the bypass. In addition, the road at the very top of the hill has been scraped down by 10 to 15 feet in places, reducing the steepness of the slope and leaving an embankment on either side of Main Street where the hill crests and starts down again. On the west side of the embankment stands a classic old white New England church, aptly known as The Church on the Hill, whose domed steeple has, for nearly two centuries, been the most renowned landmark in town.

On the embankment opposite the Church stands one of the more magnificent of all the historic Lenox mansions, a structure that traces its origins to the very beginnings of the town and was once the home of one of the original founders of Lenox. The house, which sits on two acres of land overlooking the village, has been added to and expanded over its 230 years of existence but, in the process, has never lost its charm and elegance nor its historic significance. Once a colonial stage coach stop and tavern, and for most of it's existence a private home, it was now known as the Birchwood Inn. And this was the final destination of the strange little convoy of vehicles that made its way north on Main Street in the late afternoon at the end of June 1991.

June 28, 1991
Dear Chris & Tom,

The gypsy caravan was something to see as we drove from our old home in Arlington to the Birchwood Inn yesterday. I led the way in a 15' U-Haul van that had seen it's best days about 100,000 miles ago. Joan was right behind in her Maxima which was packed not with personal luggage and last-minute leftovers, but with our two cats, Chablis and Cognac, and all the special care items that we think makes the cats love us. Finally, bringing up the rear were our friends, Claudia and Jack Hickey, who volunteered to drive my Honda Prelude up to Lenox, carrying our luggage and the last-minute leftovers. I think they thought that it was such a hare-brained scheme that they needed to be present to certify for themselves that we had lost all touch with reality.

The trip up was relatively uneventful even though there were more than a few times that I had serious doubts whether the truck was going to make it. The truck rental company advertised a "comfortable, air conditioned cab with AM/FM stereo". Unfortunately, the air conditioning didn't work and the engine and exhaust noise was so loud it was impossible to hear the radio, even at full volume. I also became a bit concerned shortly after getting on the Garden State Parkway in New Jersey when I saw a sign "no trucks". But just ahead of me at the toll booth there were two recreational vehicles about a half a block long, so I figured I was OK. At least that's what I planned to tell the state trooper if I were stopped. Anyway, we chugged along in trail averaging about 50 mph and made it safely in a little over nine hours, including a couple of quick pit-stops.

Dan was waiting for us when we pulled into the driveway, but the folks who were selling the Inn were in the process of getting the last of their personal things relocated to wherever they were moving. The truck was filled with boxes, for the most part, which contained everything from our personal clothing to the pots, pans and utensils and decorative things that would put our personal signature on the Inn. We tried to label the boxes so we could put our hands on what we would need right away, but that plan suffered from too many items in the boxes and not enough time or space on the outside to list all the details. Well, at least we wouldn't open a box of Christmas decorations in hopes of finding an omelet pan.

We quickly discovered that this was the least of our problems. Turns out that because of the move out by the sellers, we couldn't unload the boxes directly into the area where they would be used. We would have to put them somewhere else or leave them on the truck. About the time we reached that conclusion, the full impact hit us. Tomorrow this place was going to be ours. We needed access to the essentials pretty quickly because there were guests due in less than 24-hours and we were going to be their hosts.

While it meant double or triple handling, it appeared that the only solution was to unload the truck through the bulkhead hatch directly into the basement. Even though it was after five in the afternoon, it was still pretty warm and we weren't exactly fresh after the day's drive. But there was no choice so the unloading began. Trouble was, there had been a thunderstorm the night before, and the basement floor had about a half inch of water on it—not real good conditions for storing cardboard boxes containing delicate things. It obviously wasn't the first time the leaks had occurred, despite assurances in the sales contract that the basement was dry. The smell of mildew was strong and the air was dank and humid. A number of wooden pallets were scattered around so we were able to put the boxes on them, above the waterline, as a temporary solution. But they clearly couldn't stay there very long. Oh well, we'd face that unexpected problem later. But how many more are there going to be?

Claudia played Good Samaritan and went after pizza so that Dan, Jack and I could take intermittent bites while we finished unloading. Finally, just about the time that our energy ran out, we deposited the final carton in the basement, sealed the hatch and closed up the truck. We were hot, sweaty and exhausted. It was nearly 10:00 PM on a day that had started 16 hours earlier. But the first major step had been taken and we were on our way to becoming innkeepers.

Last night was not exactly what I would describe as restful. It reminded me somewhat of the night before our wedding. Like the wedding eve, we were about to make a total commitment, and there were hundreds of unanswerable questions racing through my mind. Were we adequately prepared for what we faced? Would the certainty and dedication that we feel now be able to carry us through the hard times? Would we know what to do when the time came? Well, the decision was already made and we were too far down the road to turn back now. Finally, I recalled the advice of a former boss of mine, "Once a decision is made, never look back," and that was what I needed to allow my mind to relax and get some sleep. And sure enough, it was a bright and sunny day when we awoke at 5:30 AM.

The bank from which we secured our commercial mortgage was to be the site of the closing at 10:00 this morning so Joan and I decided we had a few hours before then to devote to finding the essentials we needed to get underway. Fortunately, Dan had purchased a few things for breakfast so, at least, we didn't have to do shopping first thing in the morning. And besides, we didn't know where the stores were.

All the time we were in the basement wrestling boxes around, I kept looking around and spotting things that needed to be done. I suspect that I am already into a mode of looking at everything through that critical "what's wrong?" filter that will continue as long as we own the Inn. And of course, the panacea of the previous night, "never look back", had worn off by that time and I was back to pondering our commitment and ability to be exceptional innkeepers. That proved to be a bigger waste of nervous energy than it had the night before. But at least we found a lot of the things we needed immediately before it was time to get dressed for the "ceremony".

When Joan, Dan and I arrived at the bank, we were ushered politely into a large conference room. There were about 15 or 20 people already there. Probably, they don't make loans of well over a half million dollars every day so they drew a crowd. The only people we recognized were the sellers, Barbara Kolodkin, our realtor, Bill Sabin, our lawyer, and Bill Davis, our loan officer from the bank. Another couple whom we didn't recognize turned out to be "silent partners" of the sellers who later proved to be not all that silent today. The rest were bank officials and lawyers, about ten of them. I was immediately reminded of the old joke about how many lawyers it takes to change a light bulb—which turned out not to be so funny when I realized that someone, probably us, was paying for their esteemed presence.

The proceedings were exacting and ponderous, with the silent partner interrupting frequently for "clarifications". We found out in due course that he not only owned a substantial percentage of the Inn but was also a lawyer, with his practice on Madison Avenue in New York City. Though that increased the pucker factor just a little, as the morning went on I was very impressed with the way that our "country lawyer" from the near-by small town of Williamstown was his match every step of the way. The second-hand recommendation for professional services that we had received while negotiating for the Inn was proving to be the first good stroke of luck since we had arrived in town. After about two and a half hours, all the i's were dotted and the t's crossed, and we came out with just about what we had planned on—the ownership of the Birchwood Inn with about $35,000 left over for "contingencies".

Our realtor suggested lunch at the Church Street Cafe, the restaurant she thought was the best in town, and since she was treating, we accepted. It was as though a great burden had been lifted from everyone's shoulders after we were seated. After so many minor glitches for the past three months, this morning everyone seemed to harbor a suppressed fear that something was going to happen at the last minute to throw the whole deal off track. But now the talk changed from contract details to more ordinary discussions about the *town, the up-coming Tanglewood season and the feeling of relief that had begun to permit all of us to relax. Maybe the bottles of wine that came with lunch helped the mood of contentment a little too. Then suddenly, it hit the three of us at about the same time: What in hell were we doing sitting there and feeling so relieved and content about? We had loads of work to do, guests on the way, and it was time to get back to work.*

The Inn had been left open with no one in attendance when we headed off for the closing. It was the seller's when we left and it would be ours when we returned, so I guess no one was quite sure who was in charge. Fortunately, Lenox is one of the few remaining places in the country where you never have to lock your door or the car, and when we got back, everything was in order.

Then we heard voices from the front porch. It was Patti and Bill Smith, our first official guests as the Birchwood innkeepers. When they found no one around after their arrival, they decided to make themselves at home and wait until someone showed up. And within the next two hours, eight more guests arrived. Thank God for Dan's experience in running a front desk operation at a major hotel or Joan and I would still be fumbling our way through the whole process. So far, no one seemed to know that we were the newest kids on the block, and we were unquestionably in business.

Without a doubt, Friday, the 28th of June 1991 will be forever etched on our memories as the day our lives changed forever. Say a prayer that we will be successful. The confidence that we expressed to you when you made it possible for us to buy the Inn is still there, but there's not quite as much bravado behind it.

Cheers,
Dick

And thus began our careers as innkeepers. As we look back on these events today, it was a huge jumble of emotions, stresses and confusion. We were in a totally new environment. We hadn't even learned where each individual guest room was, let alone gained any familiarity with all the nooks and crannies of the old house. Worse than that, here it was the first day of the first weekend of the Tanglewood season, and we didn't even know where the Tanglewood grounds were, let alone all the other cultural attractions of the immediate area. While we intuitively knew what we should do, and we had rehearsed our roles rather thoroughly in our minds, applying those plans and ideals had yet to take place and we were nervous if not downright scared. But I'm getting ahead of the story.

The beginnings go back to the first of the year, actually December of 1990 to be exact. I had retired from the Air Force three years earlier, and had taken a position as a vice president in a start-up engineering and management consultant firm in the Washington, DC, area. My former boss, Charlie Gabriel, whom I had worked for as his executive assistant when he was the Chief of Staff of the Air Force, had recruited me for the job. Our relationship was far more than professional, though it was that, through and through. But in addition we were close friends with a deep and abiding respect for one another. Clearly, working with Charlie was going to be a dream second career, and while that proved to be true at the outset, that didn't last very long—for either of us.

The president and founder of our little company had some different ideas about the mission of the company than we did. He viewed our role as one of selling—selling our company to new clients and selling our existing clients' products to the U.S. government, primarily the Department of Defense. While he certainly had correct expectations for the first goal, we were strictly prohibited, as former senior military officers, from engaging in the latter. But more importantly, the last thing either of us aspired to when we retired from the Air Force was to be salesmen.

When it became increasingly clear that Charlie Gabriel (and I, to a far lesser extent) was, in reality, more important to the company for who—rather than what—he knew, it was time for his parting of the ways. After three years with the company, Charlie left at the end of the summer and I was soon to follow, leaving the company a few months later, effective the 31st of December 1990. Not surprisingly, Joan and I found ourselves facing the dilemma of "what next". But for this second time around, we were determined that we would be better prepared.

There were only two hard and fast criteria for my second post-retirement career search: the new position would have to be something that I knew in advance would both stimulate and challenge me, and after facing up to the realities of the previous three years, I was determined to have nothing to do with "selling", especially for the aerospace and defense industries. As a logical point of departure, my first focus was on academia. After all, I had been the president of an accredited, doctoral level degree granting institution in my final Air Force assignment. Why not? And the decision immediately seemed to be a prudent one.

Virtually the first position I applied for turned out to be an apparent winner. In response to my application as the director of their short-course executive management program, one of the more prestigious of the Ivy League schools invited Joan and me for a three-day, whirlwind tour of the campus and a series of interviews and social activities with college deans and the university executives. The dean of the business school in which the program was to be established assured me at the end of the three days that the position was mine, but he hadn't reckoned with the faculty senate.

In what was a huge disappointment for both the dean and us, he called me a week later to inform me apologetically that the faculty senate had vetoed my appointment because they felt that a retired general did not fit in with the image of the university which they wished to portray. So much for the liberal exchange of ideas and perspectives that are supposed to mark the academic community. The emergence of "political correctness" on university campuses—and perhaps an enduring anti-military hangover from the Vietnam War—quickly made it clear that professional military people with presumably conservative views had no place in these sorts of endeavors.

So now where to turn? In a mood somewhere between despondency and resignation, I said to Joan one evening, "Well, you gave up a professional teaching career to follow me around the world for the last thirty years, what do you think you'd like to do?" She laughed off my comment and the conversation drifted elsewhere, but she didn't forget what I said. Two days later, over a glass of wine before dinner, she had her answer.

She had contacted an innkeeper on the coast of Maine, simply because she learned that he was an Annapolis graduate, like me, and had retired from a long and successful military career. Though it was not characteristic of something she might normally do, she had called to ask the couple's advice on getting into the innkeeping business. They assured her that it wasn't for everyone and although they liked what they were doing a great deal, they advised her not to go into the business without a lot of research and preparation. Their long conversation ended with a recommendation that we attend a four-day seminar on purchasing and operating a country inn, conducted by a small company from Brattleoro, Vermont. And it just so happened that the next offering of their seminar was scheduled the following week at a resort in the Pocono Mountains of eastern Pennsylvania. And, as Joan assured me, while there was still an opportunity to cancel, there was space for only one couple left in the up-coming seminar, and she had reserved it for us. Our fate had been sealed. All we needed was money!

*   *   *

March 16, 1991
Dear Chris and Tom,

We can't tell you how grateful we are for your willingness to invest in our new venture. As wacky as it may sound, I'm convinced that we're going to make a success of it, and perhaps more importantly, we're going to enjoy it as well.

*Probably the most touching (and gratifying) aspect of your decision is your choice to ignore the advice of your lawyer. I suspect that if the roles were reversed and my lawyer had asked for all the conditions and guarantees that yours did, it would be a tough decision to turn my back on that advice—that is, until you reminded me of what our professional life has been all about. I'm referring to your comment that, "He may know the law and how to advise his clients, but he isn't familiar with the trust and friendship that exists among Air Force officers." Few values in life are more important. We'll never betray that trust, and you can bet **my** life on it.*

We have made a couple of forays out into the Blue Ridge Mountains and the Shenandoah Valley to look at a few B&Bs but they are not our cup of tea. One was a combination winery and B&B, but I suspect that it's a more a winery that rents out rooms occasionally. Not that making vino wouldn't be interesting, but that place illustrates the problem with the whole area: it's not a destination. If we just wanted to rent rooms to people passing through, we'd buy the Seven Dwarfs Motel on Route 66, but that's just short of running a flop house on the Bowery to our minds.

So, our first real decision is to begin to spread the field and look only at those areas that attract people for what the location has to offer. The guy who ran the seminar that we attended last October, sends out information on inns for sale to his "promising students". (I guess those are the 20% that haven't totally rejected the idea of innkeeping after completing his course.) At any rate, he recently sent us a brochure on an inn in Southampton, NY—a very popular summer community way out on the eastern end of Long Island. At the bottom of the cover sheet, he wrote in longhand, "I'm sending you this because it's in your price range but I really don't think you'd find that you fit in there very well." Not sure what he means by that—whether we're too poor or whether we shouldn't expect to find many former fighter pilots among the potential clientele.

Joan has made reservations for us to fly out to Santa Fe in about ten days, a place that is rated very highly for potential B&B owners. We have liked the area a lot whenever we've passed through, and it has a wonderful combination of culture, recreational activities and scenery. Meanwhile, we're headed up to New England this weekend to Lenox, a small town in western Massachusetts. Neither one of us is particularly anxious to go back to our home state—Taxachusetts, as the natives call it. But Lenox is the summer home of the Boston Symphony Orchestra and, coupled with the world's best fall foliage and the opportunity for decent skiing in the winter, it is clearly a destination. We'll keep you posted on our progress.

One late-breaking news bulletin. Dan just told us that if we are going to buy an inn, he wanted us to count him in too. He said he'll give up his job with the Sheraton chain to come with us. Looks like there will now be three members of the Toner family who have lost their marbles, but now, at least one knows something about the hospitality business.

All the best,
Dick

Military life can be the most rewarding and exciting of careers, if that's the sort of thing that you like, and it can be many things to many people. But one thing it's not, for anyone: a way to get rich. And rich we were not.

We had saved as much as we could over the years, but 24 moves to six countries and 12 states within the U.S. over thirty years takes it's toll on family savings—not to mention the expense of raising three children. We had done fairly well with our two incomes after my military retirement. But if we were going to be able to buy the sort of inn that we pictured in our minds' eyes, we were going to have to find some investors. We needed more than we had in savings just to get enough money to qualify for the commercial bank loan if we were to buy the sort of inn we had envisioned.

In the seminar, we had learned that a couple who wanted to operate an inn themselves, with a minimum number of part-time employees, was pretty well limited to a maximum of 12 guest rooms. It would be beyond their capability to handle any more, effectively, without hiring full-time employees. On the other hand, under normal occupancy rates, the same experts say that this couple would need a minimum of eight guest rooms to break even, financially. When Dan decided to join us, that added to our family work force and convinced us to go for the high side. So we had the target bracketed, and this was what we had in mind when we first arrived in Lenox.

The place that we went to look at was right out at the extreme: 12 guest rooms, an active business and a good location. But it just wasn't "us". Then we met Barbara Kolodkin, a realtor we contacted as a back-up in case the first inn we saw didn't get our juices flowing. As we drove with her up Main Street, leading north out of town, there it sat on the top of the hill—the Birchwood Inn, a gorgeous old white colonial with green shutters and green awnings. Joan and I looked at each other and something clicked. The inside would have to be pretty disappointing for us not to fall in love with it. It was the image in our mind's eyes come to life. The huge porch extended across most of the front of the house and it beckoned warmly with its charm. We couldn't wait to see the inside.

If anything, the interior was even more charming. A huge, 800 square foot library with an enormous fireplace covering most of the end wall was down two steps right off to the right of the entrance hallway. To the left was a smaller den leading to a lovely dining room that seated twenty comfortably at separate tables for two or four. Behind the swinging door in the dining room was good sized butler's pantry and beyond that, a marvelous, large kitchen with a center food preparation island, endless amounts of shelf and storage space and a massive old gas range with six burners and two huge ovens.

Though we didn't know it then, this was to be our home for the next eight years. The place needed a lot of sprucing up—and then some—and the business had waned to almost nothing over the previous two years. On top of that, the asking price of $900,000 gagged us. But Barbara knew that the inn had been on the market for almost three years and she figured she could put a deal together with some inspired negotiating.

On the way back home, we made a decision. We would spend the next week or so trying to cobble together the additional investment money that we'd need from friends and family. We thought it would take about a quarter of a million dollars and, even if we sold or liquidated most of everything we owned, we would be nearly $100,000 short. But if we succeeded in raising the money, we'd come back in ten days and make an offer. We were so preoccupied with our plans and all the excitement, I turned north instead of south on I-91 and we were nearly to the Vermont border before we turned around and headed south toward our home in Virginia. Now the juices were clearly flowing!

*   *   *

July 7, 1999
Dear Chris & Tom,

Our first ten days have come and gone and we need to give thanks for small favors that we survived. We had a full house, on the weekends at least, with more than half the guests turning out to be walk-ins—people who arrive in town without reservations, wonder why it's so crowded and expect to be able to just walk in any place and get a room. Unfortunately for us, the former owners did no advertising and had no one at the inn to take reservations for most of the past six months. So we have very few advance bookings. Fortunately for us, virtually all of the inns are already fully booked for the Tanglewood season and one of the few places for walk-ins to come is to our place—and the other innkeepers are kind enough to send them to us. However, the walk-ins don't always turn out to be the best sort of folks, a fact that we can readily attest to after two weekends.

New Yorkers have a reputation around the world for being rude, arrogant, demanding and not very pleasant people to be around—except if you're another New Yorker. I suspect the reputation is similar to the belief shared by some Americans who dislike the French because they went to Paris once and were treated rudely—a small sampling to say the least, but a repute that seems to stick, nonetheless. And while I know it's unfair to generalize like that, the ones we had this weekend more than lived up to their advance billing.

The largest ski resort in the area has a training program each fall for their new staff and the title of the very first session is, "How to Deal with the Sharks". The sharks, of course, are the small minority of people from the New York metro area who are responsible for the ugly reputation. So, sharks it is from now on.

At the start of this past weekend, the worst of the worst sharks arrived: two brothers—one of whom turned out to be a dentist and the other a psychologist. The dentist lives on Long Island and the shrink in North Jersey and this was a mini-reunion for them and their wives. They insisted over the phone on rooms that were adjacent to one another. Despite the fact that we told them in advance that the only adjacent rooms we had were on the third floor, they complained loud and long after they arrived because they had to go up two flights of stairs. They also demanded that "someone" carry their luggage to the rooms. After looking around and finding no volunteers, it appeared that Dan and I were elected.

Dan made one more trip than I and when he came down the stairs into the kitchen—our sanctuary—he was carrying an antique, wrought-iron floor lamp and steam was figuratively coming out of his ears and nose. Apparently, the dentist's wife turned on the light, discovered that the bulb had burned out, pulled the plug out of the wall by the chord, and shouted at Dan, "Get this damned light out of here and don't you dare bring it back until it works". No thank you or even an acknowledgment for bringing their five heavy bags up to their rooms. When he halfway calmed down, he said, with lamp still in hand, "What I should have done was wrap this goddam thing around her neck." We all laughed so hard at his comment that it snapped him out of the fury. But that would hardly be the end of them.

Within minutes the two women were at the Dutch door leading from the entryway into the butler's pantry with seemingly an unending list of complaints. The rooms didn't connect (none of them do); the room was too dark (probably because the floor lamp was gone); it was too hot up there (the temperature was 74°); and on and on. But even if the complaints had been legitimate, the nasty way that they were made, both in tone and phrasing, plus the side comments between them that were personally derogatory to all of us, was enough to want to throw them out of the Inn. Finally, they ran out of bitches and the four of them headed out the door to wander around the village.

Just before 5:00 PM, the three of us were in the kitchen preparing to serve wine and cheese when the call bell at the Dutch door rang—ding, ding, ding, ding, ding,—as if we couldn't hear one or two rings. I was closest and glanced up to see our favorite Mrs. Dentist standing there. I stiffened my back, braced for the worst, and asked her as cordially as I could if I could help her. In an equally sweet voice, she said she had a favor to ask. Apparently, their mission when they went into the village was for her to break away and order a cake for a surprise birthday party for her husband the next day. But she failed to get away from him and, showing the first signs of civility since we had met them, she asked me if we would handle the arrangements. I said yes and we agreed that we'd have the celebration at the same time the following day.

When I told Joan and Dan, he and I had the same thought. Let's get a week-old cake from the Salvation Army soup kitchen, everyone take turns spitting on it and then we'll serve it to them. Joan, of course, would hear none of it—even in jest—and instead suggested that this was our chance to shine. "Leave the arrangements to me," she said, and her grin began spreading from ear to ear.

The next day, we served wine and cheese to all the guests and, in an aside, confirmed with the dentist's wife that she wanted us to bring the cake into the library with all the other guests rather than have a separate "party" in the dining room. With that, we went back to the kitchen, put on party hats, lit the candles on the cake, and headed into the library. Joan carried the bouquet of balloons in one hand and a bouquet of flowers and a card in the other; I carried the cake, on which was written, "Happy Birthday David"; while Dan carried our silver champagne bucket with a chilled bottle of Korbel and four iced flutes. As we came around the corner and started down the two steps into the library, we lustily broke out singing "Happy Birthday to You" which all of the other guests immediately joined, as if on cue.

David was clearly surprised and touched. The other three just glowed, obviously expecting a more perfunctory showing from the tawdry innkeepers. The other guests came by in twos and threes and wished Doc a happy birthday, with a genuine warmth that would have made you think that they had known one another for years. The four of them became a bit misty-eyed when they read the card that Joan had very carefully selected. The birthday boy insisted that we get three more glasses and join them in a toast. Before they went out to dinner that evening, each came by individually to the Dutch door to thank us for such a thoughtful remembrance of his birthday. With a twinkle in her eye, Joan reminded both Dan and me of the old adage about flies preferring honey to vinegar.

The following morning, Doc was not present when the other three came down to breakfast. When Joan went into the dining room to take their order, she jokingly asked if the missing birthday boy had continued to celebrate a little too much. His wife assured us that he was just a little off his form this morning but would be down in a few minutes.

Suddenly we heard a resounding thud from upstairs, and I knew instantly that someone had fallen and fallen hard. I took off running up the stairs to the third floor and when I reached eye level to the top of the flight, here was Doc lying in a pool of his own vomit, his body racked by spasms that obviously spelled an epileptic seizure. As quickly as I could, I moved him away from the top of the stairs—one leg was actually hanging over the top stair so he had come very close to falling down the flight when the seizure hit him. Then I checked to see if his breathing passage was clear. About that time, his wife came up the stairs and I told her that I was afraid that he was having a seizure.

She seemed amazingly nonchalant about the whole thing and proceeded to tell me that he was due for one—it had been three months since his last. As strange as her behavior appeared at first, she seemed to know what she was doing and had very skillfully assumed control of the situation. When I suggested calling an ambulance to move him to the hospital, she said, "Absolutely not!" She went on to say that he refused to consult a physician or get medication for the seizures because he was "afraid that he wouldn't be able to practice dentistry any more if his problems became public knowledge." Now won't that give you a sense of confidence the next time you visit a new dentist.

He seemed to begin his recovery amazingly quickly, based on my limited past experience with epilepsy. After we moved him back into the bedroom, she offered to clean up the mess, but I told her not to worry. She should take care of her husband and we'd take care of the clean up, to which she gratefully agreed. Less than a half hour later she was back down to finish her breakfast. She told Joan that he was resting comfortably, that he usually slept for four or five hours after an incident like that, and she requested a late checkout. An hour later, she came to the door and asked us to keep an ear out for her husband—the three of them were going to wander around our lovely village for a couple of hours and then have lunch.

When the four of them were finally checking out about 3:00 yesterday afternoon—the dentist looking as fit as he had when they arrived—I pulled his brother aside and very emphatically suggested to him that he needed to talk some sense into this guy. It probably was none of my business but the fact that the families treated his condition as a rather routine situation was, to me, absolutely bizarre. Not only was he seriously jeopardizing his own health, but he probably was a considerable threat to his patients as well. Brother Shrink said he agreed with me and they'd discuss it on the way home. Then to our utter astonishment, they all stopped in the middle of the parking area. The dentist's wife apologized profoundly for being a complete bitch when they arrived and thanked us profusely for the kind and considerate treatment they received—even though, as she said, they didn't deserve it. Then, to further add to our surprise, both ladies, with tears in their eyes gave each of us a kiss and the men followed with bear hugs. Then off to New York they went.

We learned a couple of valuable lessons from that experience. First, in the future, we'll give New Yorkers a while to calm down after their arrival before judging them. Apparently they exist in such a dog-eat-dog world, they don't know how to act when they're thrust into a more civil society and it takes them time to adjust. And second, we discovered there are great personal rewards to be gained from going out of our way to make people happy, even though we might need to overcome some initial resistance to our efforts to be warm and hospitable. We look forward to making many more people happy many more times. I think we're going to enjoy this adventure, after all.

All the best,
Dick

After we had added a few more similar experiences to that one, we began to get our feet wet, build up our confidence and settle down into the routine of being innkeepers. Having taken over the Inn the same day that the high season began was not the best possible timing for our new career. It reminded me of learning to swim by being thrown out of a boat in middle of the North Atlantic. But we were all still swimming after the first ten days and the confused daze that had settled over us at the outset, particularly Joan and me, had begun to lift. But it wasn't to be a completely smooth transition by any means.

From the very first morning, a minor conflict reared its head. Despite the fact that the three of us had talked for hours on end and planned intensely for our new career back in Virginia, there had been one very important oversight. Joan and Dan were under the impression that we were going to rotate assignments, probably on a daily basis. My understanding was that we would each have our own jobs to do and, while each should know how to fill in for the other, we would retain a primary function all the time.

The fundamental question was, "Who's going to be the cook?" and as luck would have it, we all wanted that job. Joan had broken her leg in a terrible skiing accident four years previously and, despite five major surgeries and a number of bone grafts, her tibia—the shin bone—had still not healed. She wore a brace and could walk fairly well, but because of her condition, I had done all the cooking and related chores for the two of us ever since the accident. Further, we had both attended a week-long course at the La Varene Ecole de Cuisine in Paris about fifteen years previously. And despite public impressions that all generals and admirals have hosts of enlisted servants, we frequently entertained official guests in our homes—without financial assistance or aides to help—and I generally did all the cooking. It was only logical and fair that I should continue that role.

But Dan had ideas of his own. He had majored in hotel management in college, had been at the operational level in the hotel business for a decade, and had pitched in wherever he was needed. He had accumulated considerable experience in the food service aspect of the business, ranging from food preparation to "plating up" dinners for 500 or more guests. I may have been pretty good at doing our own meals, or even a formal sit-down dinner for 12, but what did I know about cooking and serving breakfast for 25 or more people. Clearly, he had the experience to be the cook.

Joan was, as usual, the moderating influence. She didn't think anyone should be the cook all the time. We should take turns and share the duty that all of us apparently wanted and expected to do. We'd rotate assignments and, that way, everyone could take the good with the bad. But Dan and I suddenly closed ranks. No way either of us was going to be the head waitress, and besides, she was the one who wanted the pleasure of interacting with the guests, and what better way than greeting them each morning when they came to breakfast.

I patiently explained to both of them that we were going to be as democratic as possible in running this business. We would try to compromise on all differences of opinion and work things out through discussion. But, dammit, when we came to loggerheads and there was clearly no room for compromise, as the senior officer present, I would break all impasses and make the final decisions. There were a few long faces for an hour or two, but that's the way we ended up. Joan would be the waitress. Dan, with his extensive overall experience in the business, would run the front desk operation and supervise the housekeeping activities. And I would be the cook!

However, Dan didn't abandon the kitchen and, in fact, established a tradition that was to be one of our hallmarks at the Birchwood Inn for the duration of our ownership. He had always been artistic, even as a youngster, but we didn't know that this applied to food service as well. He began putting together fruit garnishes for the plates on which the main breakfast course was to be served. And they were beautiful. He often used five or six different types of fruit, creating a work of art on the far edge of the plates of delicately cut and shaped pieces which, when assembled, were as good as we'd ever seen in some of the finest restaurants in the world. The guests often ooh'd and aah'd when Joan served them, and it clearly wasn't my omelet or pancakes that drew the reaction. And she was sure to give Dan the appropriate feedback. Serendipitously, we had reached a workable compromise on the cooking chores and we were all settling in to a smooth routine.

*   *   *

July 15, 1991
Dear Chris and Tom,

I got so carried away in my last letter telling you about the dentist and all the goings-on surrounding their visit that I forgot to tell you about the two young women from Montreal who were with us on our very first weekend. They were booked by the former owners and apparently had come to the Inn previously on at least two or three occasions. They had reserved one of our very large, premiere rooms with a fireplace, a full bath with a soaking tub and queen canopy bed. From what they said, this was the room that they requested each time they came. They were very nice, spent most of their time at the concerts or involved in recreational activities and were absolutely no trouble at all.

When they were checking out, one of them pulled me aside, reached in her backpack and took out a can of Bon Ami. In case you don't recall, that's an old cleansing or scouring powder that was a big seller when we were young, but I don't think it's even available in the States any more. Apparently it still is in French-speaking Canada. After she showed me the can, she told me that they love the Inn, and especially like that room, but the bath has always been so dirty that they habitually brought cleaning compounds and equipment and thoroughly cleaned the bath themselves so they could feel comfortable using it.

It was the type of comment, of course, that both embarrasses and makes the hair stand up on the back of your neck. I apologized as best I could, but refrained from telling her that we had already discovered the deplorable condition of the baths, in particular, but also the house in general. It was very dirty—a fact that we doubtless overlooked when we were looking at things through our rose-colored glasses. Since we had too much to do with unpacking boxes and the like, we had already solicited bids from a couple of small local cleaning companies who did major projects in offices and hotels. The one we selected was scheduled to start a top to bottom, thorough cleaning the following day.

Not sure why I didn't mention it to her, but it may have been because they were scheduled to come back again this past weekend, only this time, they were to be joined by their husbands. Apparently, the men had come down from Montreal and they all continued on from Lenox to Cape Cod where they spent the past ten days before coming back to stay with us. Once again, all four were ideal guests— very active playing tennis and biking during the daytime and they attended the Boston Symphony concerts each evening. We did get an occasional chance to talk with them all, and the more we got to know them, the more we liked them.

When check-out time came on Sunday morning, all four of them came to the desk and after the credit cards were processed, the infamous back pack was opened again. But this time, a gift wrapped package came out and one of them handed it to me. They insisted that I open it in their presence and when I did, here was the partially used can of Bon Ami in the box with a card that read, "The place looks beautiful and we won't be needing this any more. All good wishes for success after such a positive start." Wasn't that a thoughtful way for them to undo the not so subtle innuendo of two weeks ago. Looks like we're doing some things right at least.

We'll be in touch, Dick

Shortly after we had closed on the purchase of the Inn, Charlie Gabriel had called me to see how things were going. I told him all was going well—in fact I had already made my first bed and cleaned my first toilet. "C'mon," he said, "I know you've done that many times before." I assured him that, indeed I had been doing these household chores since I was a little kid, "....but never professionally." Housekeeping was a subject on which we had complete agreement—none of us were going to be professionals. That was the only function at the Inn for which we would hire part-time help.

Oh, yes indeed, we would have housekeepers. There was no misunderstanding the prior planning on this function. The one subject on which there was unquestioned agreement was the fact that we would do rooms, or any of the other housekeeping chores that were necessary, but only as an emergency last resort. We were going to hire housekeepers—even though we weren't yet sure what shape and form that part-time, temporary staff would take. As it turned out, one of the few beneficial references that the previous owners had left us were the names of a group of high school girls who had very limited housekeeping experience but an obvious desire and willingness to work. They turned out to be lifesavers that first summer.

There were actually five of them—Andrea, Lisa, Sarah, Shannon, and Sherrie—all of whom came from Pittsfield, the county seat of the Berkshires, and all of whom were classmates and close friends, about to enter their sophomore year at Pittsfield High School. We were soon to learn that the five girls had already emerged as class leaders; each was a standout athlete and each an honor roll scholar. They knew the meaning of hard work and it quickly became clear that they hadn't reached the early levels of success that they had without being responsible and knowing how to apply themselves. What better combination could we hope for?

And they showed their resourcefulness right at the outset. We needed only two or three of them to work on a daily basis, depending on the guest load. Generally, they spent three or four hours a day with us so most of them had other part-time jobs as well. It had all the makings of a scheduling nightmare. But there was no need to worry about scheduling them for work. They would take care of that themselves, to include getting a substitute if someone were sick, had gone on a family vacation or, for some reason, couldn't show up when scheduled. And they handled the scheduling beautifully, or at least I should say that Sarah did. But it took cooperation and a sense of responsibility on the part of each of them. For the three ensuing summer seasons that they were to work for us, we were never disappointed in their reliability, dependability and integrity. Knowing them greatly restored our trust in the younger generation and our hopes for the future.

But there came a time in that first August that the need for more permanent help became obvious. Four of the five girls were expected to start on the varsity girls' soccer team and Sarah had already played at the number four position as a freshman on the girls' varsity tennis team. Pre-season practice was to start the final week in August and they were all fully committed for the weekdays after that. We needed to hire someone who could take over right away and would stay with us on a regular basis, year round.

Advertisements in the paper brought a flurry of phone calls from applicants, a response that was not surprising because the Berkshires were, at the time, an economically depressed area and the unemployment rate was in the teens. We could afford to be selective. Dan volunteered to do the interviewing and after meeting with about four or five candidates, he became a bit pessimistic about our prospects. Then along came Paula. She was an attractive woman in her early thirties, immaculate in appearance, experienced as an assembly line worker in one of the many mom and pop plastics plants in Pittsfield but also a homemaker with two teen age children. If her appearance were any indicator, she was just the person we were looking for.

I think Dan recommended that we hire her on the basis of one statement only. She told him, "I may take a couple of minutes longer to clean a bathroom than you might like, but you will know without a doubt that it will be spotless when I finish." And it was. She was absolutely meticulous in what she did, and despite her advance warning, she also proved to be equally efficient and thorough. So much so, that we found ourselves checking the guest rooms less frequently because we were fully confident that they'd be close to perfect.

As we got to know Paula better, we found that she had wanted to leave her plastics job because it was a family business and she felt that she was being taken advantage of. In addition, as we were to discover, her husband, who was a manager and co-worker, had a wandering eye and their marriage was in serious trouble. Whether or not those circumstances were related in any way, it also soon became obvious to us that she was painfully shy and had a very low sense of self-esteem. She even blushed and hung her head when given a compliment. Over the next months we set out to try to draw her out of her shell and to build up her confidence. But that's getting ahead of the story.

*   *   *

July 20, 1991
Dear Chris & Tom,

This is clearly going to be an experience, the likes of which we've never had before. As I mentioned previously, we had virtually no bookings for the summer when we arrived, while most of the other inns are completely reserved for every weekend in the summer and most of the weekdays to boot. As a result, the walk-ins, who make up our guest lists most of the time, generally seem to be a pretty motley bunch of strange people—or at least we hope they're not characteristic of the regular clientele. I sure hope they don't get much stranger the lady who dropped in this morning.

We concluded right at the start that it's going to be very, very difficult to have any personal time. And I'm not talking about the opportunity to go off in a secluded nook and meditate, or the chance to go to the gym for an invigorating workout. Just for example, today was our 34th wedding anniversary and we celebrated it by doing what we do every day. Working! Joan was even too tired at the end of the day to crack the bottle of champagne that Dan had thoughtfully given to us, and she's sound asleep now as I write.

No, I'm talking about having the time for something as basic as going to the john. First of all, with the guest demands in the morning being what they are, just the simple act of getting away for five minutes appears to be a luxury. Between doing the final preparations, cooking and serving breakfast for the first four and a half hours, the day begins with a singularly restrictive quality to it. Then, just about the time that the last guests show up for breakfast, the first ones who ate decide that they're going to check out—and Joan is not yet willing to go within arm's length of the mini-computer that processes the credit cards. But there I go digressing again.

This morning, the gods were smiling and my urge to go and the time to devote to it just happened to coincide. Our "owners' quarters", which we have affectionately dubbed The Hovel, are laid out in the European style with the toilet enclosed in a separate "water closet" which has a privacy door. However, since Joan was in the inn with the guests and it was a bit on the warm side, I just left the door wide open. I had just barely settled in for my morning constitutional when I heard someone open the outside door to our quarters, which has a very visible "private" sign on it. No sweat, I thought, Joan is probably just coming over to tell me that one of the guests is ready to check out. So much for a little peace and quiet.

Suddenly, I looked up from my crossword puzzle and here, standing directly in front of me, not three feet away, was a woman whom I had never seen before in my life. Without blinking an eye or showing the slightest loss of aplomb, she said, "Hi, do you have a vacancy?"

I guess it must have been my puritanical upbringing, but I had all I could do to keep from diving into the toilet and pulling the cover down on top of me—and there wasn't even anything showing that should embarrass me. But as flustered as I was, I still managed to see the absurd humor in the situation. Contrary to that invariable after-thought that we all seem to get—you know, the "Jeez, what I should have said was...."—the very first thing that popped into my head was the right answer. I looked her straight in the eye and said. "I'm sorry, ma'am, but this is a one-holer!"

With equal composure, she calmly replied, "Thanks anyway. I'll try again some time!" And with that she walked out the door and, evidently, got into her car and drove out of the driveway. I'll probably never know if she knew what I was doing or where she was, but I hope it's not a forecast of things to come.

But getting back to more normal events again, we had a pleasant surprise in the middle of this past week. Tom Anderson's [a mutual friend from Air Force days] *brother, Bill, and his wife, Betty, called to see if we could squeeze them in for a couple of days. They were in Sturbridge, Massachusetts, about an hour from here, where Bill was attending a medical convention and they were enjoying New England so much they thought they'd stay a day or so longer. We were concerned in advance of beginning this adventure that we wouldn't have much chance to spend with personal friends who came to visit. And we were right, but we split a nice bottle of wine before they went out to dinner, and it was very truly enjoyable to see them again. When they were leaving, Betty presented us with a little "inn-warming" gift that, I think, will become more meaningful each day.*

In a nicely wrapped package, there were four small books, all with different cover designs, which blended beautifully with the decor of our rooms. The pages of each book were lined but blank. She told us that she and Bill had stayed in a B&B in San Francisco and they found a similar book in their room there. With it was a nice little note from the innkeepers, which invited them to record their memories of their stay and to insert any other comments that they thought appropriate. Betty had already put a very gracious message in the book that she had chosen to go into the room where they stayed. She also told us where she bought the books so that we can put them in every room, if we wish. It was a most thoughtful thing to do. We hope all the memories will be pleasant.

Time for me to join my frau and get a decent night's sleep. Enjoy your potty time whenever you choose—and I'll be envious of you when you do.

Warmest regards,
Dick

My brief mention of The Hovel probably deserves a more substantial bit of amplification. In the initial description of the ground floor, I made no mention of one part of the building—the area behind the kitchen. Prior to 1951, this stately old mansion had been a private home, owned for the previous 75 years by the Dana family. The Danas were quite wealthy and, as was the custom of most affluent families of the nineteenth and early twentieth centuries, they had a number of domestic servants. At that time, the domestics had small bedrooms on the third floor of the mansion and the family bedrooms were on the second floor.

During the day, those same servants had two "day rooms" connected to the kitchen where they could spend their time when not working, and the rooms also served as their dining room where they took their meals. Each was 12' by 12' and they were separated by a narrow alcove containing a closet and the toilet. In addition, there was a small sink for washing up in one of the rooms. This explains why the toilet was a European style W.C. since the servants probably were of both sexes and it is unlikely that they were all related. These two rooms had been converted to "innkeepers' quarters" when the mansion became an Inn. With the exception of converting the small closet between the rooms into a stall shower and closing off two doors to the kitchen, the rooms were probably much the same as they had been in the halcyon days of the mansion. The door to the kitchen was also sealed off, so it is necessary to go outside to a small porch in order to go from the kitchen to The Hovel.

All the other bedrooms in the mansion were guest rooms, and therefore revenue producing rooms, so it was clear that any of those rooms that were converted to living quarters for us meant an automatic decrease in potential revenue, particularly in the summer. At a time when cash flow was essential, we agreed to forgo the comfort of a normal bedroom and we would live in The Hovel. That's right, all three of us, plus the two cats. Fortunately there was a privacy door between the rooms, so Dan took the outer room—the one adjacent to the outside access door. We had a double bed in our room—actually a box spring and a mattress on a frame—but because of space limitations, Dan was forced to sleep on a futon that was folded up and stored in a corner each day.

Since the one closet between the rooms had been converted to a shower, there was no place to hang any clothing. But thirty years of military life had taught us to be resourceful when it was not at all unusual to live in a mansion during one assignment and a shack the next. A couple of portable clothes racks and a set or two of steel storage shelves from Kmart would get us through the summer. Our rooms violated the "square feet per person" criteria for inmates at a maximum security Federal prison but we were determined that we could handle it. So that's how we lived during those early days at the Inn. We weren't living in luxury, by any means, but it would do until winter came along and we could make alternate arrangements—or at least that's the line of reasoning we tried to use to convince ourselves.

*   *   *

July 29, 1991
Dear Chris & Tom,

Oh lordy, I knew it was bound to happen some day but I didn't think it would be quite so soon or so violent. Dan and I had a knock-down, drag-out argument this morning and it ended, for all intents and purposes, in hysteria.

When we decided to make this a family enterprise and Dan came into the business with us, I knew from past experience that the situation was fraught with all sorts of emotion. I vowed to myself that I was going to try to be as agreeable as I could and would be especially watchful about not being authoritative—a difficult challenge since the exercise of authority has been part and parcel of our lives as military officers, as you well know. I'm sure Dan was also intuitively aware of the inherent danger of trying to transition seamlessly from being a son to being a business partner and he probably made a vow of his own not to let things erupt when the going got tough. But erupt they did.

The reasons why are stupid—just as they usually are—but that didn't lessen the rancor that was expressed. Since he's a bachelor, a tad younger than we and is endowed with a bit more stamina, he has been going out a couple of nights each week looking for a little social life—and I don't blame him a bit for doing so. I guess last night, he found some very social life and didn't get home until after 3:00 AM (our knowing the time is probably one of the hazards he will face, having to share a small suite with his parents). He had probably enjoyed a few more than a couple beers during the evening, as well. Anyway, when the alarm went off at 5:45, he didn't stir, and as we stepped over him to go over to start breakfast preparations, he still hadn't budged.

As we got closer and closer to the time for serving the guests, and he still wasn't there, I began to prepare the garnish for the plates, simply following what I had watched him do previously. At the same time, I was gritting my teeth over sense of responsibility, duty first, and all the other principles that we've both preached since our kids were small. Instead I should have just gone over and told him to stay in bed, we'd handle things today. But I didn't.

Finally, he came into the kitchen around 8:45, after about six guests had been served, and he didn't say a word. He looked a little hung over and probably wasn't in a very good mood to begin with. He glanced around the kitchen, then gave me a sidelong glower and said, "First you hog the cooking to yourself, and now you've taken over the only thing that I really enjoy doing around here."

You didn't have to be there to predict my response. Though I tried to be calm and express myself in a reasonable manner, I probably didn't sound all that reasonable and he certainly didn't take it that way. Before you know it, we were having at one another hammer and tong, and all the frustrations over the first month in business were coming out. He thought that I was being too autocratic and treating him like a child, and I told him that he needed to take more initiative if he didn't want to be told what to do.

About that time, Joan came back into the kitchen with a panicked look on her face. She had heard us from the dining room and knew this wasn't just a cross word or two. We were having at one another with great gusto. After trying a number of times to talk a little reason into our heads—and eventually being told to shut the hell up, this had nothing to do with her—she went over to the large butcher block table at the far end of the kitchen and put her head down and began to sob. Neither of us paid any attention to her because we were still working hard at getting another zinger in. Finally, I watched as her head slowly lifted from the table, her face terribly contorted in anguish, and she began shouting at the top of her voice, "Stop it, stop it, I can't stand it." And with that she became hysterical.

Dan and I instantly froze and watched incredulously as she began screaming at both of us, as well as the world. Some of what she said was unintelligible and some was sheer frustration over the pressures of not enough cash flow, the unpleasantness of so many guests, the tremendous workload of clean-up and repair that we hadn't anticipated, and on and on. Finally, still screaming at the top of her voice, she got up from the table, seemingly with the intention of going over to The Hovel to try to recover.

Then what to our wondering eyes should appear but the town Health Inspector, coming to make his initial inspection to see if we merited having a food service license. Can you imagine any worse timing? Well, I don't know how she did it, but she managed to change directions in mid flight and headed for the walk-in pantry that was in the opposite direction. Dan busied himself with head down at the computer desk in the opposite corner while I greeted the inspector as if this was the best day of our lives. Max is a very nice guy with a very wry sense of humor, and the first thing of substance that he said to me was something to the effect of, "What makes you think that you're qualified to serve food to the public?" I saw the twinkle in his eye and knew it was a mirthful comment so I responded with something like, "because I've been eating regularly for the past 57 years and I know good food when I see it."

Well that's all Joan needed. Here I was, first destroying family tranquility forever and if that wasn't bad enough, I was going to put us out of business after we had sunk every penny we owned into this place. She very deftly slipped out of the pantry, through the kitchen and out the door into The Hovel. I suspect she probably shed a lot more tears after she got there, but my immediate responsibility was to escort Max wherever he wanted to go. The short story is that Max refused a cup of coffee because he didn't want anyone saying that he was "on the take". He and I exchanged a few more quips and finally he said, "This place looks great. Just keep it that way. See you again next year."

When he was gone, Dan looked at me a little sheepishly and said, "Do you think we'd better check on Mom?" We did, of course, and in a matter of a short time, we were all holding hands and promising never to let that happen again. There were a few tears all around but this time they were tears of relief, not anguish.

As I look back on that incident this evening as I write, I think it was probably good that it happened. It certainly had a cathartic effect on all of us, while giving each of us a chance to get a few things off our chests that had been festering. It's not the best way to handle frustration and pent up anger, but it is an effective way to do so. We all profoundly apologized to one another and though I have a very uncomfortable feeling that it's not the last time that there will be disagreements and angry words, I think we're all committed to avoiding the extreme of today's outburst. None of us wants to go through anything like that again.

Thanks for letting me dump on you. Retelling the incident helps to spotlight the special responsibility that I have to both Joan and Dan and to firm up my resolve to try harder. It also helps to get a little of my guilt out into the open. Don't worry, we're all fine now and the next letter will be a lot more pleasant.

Bless you both,
Dick

And we never did go through that sort of thing again, but to say that there was complete harmony from then on would be stretching the truth considerably. There were certainly those occasions when we didn't see eye to eye on all sorts of issues, but we had all agreed that someone had to make the decisions when we couldn't compromise and there were no further problems with the fact I would be the arbitrator in those situations. The range of decisions was rather broad and might be related to maintenance projects one day, or the advertising plan the next.

One of the enduring difficulties was the conflict between investing in the ambiance of the guestrooms and public areas as opposed to doing maintenance projects that were vital to the structural integrity of the property but weren't necessarily visible or important to the guests. Joan had always enjoyed putting her signature on every place where we had lived in the past, and she had both a wonderful talent and classic taste for doing so. While she probably never even articulated the sentiment to herself, more than likely one of the major attractions of innkeeping to her was the prospect of making the various rooms of the Inn more elegant and decorous. It was not her fondest wish to have to sacrifice or defer some projects that clearly would have made the place more attractive because the front porch steps were unsafe and needed to be replaced. And while she presented the merits of her side of the issue with unquestioned passion and clarity, she was always gracious about accepting the reality of priorities.

The odds were stacked against her as well. Dan had worked summers while he was in college building houses and doing similar structural work, so he was very attuned to the neglected condition of the buildings. He and I essentially joined together during those early days to talk Joan out of most of the decorative projects because we were especially concerned with the state of maintenance of the property. What bothered us most were the chimneys of the main house. They were in bad need of repair and while he and I did virtually all of the routine maintenance—from rebuilding all the porches to doing the routine electrical, plumbing and interior and exterior painting work—these larger projects were beyond our ability. If for no other reason than the fact that we had neither the equipment nor the time to do them. The roof and the five chimneys were to become the albatross that we carried with us for most of the time we owned the Inn, but fortunately they held up sufficiently well until we were able to get to them.

The division of labor and the projects that we enjoyed doing also became a bone of contention, but never anything to rival my usurpation of Dan's preparation of the garnish. While we laugh heartily about those differences of opinion today, muffins, of all things, were also a source of discord. Joan liked the idea of doing the unusual, like making cranberry sour cream walnut muffins, and she wanted to do a different type of exotic muffin every day so that the guests would be surprised and impressed. Dan, on the other hand, had some specialties that he had picked up in his past life. A banana muffin, with or without nuts, was his particular favorite and the guests (and the housekeepers) seemed to agree. I was more inclined toward the old traditionals, like corn, but the other two felt they were too ordinary. So to settle this issue, we took turns making muffins—each to his own.

The ludicrous aspect of this approach hit each one of us gradually and at about the same time. Here we were with the oven on practically all day long, with the temperature in the kitchen usually well in excess of 95°, each taking turns at the bowl and the mixer, each making specialty muffins—one dozen at a time. Valuable time that could have been spent doing many other things was being wasted on making muffins all day and we never could catch up with the demand each morning at breakfast. Usually, with a fairly full house, most of the individually crafted muffins were consumed each morning. But what do you do with one or two leftover cranberry sour cream walnut muffins at the end of the day?

The solution was not easy in coming, but eventually we arrived at it. First we tried buying muffins from the local supermarket (good looking but tasteless) and then buying them from the little bakery in town (good looking and tasty but we could have served steak for less). Throughout our tenure at the Birchwood, we bought the high volume food items from various local wholesale provisioners, so we decided to ask the salesman who took our weekly order for his suggestions.

He had just the thing for us. Next week they delivered a five gallon drum of frozen blueberry muffin mix to our back door. It took about three days to thaw, taking up valuable refrigerator space in the process, but once it thawed, it turned to gooey soup. With the capacity of our ovens, we could make eight dozen at a time and then freeze them, but that certainly limited the variety available to the guests. This week you get blueberry; next week you get bran. Obviously, this, too, was not going to work.

Our solution came from General Mills. We discovered that they produced a large variety of dry muffin mixes for commercial use. Each box made exactly four dozen 3-ounce muffins that could be frozen and thawed each morning for use as needed, coming out of the oven just as if they were fresh. We experimented on our guests to determine their preferences, and eventually resolved to have four types each morning: blueberry, corn, bran and orange-cranberry. Instantly, our days became less hectic. The conflict over when and who would make muffins had disappeared. Now our only challenge arose when one of the guests said, as they frequently did, "Those muffins were delicious. Do you give out your recipes?" We had been liberated. Now we had more time for preparing gourmet picnic suppers!! Oh yes, that was to be another of our great projects.

Cash flow—the balance between income and expenses—is always a serious concern in a start-up business and we were right in there, concerned with the best of them. So prior to even closing on the sale of the Inn—when we were writing the business plan to secure bank funding, to be precise—we had a number of brainstorming sessions to determine how to make some extra income. One of the first ideas that we came up with was to do picnic suppers for the guests to take with them to Tanglewood. One of the wonderful treats of Tanglewood was to sit on the lawn near The Shed, the open-air amphitheater where the Boston Symphony Orchestra played, and enjoy a concert and a picnic supper under the stars. We knew how to prepare picnics and what better way could we ask for to make a few extra dollars. Of course, they'd have to be done right.

To do it right, we needed to begin with some investments. We would need picnic hampers that were worthy of the name and up to the standards of the Birchwood. And the guests would certainly need carriage robes to sit on while they ate, plus quality food containers, glasses and flatware. A dozen sets of each wouldn't be too many if all the guests were to picnic at once (which they never did).

Then, more importantly, we would need a menu. This was not going to be two baloney sandwiches on rye and a Twinkie. This was going to be a special, homemade selection of specialties with a variety of choices that would appeal to any taste as well as those with religious or dietary restrictions. For starters, there would be such selections as gazpacho with shrimp and avocado, cold melon with prosciutto or vichyssoises à la Russe. Then, for the main course, there were sliced meat and cheese platters or cold fried chicken or maybe even a cold vegetable lasagna with a choice of humus, pasta or potato salad or perhaps a mozzarella and tomato salad with basil vinaigrette as an accompaniment. And not to be outdone by the other courses, dessert could be a cappuccino mousse or petit fours with strawberry sauce or a freshly-made fruit cup.

We would even purchase and chill a wine of their choice, at cost, (we were not a full-service hotel so could not have our own liquor or beer and wine license) or we would chill bottles that they had purchased themselves. There was one choice from menu one and one from menu two and what did they want with each, and on and on. The permutations and combinations were seemingly endless and the choices could confuse a waiter in a Chinese restaurant.

So every day, as soon as breakfast was out of the way, we began the preparations for that evening's picnics. The guests needed to order by 10:00 AM, and we had printed up what, to us, were simple order forms. Unfortunately, they weren't. People don't like to read instructions to begin with, and many that do, seem not to understand what they've read. One of us spent at least a half hour every day chasing around looking for guests to clarify their order. But even when the order was correct, there was one absolutely unshakeable axiom. In a group of four people, no two of them would ever order the same thing. There was one gazpacho with fried chicken and potato salad while another had vichyssoise with lasagna and humus. It never failed. And inevitably, there was the guest who came at four in the afternoon to say that she had really meant to order this morning but her boyfriend didn't remind her and couldn't we p-u-h-l-e-a-s-e do just two more picnics?

So here we found ourselves at four in the afternoon each day, cubing blocks of cheese and making up a chip and dip platter for the 5:00 PM wine and cheese serving. And all the while we were preoccupied thinking that we had sixteen picnics—each one distinctly different—that had been ordered for 5:30 and how in the world were going to be able to do both. Somehow we managed and never missed—even though the guests might be an hour late picking up their order because they were enjoying the wine and cheese so much.

The greatest irony of the whole picnic saga was that we never made any money on that venture. The quality of what we made was first class and that took first class ingredients. Amortizing the cost of the hampers and the carriage robes would probably take another five years at the margin that we charged for the picnics. And we were competing with the delis and sandwich shops in the village, so we had to keep those margins low—so low that we never charged for our own labor. We had to be there anyway didn't we?

In our fourth summer, we decided that it was too much work with minimal return, even though we had refined the process considerably. Some of the guests, who had by this time become regular returnees, were outspokenly disappointed. One couple told us that the picnics were the principal reason they stayed with us and they weren't coming back. We missed them but we never missed picnic preparation. Another great liberating move had been made.

*   *   *

August 3, 1991
Dear Chris & Tom,

This will be a real quick note. I forgot to tell you one of the more pleasant tales of our adventures and if I wait any longer, I'll probably forget it completely. (The gerontologists say that it can't be senility quite yet, but I'm beginning to have my doubts.)

About a year ago, I was "elected" by my Naval Academy classmates to chair the 35th homecoming celebration that will be held in Annapolis in October 1992. I actually enjoy a challenge like that so it was more an honor than a burden. I had already completed some of the basic preparations even though the event is still more than a year away. We had set up the various committees, given out some marching orders to each and even booked a major hotel in Annapolis for the weekend.

Then Joan and I bought the Inn. There was no way that I could still run the affair from 500 miles away so I sent a letter of resignation (and an embarrassed apology for not meeting a commitment) to the class president and his executive committee. Much to my surprise, my letter was published in our class column in SHIPMATE, the alumni association magazine. Along with my letter were the class officers' wishes for success and a suggestion to all our classmates that they had a spot to stay if they visited New England. A very nice gesture—and an unexpected plug. And therein lies the tale.

A few weeks back, Richard Adams, one of my classmates, and his wife, Nancy, made reservations to come and celebrate their 34th wedding anniversary, the first classmate to come to the Inn. I was particularly impressed because they came from the Buffalo area, a good five or six hour drive away. On the actual anniversary day, Nancy and Dick (which is what we used to call him when we were kids) invited Dan and me to join them on the front porch for a celebratory glass of champagne. (Joan was in Boston where her favorite uncle had just had a stroke and was in serious condition.)

Anyway, we rather quickly finished the champagne when Dick reached under his chair to a backpack and out came a second bottle. Well the conversation was so lively and interesting that we dispatched the second one in quick fashion as well. Suddenly, Dick got up from his chair, excused himself and headed out to the parking area to his car. My gawd, I thought to myself, he's gone after another bottle, and we'll all be wiped out for the evening. But instead, he came back carrying an oar, of all things, over his shoulder. We had been talking about their boating adventures on Lake Erie minutes before, but I wasn't quite sure what this was all about.

When he came back to the porch, he stood beside his chair, with the oar pointing to the ceiling as if he had just won the Olympic single sculls gold medal, and he made a little speech which went something like this.

"We all know you're one of those 'traitors' who went into the Air Force on graduation day, but we all love you anyway and you still have plenty of Navy blue running through your veins. So on behalf of the class, I'm going to give you a proper Navy retirement. It's said that when a sailor has had enough of the sea, he puts an oar over his shoulder and begins to walk inland. At the first

village that he comes to where someone says to him, 'What is that?' he knows he's gone far enough and that's where he should settle."

With that, he rotated the oar 180° and here, written across the blade was, "What is that?" I was truly touched and can't think of a nicer inn-warming gift. There was no better way for the Adamses, in particular, and the class, by extension, to tell me that the bonds of friendship and those forged by the experiences we shared as young men are far stronger than any rivalry over what color uniform we might have worn after graduation.

Today I mounted the oar over the doorway between the den and the dining room. I'm looking forward to telling the tale over and over when guests ask, "What is that?"

Yours, in blue and gold—and silver,
Dick

The oar stayed over that doorway for seven more years and, much to our amazement, only a handful of guests ever expressed curiosity about it. But it developed a tradition of its own that has lived on. When Nancy and Dick made the presentation, I asked him to sign the reverse side of the oar blade and promised them that the story would be passed on and the signature repeated each time a classmate came to visit. That tradition continued until we had visits from some very close friends from Air Force days. Most were not classmates in the true sense of the term but were, instead, graduates of the Air Force Academy and West Point, or had entered through some other commissioning source. So in the true sense of "jointness" to which the armed forces have all evolved during our years of service, the tradition was properly expanded to include all our military friends.

Today, the oar still hangs in a special place in our home. The reverse side of the blade has since been completely filled with the names of those visitors with whom we proudly served in years past and with whom we share, to this day, the bonds of trust, respect and true friendship that are seldom equaled.

*   *   *

August 8, 1991
Dear Chris & Tom,

Thanks for your call and especially your words of encouragement. Even at our age, a pep talk can be important. I hadn't realized until you spoke that we hadn't given you a detailed description of the Inn and we apologize for that. So, to correct that oversight, here is a quick rundown. I've mixed in a little history of the place as well, since it's also important to see the property in that light.

Our Inn is the only privately owned structure in Lenox that is on the National Register of Historic Places. It's on a hill, about a half mile north of the town center. It's within easy walking distance of restaurants and specialty shops that you usually find in a tourist town like this. And it's less than two miles from the Tanglewood grounds.

The land on which the Inn sits was the first home site deeded by the corporators of the town in 1764. A very large plot was awarded to Israel Dewey who began construction of his home shortly thereafter. While town records are somewhat vague on the progress of construction, the basic core of the building must have been completed by 1767 because the first Lenox Town Meeting was held here in March of that year. At that meeting, the town government that was established is still in operation to this day.

In 1798, the property was purchased by one Zaddock Hubbard. He enlarged the original building somewhat and turned it into a coach stop called the Hubbard Tavern. It remained a tavern until 1816 when the property again became a private home, as it remained for the next 140 years. The Dana family was the most noted of the owners, making it their home from 1885 to 1953. They enlarged and modernized the structure to its present day configuration. In the custom of the day, their home was known as Birchwood, and that name is preserved in the current name of the Inn.

After the Danas sold the mansion, it was converted into a half-way house for mentally disabled World War II veterans and it remained so until 1981 when Paul and Gail Macdonald undertook a massive restoration project and converted the property to an inn. As new owners, they also initiated action to have the Birchwood placed on the National Register of Historic Places, and in conjunction with the town historical commission, they succeeded in having the central village area of Lenox designated a historic district. The Inn opened to the public in 1982 and it has been in continuous operation since then.

Enough for the history. The principal structure on the property is a three-story, wood-frame mansion with ten guest rooms, eight of which have private baths with two other smaller (and cheaper) rooms that share a bath. As I seem to recall telling you some time ago, the very large, elegant library is the centerpiece of the ground floor. The rest of the public area consists of a smaller den/TV room and a bright, comfortable dining room. The remainder of the ground floor houses the serving pantry, the kitchen and, of course, The Hovel.

The second floor contains six guest rooms, three large and comfortable rooms which we have designated as "luxury" rooms, our most expensive, and three "standard" rooms, the mid-priced accommodations, all of which have a private bath. The third floor has four guest rooms, two standard rooms and two "economy" rooms, small but comfortable rooms which share a bath with one another and are, of course, our least expensive accommodations.

A two-story, wood-frame carriage house with two, two-room guest suites, each with private bath, is across the driveway from the kitchen. The property totals two acres and is beautifully landscaped with traditional New England stone fences, attractive formal flower gardens, and shrubs and trees which show off the home to its best advantage during each of the four seasons.

Well there you have it. Sorry I was so lax in not sending you this information before, but there are times these days when I wonder if my head is on straight. Joan sends her love.

All the best,
Dick

The carriage house was to remain an enigma for most of the time that we owned the property. The Macdonalds apparently viewed the building differently than they did the mansion itself. The main building was set up for guests who might stay for one or a few nights but the carriage house was designed and appointed with longer stays in mind. Each unit was a suite with kitchen facilities and the furnishings (range, refrigerator, microwave, etc.) that would permit the guests to prepare all their meals if that were their choice. A stay of a week or even a month could easily be accommodated in either suite. And in many respects, one of the suites could also serve as preferable innkeepers quarters.

For the three years that the interim owners (between the Macdonalds and us) owned the place, it was likely occupied as a long term rental most of the time. Unfortunately, that long term occupancy must have been by rather unkempt people because the suites, particularly the one on the ground floor, were in deplorable condition and looked like they hadn't been cleaned for years.

The cleaning team which we had hired during our first month at the Inn finished their work on the 8,200 square foot mansion in a couple of days. They spent almost an equal amount of time trying to bring back the two 300 square foot suites to a condition that we found acceptable for guests.

Joan also worked her magic on the two suites, buying a few decorative pieces of furniture to dress them up and making dry-flower arrangements and wall hangings that put a fresh new look into the rooms.

But from our experience with the first guests who stayed there, either we (and the cleaning crew) had failed miserably, or these guests had very different standards than ours.

*   *   *

August 15, 1991
Dear Chris & Tom,

We just had another shark attack. A young couple, probably in their late twenties or early thirties, reserved one of the suites in the carriage house and their brief stay was a combination of theatrical wizardry and Machiavellian intrigue.

They arrived late last Friday afternoon, and seemed like rather nice, friendly people. Generally, when guests arrive, we have them sign the registration card, give them a quick tour of the public areas, tell them about breakfast and afternoon wine and cheese, and then we give them any information they need to know about their particular accommodations. All went well and they had arrived in time to unload their car and still get over to the front porch for a quick snack and a glass of wine. I guess they went to the concert that evening, and when they came to breakfast the following morning, everything still seemed perfectly normal.

About two o'clock on Saturday afternoon, we noticed that they had returned to the carriage house and shortly thereafter, the young man came over to the Dutch door and politely rang the bell. I went to see what he needed and in a rather matter of fact way, he said that they were sorry, but they had decided to leave. I told him that I was sorry too. But because they had booked for Friday, Saturday and Sunday and we had turned many others away after committing the rooms to them, I was going to have to charge them for the three nights. Our policy was quite clearly written in our brochure, which they had received in the mail, as well as literature that was at the front desk.

You could see anger rising in him when I told him that, and he puffed up like a bullfrog. With his voice raised to about double the decibel count, he claimed, "By God, I won't pay you a cent for the next two nights and, in fact, I want my money back for last night because that place is a pig sty. It's an insult to keep pigs there, let alone paying guests."

I'm not easily shaken in a situation like that, and we had been well aware that the suites weren't all that we wanted them to be. But his was a ludicrous assertion and I could feel my anger rising at the continuing insults. I managed to hang on, however, and said that I would wait until Monday to process the charge against them, and if we happened to rent the rooms in the meantime, there would be no charge for Sunday. With that, he literally spat on the floor, turned on his heels and went back to the carriage house.

We thought for a while that they had thought better of the situation but after a half hour or so, he began to move their luggage out to the car. About that same time, I saw the young woman headed for the mansion and expected that she was coming to check out. Instead, she was coming to the Dutch door with fire in her eyes. As she and I met there, she started screaming at the top of her voice, beginning with something sweet like, "You goddam sonofabitch, who the hell do you think you are?" And then she went on and on in the same manner, with even saltier language, moving from side to side in the limited space where she was, and waving her arms frantically.

Her movements were not randomly made but instead, as I was to discover, they had a very definite purpose. A short while later, I glanced beyond her and saw her husband dart by the end of the little alcove toward the front desk. Seconds later, he flew by in the opposite direction while she continued screaming like a harridan. Moments after that, I heard a car horn sound outside the entrance door. The lady, and I use the term with intended sarcasm, stopped her harangue instantly, turned on her heels and fled out the door. I was able to get back into the kitchen just quickly enough to watch them drive out the driveway—laughing gleefully.

It was clearly an act that deserved to be on Broadway, and I began to tell Joan and Dan the details of what had just happened. They had heard her rantings, of course, but missed the by-play of the husband and the timing of her departure. Suddenly, it occurred to me that there must have been a purpose to his sneaking into the main house as he had. I went out to the front desk to see if anything was amiss. The key slot for their room, which should have contained the registration card with his credit card number and signature, was empty. The nice couple from Bronxville, New York, had just executed one of the neatest scams that you can imagine. However, little did they know that we had the credit card number recorded in our log book and we would charge them anyway.

Just about the time that we thought we were beginning to get some decent people as our guests, something like that had to happen. We were still getting the occasional bit of rudeness and a number of the guests were not at all as friendly and nice as Joan had anticipated, but this was the first case of out and out dishonesty that we had encountered. Oh well, as they say, it takes all kinds. But we'd just as soon do without that kind, thank you. Aren't you glad that you're silent partners instead of active ones?

All the best,
Dick

The story of the stolen registration card didn't end there, however, and we were to learn a most valuable lesson from the experience. As promised, we waited until the following Monday. No one came to book the room for either Saturday or Sunday, so we went ahead and processed the charges against the scam artists. Perhaps we might have forgiven the charge, knowing that the suites still weren't quite up to the standards that we wanted, and, giving them the benefit of the doubt, they actually might have been dissatisfied with the accommodations. However, after they pulled the act that they did, we were ready to exact our pound of flesh.

Although the credit card processed properly—at least it apparently wasn't stolen—about a month later we received a "chargeback" inquiry from our credit card processing company. These inquiries are evidently fairly common for any business that takes credit cards, but it was the first one we had seen. The inquiry stated the reason why the charge was being challenged and gave us four working days to respond. We would have to prove that the charge was valid or they would dun our bank account for the total amount that we had charged to the scammer's account, or about $450 in this case. The rationale that had been given by the cardholder was that they had never even been to Lenox, let alone stayed at the Birchwood Inn. In other words, they were saying to us, "Prove that we were there or we're going to get our money back."

First, I wrote a long letter to the credit card company explaining what had happened, but I wasn't satisfied that the letter would be adequate to fully illustrate the dastardliness of their deeds. So I called the arbitrator at their credit card company directly. After a conversation lasting nearly half an hour it quickly became clear that we had been had. Since we had no signature on the registration card or any other positive proof that they ever came within 50 miles of our Inn, we were up the proverbial creek. The card holder is always given the benefit of the doubt in a case where "big business" appears to be taking advantage of him or her.

The woman to whom I spoke at the Visa headquarters actually believed my story but she was sorry that, without proof to the contrary, she and her colleagues were obliged to deny such charges. She told me that she would flag their account to safeguard against a series of these scams, but the couple probably had about fifty credit cards and used each one only once. She made a number of suggestions to prevent a recurrence, such as enclosing the front desk and keeping it locked when none of us was present. She also warned that the way we were taking advance deposits was subject to the same sort of fraud and advised that we get a written signature from the card holder authorizing the charge. But this was not our idea of the way we wanted to do business, naive as it might be, and we never did change our procedures appreciably to guard against fraud—although we did take some extra precautions when situations seemed to warrant.

We were only stung one more time in the ensuing seven years, but the second was not nearly so blatant as the first. In about our fourth year, a very handsome young shark was clearly out to impress the girl of the hour—a ravishing beauty herself—and they spent an entire winter weekend cozied up in one of our most luxurious fireplace rooms. He paid his bill on checkout when, halfway out the door, he turned and asked me to reserve that same room for the following weekend. I asked him if he was sure that he'd be back, because I was going to take our usual one-night advance deposit. He said, "No sweat, go ahead and charge it."

But then he failed to show the following weekend. Perhaps the ravishing beauty found a better deal, but a month later here was another chargeback. Our friend had probably decided that it was bad enough to get jilted at the last minute, let alone to have to shell out $150 as an added insult to his injury. He told the credit card company that he had, indeed, been to the Birchwood one weekend but never said he was coming back. To cinch the deal, he accused us of fraudulently using his credit card to initiate a charge, saying that we probably thought that he wouldn't notice. I was disappointed that he lied to get his money back, and besides I should have known better by then. But I was never quite as disgusted by his actions as we were by the super sharks from Bronxville. In fact, we wonder to this day how many free weekends this handsome young couple had managed to bilk out of trusting but ingenuous business owners like us.

All in all, we consider ourselves to be quite lucky over the years with regard to fraud and chargebacks. We had only six chargebacks in the eight years that we owned the Inn, including these two most infamous examples, and for three of these, the credit card companies upheld the charges. Other inns seemed to have many more than we did, and when American Express tried to sell us chargeback insurance—isn't that a slick little money maker?—they told us that we should anticipate at least one per month at the volume of business we were doing. Perhaps we were lucky, but I always thought that I'd rather be lucky than smart any day.

*   *   *

August 21, 1991
Dear Chris & Tom,

Today was a rather slow day—only a few guests in the Inn, which is OK for weekdays, I guess, but we'd prefer to be full every day for obvious reasons. Empty rooms don't make money. About mid-afternoon, a situation arose that was a bit unnerving but something that we are likely to run into over and over as we continue in this business.

A young girl, in her early to mid teens came to the entrance and rang the door bell. When I went to answer her ring, she appeared very shy and a bit uncomfortable, so I tried to be warm and friendly and I invited her to come in. We quickly got to the point of her being there, and as we talked she seemed to gain more poise and confidence. She said that she had been attending the Belvoir Terrace School of the Dance for Young Ladies. The school is a summer program held at one of the more beautiful 19th century "cottages"—a magnificent old Tudor style mansion built by the Vanderbilt family, I believe, that was a few hundred yards to the west of us. For years, the school taught grace and refinement to young ladies at just the time in their lives that they are most receptive to such training. You might call it a form of a finishing school, at least in terms of its goals for the youngsters.

She said that her father was coming to pick her up at the end of the school term and she wanted to reserve a room for him that weekend. I told her of our accommodation offerings and asked if she knew what sort of price range he might have in mind. Her answer was quick in coming. "The very best you have," she said, which came as no surprise since the girls who attend the Belvoir Terrace programs all seem to come from affluent families.

It happened that all of our luxury rooms were open today, so I asked her if she would like to look at them and make a choice herself. After seeing all of them, she appeared to be in a quandary between rooms 1 and 4. Both rooms are very large, each about 750 square feet, with fireplaces and full private baths, of course. But the similarity ends there. Back in the days when the Dana family owned the mansion, room 1 belonged to the successive series of mistresses of the house. Each spouse occupied room 4—a strange Victorian custom to us today, but apparently the way things were done back then.

Whether by accident or design, the decor of the rooms is quite faithful to their historic antecedents. Room 1 is rather dainty and frilly with a queen canopy bed, flowery wall covering and a silk chaise, among other furnishings, in which you could easily visualize the Mrs. Dana of the day taking her afternoon rest before tea time. The fireplace is graced by an intricately carved mantel, on which Joan has placed delicate figurines and other articles that fully complement the appearance. There is an oriental carpet in front of the fireplace, but like the rest of the room, its colors and design are soft and gentle, rather than bold. Today, we'd probably call it a Laura Ashley style of ambiance.

Room 4, by contrast, is a man's room, without any question of a doubt. The furnishings are all oriental chests, dressers and trunks, most of which, we understand, had been made in and imported directly from the Far East—a historic acknowledgment of the China trade which the New England clipper ships had plied during the last century. The huge king-sized bed would have dominated a smaller room but it fits in perfectly. Joan has added a number of Japanese silk screens above the mantel and on the other walls, all of which are bold in both color and design. The wallpaper and the oriental carpets by the bed and in front of the fireplace have the rich colors and patterns that you would expect in a man's room. With the only departure from the 19th century theme for the house, this room is the sole guest room in which there is a television set. Where else but in the man's room, and of course there is an overstuffed loveseat and arm chair in front of it.

As I watched the young lady wrestle with the dilemma of which room to choose, I thought I'd give her a little help with her decision making. So I suggested that if her Dad were coming alone, room 4 would more than likely be the place that he'd want. I certainly would prefer that room. But, I went on, if your Mom is going to come with him, I'm sure that he'd be a good sport and settle on room 1 in deference to her.

She stared at the floor for just a few moments, but then took a deep breath and looked up, but not directly at me. In a firm and confident voice, she said, "It's not that way at all. He'll be bringing his boyfriend. Will you have a problem with that?" And, as she glanced to see my reaction, a few tears began to run down her cheeks.

I had all I could do to stop myself from putting my arms around her to try to make her tears go away. She was clearly embarrassed by the admission and, though she evidently had a deep love for her father, she simply couldn't seem to understand what was going on in his life. And I wasn't about to make it any more difficult for her. So I told her that it wouldn't be a problem at all and asked her to come downstairs and have a glass of lemonade while she thought it over. She did, and she eventually chose room 1.

As the child later walked out the door, it seemed that a great burden had been removed from her shoulders. Gratitude was evident in her eyes; she thanked me warmly and, with a graceful spring in her step, she headed back toward Belvoir Terrace. My heart went with her. It's a sure bet that the School of the Dance is fully succeeding in developing poise and grace in young ladies if she is any example.

After over 35 years of military life, here was a situation that I had never confronted before. But it's time for me and for us to get used to it. It's a different world out here and time to learn to live with it. Wish me luck.

Your (more liberal than he used to be) friend,
Dick

We did, of course, "get used to it" and never encountered a single problem with guests of either gender though their preferences might have been different than mine. Long before it was an official policy of the Department of Defense, we adopted a "don't ask, don't tell" approach of our own and it worked very well for us. As long as any guest, regardless of race, creed or any other social or personal distinction of their own choice didn't disrupt the harmony of our home and business, we were not about to disrupt the enjoyment of their stay. But that doesn't say that we never experienced any disruptions.

Dan had to face up to one of the more difficult situations and he had to face it alone, without any backup so to speak. And he did so brilliantly.

A man from Boston had made reservations for four rooms for the grand finale weekend of the Symphony season. He was serving as the organizer for three other couples who were coming to the Inn from all over the northeast, one from as far away as Washington, DC. He had wanted luxury rooms for each couple but some were booked when he called and he had to take whatever was available—two luxury rooms and two of our standard rooms. While these were rooms with queen or king beds and private baths, the rooms were discernibly smaller than the luxury rooms and were not quite as exquisite in decor.

But room 2 was a clear anomaly. It was probably the most elegantly decorated of all our standard rooms and, in fact, it was so lovely, we intentionally pictured it on our glossy color brochure, along with a couple of the luxury rooms. It also had a large private bath, but here's where the hooker came in. When the Inn was restored in 1981, there was only one bath on each floor and the private, attached baths had to be created out of anterooms and other adjacent spaces. All, that is, except for room 2. Here, directly across the hall, was the original bath for the second floor, a very spacious tiled room with a large antique pedestal sink and other fixtures that were in perfect working order but were nonetheless antiques.

There was absolutely no way to join the bath to the room, so it became our only room with a "detached private bath". It was clear from what the Macdonalds had told us that some people had no problem with the arrangement whatsoever, especially since we provided plush terry robes for the guests to wear on their six-foot sprint across the corridor. But others would rather go elsewhere if those were the only accommodations available. So we invariably described the bath situation clearly and in detail any time that room was booked in advance on the telephone. On rare occasions, some people didn't hear or didn't grasp the situation before they came and were surprised by it when they arrived. But they were infrequently upset once they saw the room. The man from Boston was one who didn't grasp the situation in advance and was extremely upset when he became aware of the situation on arrival, even after seeing the room.

In retrospect, it is easy to understand his anger when he discovered the detached private bath, even though we were all certain that he had been informed in advance. His pride had been hurt and his reputation was in jeopardy. Here he was, the representative who was responsible for the reservations for the whole group, and he was going to have to put someone in that room. All were professionals, either physicians or lawyers. We were to learn later that they were college classmates and close friends about 30 years previously and they were probably accustomed to going first class every time they met together for an annual reunion. So our advance man was loud and voluble with Dan when he arrived.

And it was not but a few minutes later that the others began to drift in. The man made a number of trips up and down stairs to the room, and each time he had angrier and more profane words for Dan over what "we had done to them." His wife stood by with a look of embarrassment, but probably knew better than to interject her comments at a time like that. And he was trying very hard to put on a good show for his arriving friends.

Finally Dan asked if he could interrupt the tirade briefly, and with a forced smile on his face (an example of good Sheraton training) and a steady voice, he said, "Tell you what! You give me your credit card and I'll refund your deposit right now so you can go elsewhere and get other rooms. You're upset and you're making me upset and there's no way that we should all spend a three day weekend being upset with each other".

The whole group looked at him stunned and our advance man replied angrily, "That's ridiculous! You know damned well there isn't a place within 25 miles of here that has any vacancies."

"Well, there is another choice, you know," said Dan, "You could all go back outside and come in again as if this never happened. Then put a smile on your faces and make up your minds that you're going to make the best of the circumstances and have a wonderful weekend."

They all looked at one another and began to laugh. "You know, the guy's right. Let's just forget about it and start over." With that, they flipped a coin to see who would get which rooms—the advance planner took room 2, voluntarily—and they headed off to their rooms.

After Joan and I had returned from the errands that we were doing and had just enough time to hear what had transpired from Dan, one of the men came to the Dutch door and sheepishly asked for a bucket of ice. All eight of them were going to have early cocktails in the library. When I gave him the ice, he said, "Oh, would you please tell Dan that we'd like him to join us for a drink. He's a helluva nice young man and he's got a damned good head on his shoulders."

Of course, Dan did, and in true fairy tale fashion, they had an uproariously good time for the remainder of the weekend. Not only that, they all came back as a group for the next five years on that same weekend, and even though they made their reservations much farther in advance in the ensuing years, each year when they arrived, we joked about who was going to stay in room 2. They finally stopped coming as a group when, according to one of the couples, "there were too many divorces and the new wives didn't fit in."

*   *   *

September 2, 1991
Dear Chris & Tom,

Today is Labor Day, the first real milestone that we've reached in our innkeeping careers. It's the end of the Tanglewood Festival, which actually matters not a whit to any of us other than the fact that we began our first break in the action today. The Jazz Weekend closed out the music season here at Tanglewood. Many of the other cultural attractions in the area closed down this weekend, as well. The children go back to school tomorrow, and we don't have any guests for the rest of the week.

Never thought I'd say it, but we don't want any guests right now. After having a full house or, at least, many guests in the Inn, every single day for 66 consecutive days, we're ready for a break. Even though it's a short one. We'll be half booked this coming weekend, about two-thirds filled for the following two weekends, and then it all starts again at the end of the month when the foliage season begins—or, as they say here, when the "leaf peepers" come to town.

But today was a day of rejoicing. We could even go sit in our library if we wanted to. We were alone in the Inn.

We aren't the only ones who felt relieved, however. This is apparently a day of celebration for all the innkeepers in town. And we were invited to an afternoon "return to normal" party at one of the other inns. The innkeepers, Mary and Frank Newton, have hosted this little affair for a number of years, and it has almost become a tradition. Since we're the newcomers in town, we felt quite honored being invited, and it gave us an opportunity to meet many of our new colleagues in the business. That's right, our noses have been so solidly pressed to the proverbial grindstone, we had met only a very few of the other innkeepers and that was just a hello in passing.

The backgrounds of the innkeepers who were there were fascinating. Lynn and Mario Mekinder came from Toronto where he had owned a very successful engineering and construction firm. That background certainly puts him in good shape for any modifications or additions that he wants to do on his property. Joy and Scotty Farrelly are much like us, professional vagabonds who have lived over much of Europe and North America. He retired as a senior executive with Ralston-Purina Co. and I think we're going to find them to be close friends. We certainly have the most in common with them.

We also have artists in our midst. Peggy and Dick Houdek both came from San Francisco where he was an executive with the San Francisco Opera and she was an operatic soprano, still blessed with a lovely voice, we understand. Aurora and Greg Smith are both fairly renowned painters and they own and operate one of the few full-service inns in town (i.e., with a restaurant that serves three meals per day). Barbara Kolodkin, our realtor, was there with her husband, Milton, both of whom are retired teachers in the local schools. They were former summer season innkeepers—a logical enterprise for teachers—and still rent out a couple of rooms in their home for Tanglewood visitors. Interestingly, they were the only natives of the Berkshires that were there. The host and hostess both retired from the banking business in New York City, so they probably don't even notice the sharks.

It was wonderful to share our relief with others who had been through a similar experience for the past couple of months, and of course, everyone seemed very interested in how "the new guys" fared through their first summer. We were the center stage attraction for a while, telling of our good and bad experiences, many of which I've passed on to you. The lady who came into The Hovel only to find that it was a "one-holer" got the biggest laughs. It seems that all have had experiences over the years that repeat themselves in different forms with other innkeepers, but my experience was a new one on all of them. And, as you might expect, that got the stories started.

As good an artist or innkeeper as Aurora Smith might be, she still missed her calling, in my opinion. She is the funniest woman I've ever met and I had stomach pains laughing at her stories. It seems that many of the annual attendees at Tanglewood are highly observant Orthodox Jews. Because of their restrictions on riding in cars and similar activities on Shabat, they stay at the Smith's inn so that they can walk directly across the street to the Tanglewood main entrance. The events that she related were probably not even funny as she actually experienced them, but they certainly were hilarious in the telling. I'm not sure if you remember a comedian named Myron Cohen who used to appear regularly on the Ed Sullivan Show when we were young, but Aurora reminded me of him. She told all the stories in dialect, like Cohen used to, and they were every bit as funny. I won't even attempt to relate any of them because most of the humor was in the way she told them. She was marvelous.

Toward the end of the afternoon, the conversation shifted to the subject of the Lenox Chamber of Commerce. It's a very small organization that appears to exist primarily as a referral service for the inns during the summer. They have an office in one of the old historic buildings in town and when visitors arrive in town, they usually end up there if they're looking for a place to stay. The Chamber also runs a telephone referral service and a lot of volunteers keep track of the inns that have vacancies and provide those who want to make advance reservations with the phone numbers of those inns. Both systems were a godsend to us this past summer. We probably received half of our bookings through the Chamber and it unquestionably saved our tails.

Frank Newton has been the Chamber president for the past three years and I guess the bylaws prohibit him from serving any longer—a local version of term limits—so the subject of a new president came up. Frank took a bit of a straw poll around the patio and it was like a game of hide-and-seek. Everyone that he pointed to had the same reaction, "Not me!"

Then Barbara Kolodkin said, "You know, we have a general in our midst now. He's commanded thousands of men. He certainly should be able to run our little Chamber." After some discussion pro and con among everyone there, I finally agreed that I would "think about it". I have about a month to make up my mind. I'll probably do it because we've always volunteered in every community in which we've lived. But I have an uncomfortable feeling that it's not such a good deal, especially with all the others avoiding it like the plague. We'll see.

Well it's been some day. We've made it through the summer, relatively unscathed. We've made wholesale improvements to the Inn and still managed to keep most of the guests satisfied. Many have told us that they'll be back and they were all the type that we want to have back. Give us a few days to catch our collective breath and then bring on the leaf peepers. We'll be ready.

Tired but pleased and unbowed,
Dick

To our surprise, we were to find out later that there were only a relative handful of the Lenox innkeepers at the Newton's celebration. This was our first introduction to the social life of the innkeeper community and it resulted in the discovery that the "competition" was a lot more expansive than we realized with our noses stuck to the grindstone. In all, there are 27 lodging establishments in Lenox, fifteen of which are country inns, which are actually bed and breakfast inns within the trade terminology. Like ours, country inns are full-time commercial businesses, ranging in size from about six to twenty-five rooms, most of which are open year round or just closed briefly in the off-season so that the innkeepers can take some vacation time.

The big brothers, the full service inns, are those which are essentially hotels with a 24-hour staff on duty. They have one or more restaurants that serve a minimum of three meals per day, and they offer other amenities such as spa facilities, entertainment, cocktail lounges or some combination of those features. There are six full service inns in Lenox, the most famous of which (and, arguably, throughout the world) is Canyon Ranch of the Berkshires. It is a very exclusive spa that caters to the rich and famous, and a spot that is rated annually by the *Conde Nast Traveler* magazine in the top two or three of its type in the nation—usually # 1 or # 2. Over the years, the Birchwood was to benefit greatly from Canyon Ranch's location in Lenox. Their marketing staff makes annual surveys of all the country inns in town to select those to whom they would refer their overflow guests. We were always at the top of their list and were fortunate to get a great deal of business from their referrals.

A couple of the full service inns are hybrids, if you will: smaller inns that also have a restaurant. Our introductory course on innkeeping referred to these places as "restaurants that rented rooms as a sideline" but I'm not certain that such a pejorative reference is deserved. As we were to learn later, trying to do both with limited staff is terribly hard work that drains the starch out of you.

A third category of Lenox lodging establishment is the ubiquitous motel, such as a Howard Johnson or Best Western. There are about a half dozen of them located on the main north-south roadway that bypasses the quaint downtown area known as Lenox Village. Many potential guests prefer the privacy of a motel room to the more social environment of a country inn and, as a result, the motels also have good summer occupancy rates plus a lot of business trade during the off-season.

Not included in the 27 commercial establishments—and the principal reason for the use of the term country inn rather than B&B in Lenox—is the unique local phenomenon known as the "home stay". These establishments are more in keeping with the traditional definition of the B&B, particularly as they are known in Europe. The crowds that come to Tanglewood in the summer are so great that there simply isn't adequate room in the commercial properties of the town to house everyone overnight. As a result, the town fathers saw fit, years ago, to permit homeowners to rent out rooms in private family homes to accommodate the overflow.

Despite the numbers that flock to Lenox each summer, a sense of competition was clearly not evident to us in those early days and certainly not in the ample camaraderie that we experienced at the Newton's party.

Without question, that first summer would have been far more difficult for us if it hadn't been for the generous referrals that we received from the other innkeepers, and we were most grateful for them. It appeared to us that this was one big happy community with friendliness and willing assistance the norm. Unfortunately, our initial perception of cooperation versus competition and the warmth that we experienced was not, in actuality, all that accurate.

In fact, little cliques were more prevalent than we first realized, and while there were those who chose to associate with one another rather exclusively, we choose not to isolate ourselves socially from any group.

Our first realization of the cliques can probably be traced to the arrival in town of two very nice people who bought a somewhat run down old home in the center of the village and restored it into a country inn. The couple had come from Washington, DC, where John Felton had been a journalist for National Public Radio and his wife, Marty Gottran, was a professional book editor for technical publications.

The "fix-'er-up" that they bought was an old home that had formerly been licensed as an inn but was operated more as a home stay at the time of their purchase. They went about the purchase and restoration of their new property "by the book" with respect to zoning laws, building codes, permits and the like. Unfortunately, their honesty and integrity drove a deep wedge into the innkeeper community that lasted for years.

They invested a great deal of time and money in restoring the old home and decorating it in a very comfortable, homey decor. When it was completed and ready to open for business, they were justifiably proud of their accomplishments and invited a large segment of the business community to see the results of their efforts. Instead of experiencing the warm and cordial welcome from the established inn owners that we had received, their hospitality was turned against them for the most unjust and preposterous of reasons.

Marty and John had decided to follow the contemporary style of many other innkeepers and name their guest rooms rather than number them. Using the annual Tanglewood Festival as an inspiration, they christened their inn "Amadeus House" and named their rooms after some of the most popular of the 18th and 19th century classical composers.

Unfortunately, one of established inn owners took that as a personal affront because, for many years, his rooms had been named after classical composers and these upstart newcomers were guilty of "the worst sort of commercial espionage and blatant plagiarism". Thus began an extremely childish game of public sarcasm and innuendo by this fellow that bordered on character defamation. Joan and I made our opinions known but we chose to try to be cordial with everyone and, hopefully, enemies of none.

But this was not the only hornet's nest that Marty and John found themselves in. There had been a long-standing dilemma in Lenox over the proper fire and safety codes that should be imposed on the owners of the country inns. The standards to which the large hotels were held throughout the state would not only be unreasonable for a small country inn, but the expense of making modifications and retrofits would probably put most of the inns out of business. And the town officials realized and appreciated this. But they were also fearful of possible liability should there be a disaster with no commercial fire and safety code in force—despite the knowledge that most inn owners lived on their own properties and were as reluctant as anyone to become crispy critters.

When Marty and John went to the Town Inspector of Buildings to get their permits for the restoration, they ran headlong into a whole host of requirements and expenses that they hadn't anticipated. The building inspector had decided to use their restoration as an opportunity to establish an *ad hoc* fire and safety code, mostly as a compromise between the existing situation and the more stringent hotel code. His decision was to have ramifications for the entire innkeeper community. And Marty and John had no choice but to comply if they wanted to open their inn.

But others in the town didn't see it that way. According one or two of the owners of established inns, there never would have been a problem if Marty and John hadn't been so stupid as to raise the issue in the first place. If they hadn't gone by the book, they contended, the whole town would have been saved from the arbitrariness of the building inspector. And unfortunately, too many people were convinced of the reasonableness of these rantings, further widening the gulf that was growing in that spirit of cooperation that we had initially perceived.

As we became more involved in activities outside our little world of the Birchwood, the more we became aware that conditions and circumstances in the community were hardly as idyllic as we originally thought. But we had lived in communities like this before. Perhaps we could do our part to heal the wounds and restore the feeling of amity within the business community and between the business community and the town government.

*   *   *

Part II

Getting Established

The past two and a half months had probably been one of the most challenging times of our married life. Even the time that I left the family for a year in Vietnam seemed less difficult by comparison. Despite the danger and the lengthy separation, we probably took that period in our marriage in stride because it was an integral part of my chosen career and the whole family expected that there would be times like that. Besides, I was the product of the best military training program in the world and had every confidence that I knew what I was doing. Survival was not really an issue at the forefront of my mind.

By contrast, the Inn was an entirely new experience for us, one for which we were not terribly well prepared. In the process of deciding to buy the Inn, we had convinced ourselves that we had enough experience because of the extensive entertaining that we had done, particularly in the overseas commands that I held in the latter part of my career. But that was pleasure, for the most part, and this was a business that we had staked our life savings on—plus a chunk of the savings of a few others. We had sole control over our bottom line, as well as our destinies. It was that new type of pressure that made this venture so different and considerably more difficult.

But our eventual survival through that first summer was also a source of considerable pride. In retrospect, we couldn't have picked a worse time to begin the venture than the first official weekend of the high season. A little time to get settled and get oriented both to the business and the area would have been much wiser, but that never really had been an option. From the time that we made the decision to buy the Inn to the time that we closed on the property just took too much time. And Lenox was clearly the right place for us to be, so it was either then or never.

And by golly, we had done it. We had met the most difficult challenge that we could possibly have faced—learning our new trade while the Inn was filled to capacity—and despite a number of false starts, small errors in judgment and some revised views of the innkeeping profession, we had come through quite well. And now we were ready to get our second wind and press on.

September 9, 1991
Dear Chris & Tom,

The past week has been a comparative breeze. We never thought that putting in a week of "normal" work could be so relatively relaxing. We had no one in the Inn Monday through Thursday and then over the past weekend, we had only four rooms. It's bad for cash flow but we needed the break.

The interesting part, to us, was that Dan and I spent each day painting, doing minor repairs and yard work outside, while Joan and Paula made a lot of minor changes to the rooms and public areas that had previously been put on hold. Each day was a good solid eight hours of work for all of us but the big difference was that there were no interruptions, no one to take care of or keep happy. As Dan so succinctly put it at dinner last night, "This innkeeping business wouldn't be half bad if it weren't for the guests."

We had a neighbor drop by to say hello this week as well. She is a lovely lady who lives just down the street and she told us that she intentionally delayed stopping by to welcome us because she knew we would be overburdened with work but thought this past week might be a good time to come over. Very thoughtful.

We had a very nice chat with her, took her on a brief tour of the Inn (she had always been curious) and then we all had a cup of tea. As she was leaving, she smiled and asked, "Have you felt welcomed to Lenox?" We were a bit surprised by the question but answered truthfully that we had been so busy we hadn't even given it a moment's consideration. With a wistful smile, she responded, "Well, I hope you will be, but I've lived here for forty-one years and I still don't feel welcome."

This lovely lady's parting comment brought us both up rather sharply. We haven't been privy to any of the local gossip, but perhaps she has experienced a lot of pain and bad memories during her life in Lenox. But it seems strange that it would sour her on the town itself, especially since she seemed so sweet and gracious. Perhaps it's a warning sign. We'll know in time, I guess.

And speaking of gossip, we had another visitor during the past week who is also worthy of note. Among the chores that we were doing, we decided that this might be a good time to get the heating system tuned up. Winter comes early in this part of the country. Blizzards (or nor'easters as they call them here) are not uncommon in late October, so it's best to get ready before we get surprised. While puttering around with the things we could routinely do, we discovered a leaky pipe behind the boiler.

I have never lived in a home with an enclosed, circulated hot water heating system before, so there was no way that I was going to risk accidentally draining the entire system throughout the house. And besides, although the furnace was new and relatively simple, the associated piping and electrical wiring looked like a nightmare. Instead, I decided to call in the plumbing and heating experts who, as Paul Macdonald had told us, had installed the system. So my call for help went out to the MacLean Brothers. As we were to learn later, these were two brothers who were getting on in years but were still considered the best around.

The following day, one of them (either Finlay or Donal, but he never said so I don't know for sure) walked in the back porch entrance to the kitchen. Joan was sitting at what has now become her "command post", the large butcher-block table of recent hysteria memory, doing some of her advance planning work. Mr. MacLean nodded her way with a very diffident, "Missus," and continued through the kitchen to the basement entrance, right off the butler's pantry. He didn't even break stride as he went down the stairs, through the considerable length of the basement and into the furnace room. He knew where the light switches were every step of the way (something that I'm still not completely sure of) and he obviously was completely familiar with the layout. I must have done a decent job of explaining the problem to him because, like Clement Moore's Saint Nicholas, he spoke not a word but went straight to his work.

I certainly trusted him alone in my basement and I hope he didn't think otherwise, but I stood watching him as he proceeded. Who knows, if I watch closely enough, I might be able to take care of similar problems myself in the future. He opened and closed a number of valves, too many and too fast for me to keep track, and then started to wrench open the leaky joint. After many minutes of silence, I heard his second utterance of the day, in a distinctive Yankee accent that I might have expected more if we were in Boston or Maine.

"S'pose you know all about the Dana family, eh?" he began.

"Well, actually, I know very little about them other than the years that they called this place their home," I replied, fully expecting that I was about to hear of the Danas for at least the last seventy or so years they had lived here. But not a sound from Mr. MacLean.

After he had removed the pipe joint and had cleaned off the accumulated rust and inspected it for corrosion, he continued as if there had been no break in the conversation. "Lotta skeletons in these old closets," he said, and then, after a very long pause, "but you ahn't goin' ta heah about them from me." he concluded.

He seemed satisfied that the joint and everything else was in good shape, properly reinstalled it using some plumber's Teflon tape, and then he repositioned the valves. Tools went back into his bag and, just as he had entered the basement, he briskly retraced his steps, extinguishing the lights as he went.

When we reached the kitchen again, he looked back over his shoulder at me and said, "Don't know what the cost is. We'll send along a bill one of these days." Then as if in an afterthought, he stopped, turned and faced me and said, "Bout the time you've lived heah for a hundred yeahs or so, you'll prob'bly know all about the skeletons." And with another perfunctory nod toward Joan, and a barely audible "Missus," he was out the door and into his truck.

Quite an introduction to the local folks. Should be fascinating to get to know more. But right now, we've got to get ready for leaf peepers.

Hope all is well,
Dick

Over the years, of course, we came to know a great many of the local people, particularly as I became more involved with the Chamber of Commerce and, later on, with many volunteer activities associated with the town government. For the most part, they are a wonderful group of people, solid

Yankees through and through. As I had often joked in years past when asked about growing up in New England, I was nineteen years old before I learned that Irish, Catholic and Democrat are not synonymous terms. One might be tempted to add Liberal to that equation today, but there were enough Yankee conservatives still around to counterbalance the local political philosophies.

To appreciate the people of Lenox and Berkshire County, it's probably necessary to look back on local history briefly. When the area was originally settled in the last third of the eighteenth century, it was primarily agrarian like most of the colonies. Lenox quickly grew to be the farming center of the region and it remained the county seat until the early days of the industrial revolution.

Most likely because of its tranquil beauty and idyllic surroundings, Lenox became a major American center for the literary arts during its next hundred years. It was a gathering place for some of America's most famous authors, particularly the great poets and novelists of the day. Henry Ward Beecher, Nathaniel Hawthorne, Fanny Kemble and Edith Wharton all lived and wrote in Lenox. William Cullen Bryant, Henry Wardsworth Longfellow and Herman Melville also had homes in the surrounding communities. Melville wrote *Moby Dick* at Arrowhead, his farm that lies in the beautiful countryside between Lenox and Pittsfield.

In the late nineteenth century, as industrial wealth made a new affluent class in our nation, the richest of the rich established their oceanfront "cottages" at Newport, RI, and their mountain retreats in Lenox and the surrounding towns. The income tax laws in 1914 spelled the demise of the "cottages" and Lenox went into a gradual decline. That is, until the 1930's when Dr. Serge Koussevitsky brought the Boston Symphony Orchestra to play a summer schedule of concerts in a beautiful pastoral setting overlooking Stockbridge Bowl. The summer concerts, long since known as the Tanglewood Festival, have continued for well over 60 years and they have become more popular each succeeding year. Tanglewood has also spawned the development of dance and dramatic arts theaters and many other cultural venues within the region.

With that brief background, it becomes easier to understand the attitudes and outlook of the people who live in Lenox and the Berkshires, particularly the differences and disagreements that often arise among them. In my rank amateur assessment of the town's demographics, it seems to me that are three distinct groups of people who make up the roughly 5,500 year round residents.

The solid underpinnings of the town are provided by the long-term residents, those who serve in the government, essentially control the future directions that the town takes and also own and operate the basic businesses of the town. In other parts of the country, they might be known as the "good ole boys (and girls)", but the pejorative nature of that term is not deserved here. Not surprisingly, this segment of the population owes its existence to the days of the summer cottages.

They tend largely to be of Irish or Italian heritage since the wealthy families of that era imported the finest stone masons and other building craftsmen from Italy when they were in the process of building their great homes. In like manner, the maids and butlers, the stable hands, chauffeurs and other domestic household servants often were newly immigrated Irish. It is fascinating to talk to some of the senior residents of the town who can still remember their grandparents who had been brought to Lenox for those purposes. They exude a great deal of pride in the heritage that their ancestors brought to the town, and rightly so. And for all their differences in origin, employment and other characteristics, those who can trace back their residency in Lenox two or more generations all share one thing in common: whether they believe it or not, they express a sweeping antipathy for tourists, and, unfortunately, often show that dislike.

As one of Irish heritage, I see a vestige of those early days in the vault that had been built, apparently by the Danas, in the Birchwood's basement. It has two oak doors that open in opposite directions with heavy hasps and enclosed hinges on each so that the room could be securely locked. The room was used to store the "good" china and silver and was allegedly kept under lock and key to protect the valuables from the Irish domestics. Given that this occurred during a period of severe prejudice against the Irish emigrés to New England, the NINA era as it was known (No Irish Need Apply), it is not surprising that the servants were "not to be trusted". However, looking at the qualities of citizenship, industriousness and achievement that their descendants now provide to the town, it appears that the Danas may have worried needlessly.

The second distinctive segment of the Lenox population is made up of the relative newcomers. They tend to be retirees for the most part, more affluent than most, and people who came here from the New York metro area. They originally came to the Berkshires for the cultural offerings in the summers, often with parents or grandparents, later bought second homes and eventually retired from their practices or professions "in the city" to become permanent residents of Lenox. Many are "snow birds", folks who live in Lenox for the six months of late spring, summer and early fall, but move off to Florida, primarily, during the dark days of winter.

Like many people who have the affluence and opportunity to search for an especially pleasant retirement locale, once they have settled there, many want to pull up the drawbridge behind them and exclude others from following the same path that they did. They are almost universally opposed to any growth in the area, and changes or improvements to the infrastructure or the location of new business or industry of any kind to the town are usually obstructed, harassed and fought in the courts. They like the area the way it is and any effort to change it, regardless of merit, is "bad" for the community. Their one exemption might be the introduction of a new cultural attraction to the region—but they hold themselves as the sole judges of what is culturally worthwhile.

The third segment of the population are people like Joan, Dan and me, the newest of the newcomers, who have come to Lenox for all that it offers, and more. Most come with the desire to create or take over a small business and thereby fulfill a personal goal that had always taken a back seat to a former job or profession. They are the dress or souvenir shop owners who used to be secretaries, the restaurant owners and chefs who had formerly been musicians or teachers, or they are the innkeepers who had been bankers, engineers, business executives—and career military officers.

For the most part, they are not terribly sophisticated about business theory or productivity analyses. Many probably never heard of a market survey, let alone performed one before they established their business. They simply knew that crowds of tourists came to Lenox each year and therefore it should be good place to fulfill a dream. And if the business went under after two years, which many do, they had given it a shot and their world wasn't going to come to an end.

They are, in fact, the people who make the tourist industry possible, and in a real sense, sustain the local government. Through the room occupancy taxes on the inns alone, the town treasury is enriched by over $1.25 million each year. This group tends to be the activists, the people who want their own business to succeed and recognize that related businesses must succeed as well to ensure their own survival. How to go about achieving success, however, was always subject to debate, and often rancorous as noted earlier. But with us as the archetypal example, many come and then leave when they either tire of their dream business or have to face up to failure.

As transients, in large part, in an old established town, they are never fully accepted though they aren't outcasts either. A shopkeeper might be able to serve voluntarily on a town committee or similar position, but getting elected to a town office, particularly to an important position like selectman, is out of the question. So these folks tend to stay within their own groups, socialize among themselves and rarely establish close friendships with either the solid citizens or the retired grouches.

If I've painted a picture of a fragmented community which often has difficulty deciding what it wants to be "when it grows up", and debates loudly over how to achieve the few goals that can be agreed upon, then I've painted an accurate picture. Minding your own business and doing your job as you see fit is not going to cut it. There are too many competing goals and objectives for Lenox to be a coherent municipality.

Having lived for most of our adult lives in military communities where common goals were shared and working together toward the same objectives was a way of life, we found the divisiveness and lack of common purpose to be disconcerting and not to our liking. But it was clear that getting involved was a necessary ingredient for survival, and so we did. The experience convinced us that, despite previous inclinations to retire in Lenox when we completed our innkeeping experience, we preferred to live out our years somewhere else. When we came to that conclusion, the occasional daydreams of our future began to take on a distinctive southwestern flavor.

*　　　　　*　　　　　*

September 17, 1991
Dear Chris & Tom,

It appears that a miracle may be at hand and the angel of deliverance is named Jesse Jupiter. Joan and I just returned from a visit to Massachusetts General

Hospital in Boston where we met Dr. Jesse Jupiter, the chairman of the orthopedic department at Harvard Medical School, and one of the most renowned orthopedic surgeons in the world. He has been experimenting for years on a number of radical surgical procedures with prominent surgeons in the Soviet Academy of Medicine and the miracle that he will hopefully perform is to heal Joan's leg, which she broke nearly five years ago.

One of the reasons that I retired when I did was to be able to move to the Washington, DC, area where Joan would receive proper medical care for her leg. As you well know, the facilities available and the specialists that are assigned to Walter Reed Army Hospital, the Naval Medical Center at Bethesda and Malcolm Grow USAF Medical Center are all outstanding. When we went there in 1987, we were in hopes that they could find a solution to the fact that her leg hasn't mended. Despite Herculean efforts, it just hasn't happened.

Her primary surgeon at Malcolm Grow was a young Air Force major, Dr. Frank Bonnerans. He was just a couple years out of his orthopedic residency and he not only had a very impressive set of credentials, the methodical approach that he took to try to bring about a cure for her problem was equally impressive. However, after each try—some of which were eight or more months in duration—Frank was just as frustrated as Joan was when the x-rays showed no healing. It was clearly something that bothered him. And he was most apologetic to Joan over the fact that her pain and difficulty were repeatedly in vain.

Just before we left the DC area to come north—in fact I believe that it was at Joan's last appointment with him—Dr. Bonnerans had just returned from a medical convention of orthopedic surgeons and related specialties. With Joan's prior permission, Frank had presented a paper to the convention that told of the difficulties and frustrations that they had encountered. From what he told us of his days at the convention, he apparently spent most of his time there seeking out every eminent authority in the field and listening to their views of what might be a solution.

He was delighted to learn that we were headed for Massachusetts because the person who had excited him most, and seemed to hold the key to healing her leg, was Jesse Jupiter from Harvard. Frank had taken the liberty of providing Dr. Jupiter with a copy of his paper, discussed the case in greater detail and told his colleague that he would try to convince Joan that she should make an appointment with him for a consultation.

The information that Bonnerans gave us was the brightest ray of hope that we had seen in quite some time, and we called Dr. Jupiter's office as soon as we could see our way clear to leave the Inn and travel to Boston for an appointment. From what we were to discover from the phone call, Jupiter is in such high demand for the most complex cases of this type that it is virtually impossible to see him unless the patient has a referral that undeniably warrants his attention. Apparently, Joan's case fit that category and Frank Bonnerans' paper must have been convincing, as well, because we received a call back the following day, establishing her appointment for this morning.

Massachusetts General Hospital is a bit like Harriet Beecher Stowe's Eliza—it just grew. It's a huge complex of additions and annexes to the main hospital building which have been required over the years to accommodate the many specialists who teach and consult there. Thanks to the excellent directions provided by Dr. Jupiter's staff, we found his office complex rather easily, and were immediately sent elsewhere in the complex to have more x-rays taken. After a delay of an hour or so in a waiting room filled with people who obviously had some serious problems, Joan and I were ushered into a tiny consulting room with little more in it than an examination table and a wall-mounted light for reading x-rays.

When Dr. Jupiter entered the room, he was followed by four of his orthopedic residents, two of whom had to lean in the doorway because the rest of us had already filled the small room. Jupiter introduced himself and then introduced *each of the residents, suggesting that he'd send them away if we had any objection, but making it clear that this was the best way for them to develop their professional skills. Of course, Joan had no objection, particularly after all she'd been through. He then asked Joan to describe the problem as she saw it and in so doing, he gave instant recognition to the fact that he trusted her judgment and intelligence and that she probably knew as much about her case as anyone.*

After a few moments conversation between the two of them, with a few shakes of his head and clucks of his tongue that said he understood what she had endured, he slipped the x-rays on to the light and stood studying them for less than a minute. He immediately turned around to Joan with a very broad smile on his face and said, "I can fix that!" That was it, I can fix that, and both of us became instant believers. There was so much conviction in his voice and so much surety in his demeanor that it was clear that he had no doubts and therefore, there was no reason that we should have any.

He then turned to the residents, gathered them around the x-rays, and explained exactly how he was going to fix her leg, using shorthand terminology and technical references that indicated that they had faced similar challenges. He then turned back to Joan and described briefly what he planned to do, reminding me of a fighter pilot the way he described everything with his hands. Then asked her if she thought she'd like to give it a try. It took only a brief understanding glance between the two of us for her to say she was ready. With that, he told each of the residents to plan to be part of the operating team and told us to return to the administration desk to schedule the operation. He said that it would be painful for the first few days after surgery, but they had an excellent pain management team. She should expect to be in the hospital for one day, on crutches for about six weeks but after that she should be able to walk unaided. And then he was gone.

His operating backlog is huge and the earliest that she can get in is early January. However, after a wait of nearly five years, an additional four months is not going to be a problem, particularly since Joan has limited but fairly good mobility and the pain she experiences remains at a tolerable level.

Riding back from Boston late this afternoon, we both seemed to have no doubt whatsoever that Jesse Jupiter is going to provide the solution for which we've been looking. His confidence is contagious and it certainly caught us up in his spell. Keep your fingers crossed. This may well be it.

Now the only question that needs to be resolved for January and February is who's going to be the head waitress. Maybe, between now and then, Dan and I can teach Joan to carry a tray while using crutches. It's worth a try.

All the best, Dick

Our hopes and confidence in Jesse Jupiter were fully rewarded the following January. He did just exactly what he promised to do and within the exact time frame that he had forecast. By the end of February, when we returned for her only check-up, the x-rays showed that for the first time in exactly five years, Joan had a tibia that was all in one piece and she walked without crutches, a brace or any other external support.

As he had when we had our first appointment with him, it took Dr. Jupiter only seconds to examine the x-ray and he turned, with the same confident smile on his face, to announce that, "It looks good to me. You won't ever have any trouble with it unless you get a knee replacement, and that's easily taken care of. But if anything should bother you, just give me a call or come back to see me." Joan and I were rather teary eyed in offering our gratitude, but he acknowledged our thanks humbly and stated simply, "That's exactly why I do this. Good luck." And he was gone.

Five years previously, in February of 1987, I was stationed at Wright-Patterson AFB near Dayton, Ohio. I had accumulated a lot of leave time and was faced with a "use or lose" situation so we were considering an unplanned ski trip, perhaps to Sun Valley, a place where neither of us had been but one that sounded like a great place to go. As if they had received a telepathic message, we received a call that same evening from Tom and Carol Anderson in Virginia, telling us that they were headed for Steamboat Springs, Colorado, and asking us to join them. So much for Sun Valley. We could go there some other time.

Two days later, we flew from Dayton to Chicago and changed flights directly into Steamboat where we met up with the Andersons—both couples, that is, because brother Bill and his wife, Betty, were there too. The following morning, we were on the slopes right after the lifts opened and the morning of skiing couldn't have been better. Joan formerly would not ski with me because she was very conservative (read, slow) and deliberate in the way she skied and she did not want to hold me up. But that day was different. She had made a major breakthrough earlier in the season when we went to a ski instruction week in Taos, New Mexico, and there was a quantum improvement in her ability and confidence. Skiing with her was going to be a lot more fun and that particular morning was one of the best we had ever had.

At noon, we all stopped at a very nice restaurant in the mid-mountain lodge and had an elegant, multi-course lunch, including a couple of bottles of wine. Just like the old days when we had skied together so often in Europe. All of us, that is, except Joan. She had skied so well in the morning that she wasn't going to do anything to take the edge off her new found ability and she stuck to ice water. We took a very leisurely time and it was probably more than an hour and a half later when we went back out to strap on the skis.

The sun was bright and strong as we started down the short hill toward the lift and the snow had softened up considerably while we had been inside. Half way down the hill, I stopped to wait for Joan to catch up but couldn't see her. Instead, there was a small gaggle of people gathering about 400 yards from where I stood and it appeared that someone had been hurt. Within moments, Carol skied down to join me and said that Joan had been hurt and she thought that perhaps she had broken her leg. Her suffering had begun and little did we know that it was to last for the next five years.

It began with the trip down the mountain. It was not just a simple sled or meat wagon ride, as the irreverent describe it, but it also meant that the sled had to be strapped to the chair lift to go up another slope before we could return to the base of the mountain. Though Joan was in great pain and on the verge of going into shock, the ski patrol were terrific—compassionate, careful and professional in every respect. They managed to get her to the first aid shack at the base of the mountain and shortly thereafter, we were off by ambulance to the local hospital in the village.

The orthopedist on duty just happened to be a graduate of the Air Force Academy who had left the Air Force to follow this other calling. He took one look at the x-rays and called me aside. "I'm sorry to tell you this," he began, "but this is really a very serious break and it's way beyond our capability here. She has crushed her tibial plateau, the part of the shin bone that forms the bottom half of the knee joint, and it looks like the bone is just splinters. She also has a spiral fracture of the tibia just below the knee. Both are serious problems all by themselves, but together, they're a challenge for the best there is. I suggest that we stabilize the leg here in a temporary cast, keep her in the hospital overnight in case of swelling or internal bleeding, and then you get her to a major hospital tomorrow."

And that's what we did, but it was hardly easy. I called back to Wright-Patterson, the site of one of the six general hospitals in the Air Force, and was assured that the orthopedic department would be up to the challenge.

But the first challenge was to get her there. Through an agonizing fourteen hour odyssey the following day, we managed to arrive in Cincinnati, by way of Dallas-Fort Worth, about 9:00 PM that evening. The ground and flight crews of American Airlines went overboard to try to ease her pain and difficulty on the two legs of the fight home, but their extraordinary efforts and a whole bottle of pain medication wasn't enough to dim the excruciating pain that she experienced. The slightest movement or bump caused all the splinters of bone to grate together and the resultant pain was blinding. Fortunately, an Air Force ambulance had been sent down from Dayton, with a nurse and a medical technician aboard, and that made the last hour of the trip a bit less difficult. By the time she was in bed and knocked out for the night in the hospital, it was near midnight and she was understandably near the limits of her tolerance.

The following morning, Dr. Richard Ruda, the chief of orthopedics and one of the very best orthopedic surgeons in or out of the Air Force began the preparations for what was to be a six hour surgical procedure involving two major bone grafts from her pelvis. Additionally, twenty stainless steel screws and three steel plates were used to stabilize her leg. In a later aside, Dick Ruda told me that he had started to come out at the half way point to ask my permission to amputate the leg from the knee down. It was that bad.

In addition, the accident took place at the height of the early AIDS scare, and although Joan had lost a considerable amount of blood during the procedure, Ruda elected not to give her a transfusion because of the general lack of confidence in the blood supply.

The result was two more months in the hospital, a great deal of pain from the mechanical therapy that had begun in the operating room and continued twenty-four hours per day, and a long period to rebuild the blood supply that she had lost. All would have been worth it if the surgery had been fully successful but, unfortunately, it wasn't. The tibial plateau, considered the most delicate and difficult part of the procedure, was in fact showing signs of healing and a year later the four three-inch screws that held the bottom of her knee together were removed.

But the spiral fracture simply wouldn't mend. The fibula, the small lower leg bone that parallels the tibia, was cut and shortened to see if that might foster healing but it didn't. We visited specialists in New Orleans and San Francisco for consultation. She had four more major surgical procedures, more bone grafts from her pelvis, spent eight months at one point and six months another time in fiber glass casts that extended from her toes to her hip. The casts were removed, x-rays taken and the casts refitted every six weeks, always with the same result. No sign of healing.

Throughout that time, she couldn't drive a car nor could she sit in the passenger seat of the car because of the straight-leg casts. The movie, "Driving Miss Daisy", was popular at the time so I played her Morgan Freeman while "Miss Daisy" sat in the back with her leg extended across the back seat. She was at least able to joke about it.

So it was with a special amount of grit and determination that she was willing and anxious when we decided to buy the Inn. Clearly we went into the venture with the confidence that it would heal one day, somehow or other. She had been fitted with what is called a Lenox Hill brace (no connection to our newly adopted town) which took the weight of walking off her lower leg and placed it on the lower portion of the knee. It also prevented hyperextension of the joint, and while it was cumbersome at best and she still experienced some pain, it permitted a reasonable amount of mobility. But she never complained.

Understandably, it is with obvious happiness that we recall the joyous day we were directed to Jesse Jupiter, the miracle worker. Today Joan's right leg is five-eighths of an inch shorter than the left; she can only wear flats and has to have a lift put on all her shoes; her knee is very unstable and she has difficulty walking on uneven ground. Of course, her skiing days have long since come to an abrupt end. But she rarely experiences any pain; she has excellent mobility, considering; she even dances the night away when the mood strikes—which it didn't often do when we owned the Inn. And while we sing the praises of Jesse Jupiter long and loudly to anyone who will listen, we never forget Dick Ruda. He is the man who could have despaired, who could have refused to do his utmost and who could have taken the easier choice of making her a below the knee amputee. Both of them are very high on our short list of quiet heroes we have known.

Oh yes, the head waitress job. Joan never was very enchanted with the idea of carrying a tray while hobbling of crutches, and she never even gave it a try. So Dan and I shared the duties equally. But Joan had become the expert by that time and could never be replaced. The day after Dr. Jupiter signaled the OK, she was back where she belonged and no one ever again challenged her for the position as long as we stayed at the Inn.

*   *   *

September 23, 1991
Dear Chris & Tom,

As we were often required to yell, standing on our chairs in the mess hall during plebe year at the Naval Academy, "It's Monday morning, sir, and the start of another week in which to excel, sir." Next to plebe year, this is a piece of cake, but I still need that occasional reminder that the week should be dedicated to excellence. Only trouble is, it's hard to tell when one week ends and another begins when you're on duty seven days a week.

We are about to launch off into the foliage season and are getting ready for the onslaught of leaf peepers. Like you, we've lived all over this great country and in Europe and Asia as well. If the early showings are any indication, the color of the foliage here is far and away the best in the world. Most other places have what I would call the varying shades of yellow and while they are pretty, particularly in contrast with other trees that still may be a rich shade of green, they can't compare to what we've seen here. The forests are very dense to begin with and the oaks, maples, beech, elm and locust trees are all intermingled among the evergreen firs, spruces and hemlocks.

The varying colors that they produce—deep maroons, crimsons, scarlets, bright oranges, rusts, yellows and a dozen other shades—are smeared over a seemingly never-ending canvas that is punctuated by the evergreens that are clearly determined to hold their own against the tide of color that is sweeping over them. And the amazing thing is that one single maple tree will have that whole range of colors within its branches and every hue in between. Putting them all together, side by side, is a stupefying sight. I have never been one to get very emotional over Mother Nature's annual molt of the local flora but, if the changes of this past week are any forecast of the month to come, the scenery will be spectacular. I found myself simply staring in awe at one small patch of trees near the center of town this morning as I went to fetch the newspapers. It was breathtaking.

But before the full rush of the tourists returns, Joan and Dan had an extended errand to do today and the result has been a new member of the family.

Ever since we arrived here, Dan has talked about saving up enough money to get a dog. Not just any dog. He has his heart set on a chocolate Labrador retriever. The black and yellow Labs are fairly common and are rapidly becoming the favorite dog in America, but Dan doesn't want anything except a chocolate. With the meager pittance that he draws from the business for personal expenses—as you recall, none of us is receiving a salary but Dan has no outside income as we do—he'll be an old man before he can afford a purebred dog. So Joan and I have been secretly checking the regional pet breeders to find the dog for him. We thought it particularly important to get *the newcomer accustomed to the house and become reasonably well trained before the snow flies.*

Over the weekend, we received a call from a local breeder saying that he had located a chocolate Lab at a kennel in upstate New York so the two of them took off this morning to go have a look at it. It was nearly a three-hour drive from here, just slightly west of due north, and the town that they went to was nearly up to the southern shores of Lake Champlain. Just that short distance north of here, the foliage was near peak and they apparently ooh'd and ahh'd their way for most of the trip.

When they arrived at the kennel, they found a rather strange set-up. The home of the owners was teeming with dogs of all breeds, sizes and ages. They weren't sure whether these were their own house pets or what, because the dog they went to look at was among many more that were kept in small kennels behind the house. The little Lab pup had been born in Oklahoma in mid-July and apparently shipped to this "distributor" as soon as he had been minimally weaned. He was a bit unsteady as they let him out of the cage, probably because he hadn't had any exercise since he had arrived, and the lady of the house referred to him as "a very special dog", whatever that is supposed to mean. He has all his AKC papers and there are some champion show and field trial Labs among his credentials. And, in Dan's judgment, he was just the right shade of chocolate.

He immediately went to Dan and began licking him all over, with a tail that was wagging so hard that it seemed to be moving from the shoulders back. Dan later said that he seemed to be saying, "Gosh, I've been waiting here for you. What took you so long to come?" and as Joan told me later, it was clear from that instant that we had a new member of the Toner family. Dan was smiling broadly through very moist eyes but all he could say was, "He's perfect."

On the way home, Dan sat in the back seat and held the dog who seemed like he was never going to get tired of licking the face of his new found pal. In between giggles, he and Joan began to toss names around. Obviously he'd need a name that would fit him as a full-grown Lab, fit the fact that he was about to become "an inn dog", and one that he could quickly learn for himself. A significant portion of the trip went by quickly, consumed by the naming process. Suddenly, Dan said that he had it. He'd name him Seamus, in part because a Gaelic name would honor our Irish family heritage, but largely, the phonetic pronunciation of his name—Shame-us—might provide the pup with an excuse for any misbehavior, especially in the presence of the guests.

And so Seamus and his new found friends arrived back to the Inn late this afternoon. And after a quick series of sniffs as he wandered about the kitchen—tail wagging eagerly every step of the way—he declared the place fit and acceptable, and settled down for his first nap on the newly made bed in the corner. He is truly something to see. Most all puppies are cute, and I'll ask you for a little latitude for the new, proud family, but they don't come much cuter than this guy. He's all legs, head, ears and paws and has the most dolefully expressive eyes that I've ever seen. If the size of his paws are any indication of his eventual size overall, he's going to be a real big boy.

When he awoke after his short nap, he looked at me for the first time as if to say, "Well if the other guys vouch for you, I guess you have to be OK. Bend over here and I'll give you a couple of licks on the face." I was hooked too.

The cats also had their review of the new arrival as well. Shortly after we had arrived at the Inn, we cut a small hole in the wall, a kitty passageway between a closet in the kitchen and Dan's room in the hovel. This gave the two cats the opportunity to stay in the hovel if they chose isolation or to come over to join us if they felt the need of company. It wasn't long after Seamus' arrival that both of them poked their noses out of the closet door to see who the new intruder was. Cognac, who is a Himalayan, weighs over twenty pounds and is more normally called Big Boy, gave the pup a few sidelong glances, sniffed disdainfully at the foul smell that Seamus had brought in and strolled back through the closet into the hovel.

Chablis, a Birman and a more normal sized nine pounder, decided that he was going to assert himself right off the bat and let this interloper know where he stood. He arched his back as high as he could, raised every hair straight up, opened his mouth showing fangs that I never even knew he possessed and let out a fierce series of hisses, spits and growls. Despite the fact that he's already considerably taller than the cat, Seamus was petrified at this strange apparition and immediately ran to hide behind Dan's legs. Satisfied that he had made the proper initial impression, Chablis also returned to his favorite spot in the hovel. Oh well, they'll eventually learn to live together, but I suspect that Seamus will always have a wary eye out for the little guy.

I told you before about our minds' eyes and the prior conception of the inn we wanted to own. Well, now that image is just about complete. No country inn should ever be without a dog and now Seamus has come home. We have no idea yet if he'll be difficult to train or whether he'll adapt to all the people coming and going in the Inn, but if love makes any difference, it should be a breeze. Without the slightest reason to feel so sure, we all are absolutely convinced that the family is now complete.

You will obviously hear more about Seamus as time goes by, but that will be all for today. Can't wait for you to see him.

Cheers, Dick

All the expectations and hopes for both the foliage and the new puppy were more than exceeded. There is no question in my mind but what the Berkshire Mountains, and as they extend northward to become the Green Mountains of Vermont, are the autumn foliage capitals of the world. Breathtaking is an inadequate word to use to describe the beauty, and just about the time that you think it can't get any better, you awaken the next day to find that it is. The weather also turns brisk at this time of year and cooperates fully with the rest of the vista by providing cobalt blue skies most days as the perfect contrast for the riot of colors below.

Dan had the perfect way to fully appreciate the perfect foliage about two weeks later. He had already planned our adventure with George Roberson who runs the Main Street Sports and Leisure store, had picked up a very nice bottle of chilled champagne at Joey Nejaime's wine shop and arranged with Paula to stay at the Inn and "mind the store".

"C'mon," he exulted, "we're going to enjoy this first foliage season the best way possible. We're going to take a canoe trip down the Housatonic River, past October Mountain where the leaves are at their peak."

I fully expected Joan to decline because we had too much to do, we had guests arriving or some other very practical reason. Instead, she had a picnic basket out and had stocked it with cheese and crackers and champagne glasses before I knew what happened. We drove our car down to the Housatonic in Lenoxdale, a sub-division, if you will, of Lenox, where we met George who had the canoe lashed to the top of his Ford Explorer. We left our car there, all of us piled into his vehicle and he drove us upstream to where the Housatonic wends its way through the Canoe Meadows wildlife sanctuary. There we off-loaded the boat and began our journey. George told us to leave the canoe and paddles right where we had left the car. No one would bother them and he'd pick them up later.

If ever there was a more idyllic day or way to best see the grandeur of the autumn colors, we never found it in all the time we stayed in the Berkshires. From the moment we pushed off from shore, it became an unforgettable adventure. Water birds, such as herons and cranes, were in profusion. Farther back from the water's edge, pheasant and bob white quail could be heard and occasionally flushed directly across the front of our boat. Beavers and woodchucks paddled by us in no special hurry but clearly bent on the chores they had at hand, preparing for winter.

But the brilliant rush of color that completely surrounded us clearly stole the show. It's a wonder that we didn't capsize the canoe a half dozen times. Between Joan's turning from the center of the boat to hand champagne or cheese to Dan in the stern and me in the bow, along with all of us craning of our necks to see the latest wildlife creature pass by or a new view more spectacular than the last, our stability was in constant jeopardy.

While we could probably have continued down the river until dusk, the landing at Lenoxdale came into sight all too soon. We were flushed with the excitement of scenes that few people are privileged to view and the break in the action of innkeeping could not have been more richly rewarding. Whether or not it was an unspoken agreement or just something that we intuitively felt, we never attempted to recapture the magic of that afternoon again. Though the arrival of fall foliage was always a welcomed and exhilarating event for each one of our remaining years in Lenox, we seemed to know that we had experienced the ultimate that very first year.

Seamus was equally exhilarated to see us when we returned to the Inn. He had never been apart from at least one of us since his arrival and he felt very grateful that we saw fit to come back to him. Paula had apparently had one or two unfortunate incidents with dogs in her younger life and, to put it mildly, she wasn't a dog person. She found Seamus to be cute and liked the way he seemed to be rapturously happy all the time, but only at a distance. And while she was human company for him during the few hours that we were gone, he clearly missed the petting and attention that he received constantly while we were there.

He trained very easily right from the start. Piddle or do-do accidents were rare. Dan did a good job of taking him out immediately after he ate and he was certainly intelligent enough to figure out why. But our domestic arrangements trained him to expect that he was fully equal to any human when it came time for bed in the evening. We were still sharing the hovel and the addition of a sixth "person" didn't make all that much difference. Besides, with Dan's futon on the floor, it was very easy to get into bed and if Seamus thought he was being cheated out of enough room on the futon, he had no compunctions about pushing Dan over to get his share of the bed. The bigger he became, the easier it was to assert his claim for room.

And "big" is the best way to describe him as time went by. The folks who sold us the dog had told Dan that Seamus was an example of the evolving shape and size of Labs. He was considerably longer legged than Labs appeared to be when I was younger, and his body was longer and leaner. He became remarkably well-muscled as he grew, in large part because he loved to run. Dan began by taking him to Kennedy Park, a town woodland diagonally across Main Street from the Inn, as often as he could to let him run. It soon became obvious that he couldn't keep up to the pup on foot, so Dan switched to riding on his mountain bike as Seamus sprinted ahead of him, chasing rabbits and flushing pheasant every chance he got. Though he probably would have been stunned if he ever caught up with one of them.

By the following spring, when Seamus had probably grown to 90% of his full height but had not yet begun to fill out, the mountain bike was no longer fast enough so Seamus became a road racer. We would take him up to Reservoir Road, a dirt trail that the public works department used for access to the town water supply, and let him run along the road as fast and as far as he wanted to, following him in the newly acquired Nissan Pathfinder. It was a rather majestic sight, watching this handsome canine speeding along a mountain road at a constant 20 miles per hour, uphill and down, and often not stopping until he had gone four miles or more.

If dogs can smile, that's exactly what Seamus would do after every run—usually at least twice a week—and even though he had foam coming from his mouth and the panting lasted for a half hour or more, he was never happier than when he went for a run. It got so that we couldn't utter the words "Kennedy Park" but what he would go into paroxysms of excitement, and soon after that, "K.P." became a no-no expression, as well.

In fact, Seamus liked to run so much that he occasionally would decide to take an unaccompanied jaunt. He never was allowed to go out the door by himself, partially because of the guests but also because we were located on Main Street and the traffic became fairly heavy at times. But sometimes guests would inadvertently let him out or he would occasionally sneak away as he made his rounds of the property after lunch or dinner. It usually was straight to Kennedy Park, which meant crossing Main Street, or to visit his "friends" down the street, two other chocolate Labs in whom he found some sense of kinship. Fortunately, he had the luck of the Irish and was never hurt.

When he was fully grown, he occasionally got some exercise by chasing a Frisbee that Dan and I would toss back and forth between us, letting him intercept whenever it appeared that he might lose interest. The back gardens at the Inn were terraced and bordered by New England stone fences, huge hand-set rock walls, some of which were nearly eight feet high. The longest of the walls bisected the property along its long axis and was roughly four feet high and two feet thick. As the challenge of Frisbee needed to be stepped up, Dan would get on one side of that wall and I on the other and Seamus would leap over the wall in a single bound as he chased the disk. We would often begin laughing in the middle of the game, remembering the gangly little fella who, when he first was adopted, was too frightened to step off one of smaller walls which was less than 18" high.

Though we normally restricted our pets to the private areas of the Inn, Seamus stood out far too noticeably for that to be an inviolable rule. It was not long before the sound of the call bell at the Dutch door told Seamus that someone wanted to see him. Whether they did or not, he was always the first to respond and as he grew to full height, he would put his front paws on the door shelf and look most of the guests eyeball to eyeball. If the guest happened to expect a human to respond to the bell, he or she got quite a shock when greeted by the smiling face and wagging tail of the pup.

The vast majority of the guests were delighted to see him and it wouldn't do but what he had to go out into the public areas and enjoy the attention of all there present. And he ate it up. He was a genuine showman and he performed to perfection. Guests, many of whom had left their own dogs at home, frequently requested that Seamus be permitted to spend the night with them in their guest room. We tried that once, with a very nice young couple from "the city", but Seamus decided that he missed Dan too much about 2:00 AM and he wasn't going to rest until he got back with his pal.

Whenever the attention of the guests waned, he was perfectly content to return from his trip into the spotlight and seek out his favorite spot in the kitchen. He became the ideal inn dog. He very rarely barked and then only when he was startled. Even if he did, it was one single deep-throated "woof", but certainly menacing enough to get the attention of whomever had startled him.

He and the cats quickly accommodated to one another and, in fact, he and Big Boy became good buddies. Some of our favorite photos of Inn days are of Seamus and Big Boy lying together on the carpet in front of the TV set in the kitchen, often with Big Boy's head resting on the dog's leg or shoulder. Chablis never did get very close to him, however. He was a bit of a scaredy-cat anyway and he just couldn't cotton up to that smelly old dog. Primarily they were inclined to avoid one another most of the time, but

Chablis would go through his arched-back hissing routine every month or so just to keep Seamus on his toes. Even as a fully grown, 100 pound mass of pure muscle, Seamus would back away and head in the other direction, usually to find one of us and ask with those ever expressive eyes, "Why does he keep doing that?"

The hole from the kitchen closet into the hovel was just large enough for Seamus to squeeze through as a puppy. In his rambunctious way, he loved following Big Boy everywhere he went and did so for the first few weeks. Then one day we heard him half crying and half whining only to find that his head and front paws had made it through, but his shoulders had now grown so much that he was stuck. Despite protests by the cats—we should leave things just as they are—it was time to make the hole bigger, about five times bigger, so that the pup could make it through even as he grew. All the animals could go directly from the kitchen to the hovel and return, while the humans had to go out to the porch, no matter what the weather, to access the bedrooms through the door. Now what does that tell you?

Referring to Seamus in the past tense may give the impression that there might be some sad story about to be told of his final days, but not so. He is still very much alive living with his beloved pal and still the same wonderful pup that he always was. He's getting pretty gray around the muzzle these days and he no longer has the stamina to keep up a steady 20 mph. He has never told any one of us if he misses the Inn, but we suspect that all that attention and the repeated performances might have been getting a bit old for him too. But being the old showman that he is, I'm sure he'd be back in top form in minutes, charming all the guests and smiling or winking at us when each performance was over.

*   *   *

October 10, 1991
Dear Chris and Tom,

We had a wonderful time over this past weekend, if only because of a very nice young man and the happiness that he brought to a number of people, not the least of whom was us. He started calling about a month ago to make reservations for this past weekend, but that initial call was just one of many. Originally, he was just anxious to get "the most romantic room" we had.

That was easy: room 5. It is smaller than the other luxury rooms, only about 400 square feet, but it just has a special feel to it that caused Joan to embrace it as "hers" the first time she saw it. It has a lovely antique reproduction canopy bed and a large fireplace with a colonial style mantel, again nicely decorated by Joan. The decor of the room is colonial as well, with rusts, beiges and creams forming the basis of the color scheme—a perfect complement to the colors of the foliage that command every view from the room's second floor windows. The bath is very large and dominated by an antique footed bathtub in which we had the porcelain restored shortly after our arrival. All the other plumbing fixtures and hardware in the bath are authentic antiques but in perfect working condition and appearance.

The reason for the young man's anxiety became clear after about his fourth or fifth call for reassurance. He planned to ask his long time girl friend to marry him that weekend and he wanted the event not just to be memorable but also to be unrivaled as well. Unfortunately, he wasn't especially creative and expected us to come up with the means to make his engagement a unique event. We began by making some rather ordinary suggestions. Champagne and roses in the room? Nah, everybody did that sort of thing. A special dinner at a special table in our favorite restaurant in town? Nope, that was a little better, but still not what he was looking for.

Finally, we hit on it but if we were going to pull it off, it was going to take his utmost cooperation and timing was going to be of the essence.

Near the highest point in Kennedy Park, there is a overlook of the Berkshires that stands at the edge of a precipice and permits a 180° vista of the rolling hills. From that perspective, it appears that you're looking out over a vast wilderness, but of course, you're not. Years before, some enterprising souls had cleared an area about fifty yards by twenty yards, installed a couple of rustic picnic tables and brick barbecue pits and erected a low security fence at the edge of the precipice. The little clearing is a great place for a picnic and provides a stunning view of the surrounding hills at any time of year. But at the height of the color during the foliage season, it is nothing short of magnificent.

We recommended that the young man pop the question here, but we would have to do a little bit of Cupid's work in setting the scene for him. He was to ask, when he checked in, if there was a nice place to which they could hike to see the scenery and then he was to give us twenty minutes after that to get things set up. Dan and I would then rush up to the overlook, clear all the people out if any were there, and put a silver champagne bucket on the picnic table, containing ice and a vintage bottle of Moët et Chandon White Star champagne. Two crystal champagne flutes would be iced in the bucket as well and a crystal vase containing a dozen roses would be placed next to the champagne bucket. And finally, the pièce de résistance was to be a little sign leaning against the flowers that read, "I love you, Laurie. Will you marry me?" Obviously, our young suitor was going to have to do a good acting job himself to pull this whole thing off, but he said he was willing and eager.

Dan and I stood by anxiously for most of the afternoon while the newly arriving guests checked in. Finally, he arrived and we were off like a shot, with Seamus excitedly leading the way. The pup knew something big was afoot and he was just as caught up in it as the rest of us. When we arrived at the overlook, very much out of breath, our worst fears were realized. There was a group of eight teenagers who had taken over one of the tables and looked like they were going to be camped there for the rest of the afternoon.

Using my best persuasive techniques, I told them briefly what was about to take place and asked them politely if they would mind moving off into the denser forest area until the little scheme had been hatched. I had probably underestimated the incipient romantic notions of these youngsters, so I was surprised when they, too, got caught up in the idea and agreed to move on. By the time they did, however, we were running out of time and had to race to get everything properly in place. Not that we were voyeurs or anything like that, but we decided to go just outside the clearing and crouch down there—just in case anyone were to come along and disrupt the flow of things, of course. (As a matter of fact, as we were soon to discover, the teenagers were similarly lying in wait at the other side of the clearing.)

Right on schedule, the young couple came through the path from the trail and into the clearing, and though we couldn't hear anything that was being said, it seemed obvious that he was exclaiming on the beauty of the scenery as he edged her over toward the fence. After a lot of pointing and looking over the surrounding hills, he took his cue, and "happened to notice" the things we had set up on the picnic table. He had her lead the way to the table and they seemed to be saying something like, Isn't this interesting! or, I wonder how this got here? Then she picked up the sign and read it.

Her hands flew up to her face, her shoulders began to convulse and she obviously began to weep. Then she threw her arms around him and kissed him with such passion and intensity that her answer was obvious. With that, there was a shout of approval from the teen cheering section at the far side of the clearing and they all drifted out of the woods, albeit a bit self-consciously, to offer their congratulations. They seemed to be just as tickled by the whole drama as the young couple obviously was. But the kids were discrete as well, because they quickly disappeared again to leave the couple to their celebration. We too had *seen enough and weren't about to allow our voyeurism to become known, so the three of us quietly slipped away down the hill and back to the Inn.*

When the happy young couple returned to the Inn about an hour later, carrying the vase, the bucket and glasses, the young man was just a tad misty eyed when he gave Dan the "thumbs up" sign to indicate that she had accepted. But then we already knew that, didn't we.

I think back now over the minor irritation that we all felt as he called time after time on our 800 number. A surprising number of people seem to think that "toll free" means that through AT&T's largesse, no one has to pay for the call. But of course, what is toll free to the caller is a collect call to us. Having witnessed one of the great modern romantic tales unfold before our eyes, however, I think he can call back any time he wants in the future and it would be worth every penny. To paraphrase Clint Eastwood's Dirty Harry, he made our day. Who said I was getting too old and stodgy to be romantic!

Faithfully yours,
Dick

After Betty Anderson gave us the memory books to place in a few of the guest rooms, Joan was so taken by the idea that she went and bought one for each room. I'll have to admit to a little case of baiting the hook, because Joan had me write an initial entry in each book so that it would whet the appetite of subsequent guests to follow suit. And it was clearly a good move because, within a very short time, most of the succeeding visitors were logging their own entries into the books as well. Joan often couldn't wait until a guest checked out, particularly those that we were especially fond of, so she could run up to the room to read what they had written.

Our newly engaged couple was particularly articulate in recording their memories, and wrote down every detail of the events that transpired during their stay. Dan and I were gratified by the nice words they had to say about us for having set the scene for them. Interestingly, they even thought that we had recruited the cheering section for them—a compliment that we obviously didn't deserve.

But the most interesting part of their recorded memories occurred after that special afternoon and they described what seemed like a real-time archive. It was like reading a steamy romance novel. Each had written down his or her own version of the nights after their engagement and they left little to the imagination.

We had planned to wait until the nighttime temperatures went consistently down into the low 50's or high 40's before we set up a fire in the fireplace rooms. After we activated the fireplaces, we did everything that needed to be done to prepare the way for a beautiful, romantic fire. We were not necessarily being accommodating. We were primarily interested in preventing a disaster by some nut messing around with flammable materials while not having the foggiest idea what he was doing. But our efforts were also a courtesy because all the guest needed to do was light the match and touch it to the paper. And we always left enough extra wood in the wood bin to keep the fire going for hours.

It really wasn't cool enough that first October to begin using the fireplaces quite yet, but we decided that nothing would add to the ambiance better for our newly engaged couple than to make an exception and begin laying the fires that weekend. From what was written in their memory book, we were exactly correct.

According to their very graphic entries, they decided that first night to start the fire, open a bottle of wine and get naked on the carpet in front of the fireplace. Every kiss and caress from thence forward was described in convincing detail. Every action and reaction was detailed. What went through each of their minds as this happened or what response took place was meticulously recorded. And as the fondling and embracing progressed, and the inevitable outcome resulted, the climax was described by each in what can only be termed as lurid clarity.

But that wasn't the end of it. They paused to enjoy a few sips of wine and then the whole process began again, accompanied by the same eloquent enumeration of the experience. And so it went the next day and evening. They must have each used ten pages of the book recording the most intimate aspects of their experiences, in a style that seemed to suggest that this was their private diary and no one else would ever gain access to it.

Joan was clearly shocked to read some of the passages but even more stunned that someone would be inclined to share these most intimate details with not just anyone, but with everyone. Subsequent guests didn't have the same reaction. To many of them, it became a game of Can You Top This! Guest after guest began to follow the same pattern of sharing their most deep-rooted passions and behavior with they knew not whom. But everyone clearly had read what had been written by previous occupants of the room and they were determined, through fact or fantasy, to outdo the chronicle that had been laid down before them. This was the only room in the Inn in which this phenomenon of public passion was so consistently repeated, and we began to wonder whether there was some aphrodisiacal quality about the decor or if it was simply the power of suggestion and a very active sense of imagination.

But not everyone who stayed in the room was similarly affected. A lady from New York City wrote in the memory book, "Yes this room # 5 is magical and everything that everyone has said it is. And while many lovers have obviously found the magic of their love and the fire of their passions under his beautiful canopy bed, this single woman at least got a great night's sleep."

And in a similar vein, another woman from North Jersey penned, "How well we remember the intensity and passion of our young love and the affects of champagne and a bubble bath for two. But we now have a 22 month old at home. The wonderful generosity of his grandparents, who are watching him this weekend, has given us the chance to get away by ourselves for the first time since he was born. And all I want to do is sleep."

Within the innkeeping community, there seems to be a tendency for the innkeepers to name their rooms rather than use such mundane addresses as Room 1 or Room 3. Some of the Lenox innkeepers had named their rooms after great composers, an apt tribute that fits in very nicely with the Tanglewood Festival. Others saw fit to name their rooms after their own forebears, and provide a short biography in each room explaining why their relatives were worthy of this honor.

We considered giving names to our rooms on a number of occasions, and probably had a variety of bases on which to dream up interesting and appropriate names for each room. Joan has always been a great collector of stuffed animals, especially teddy bears, and there was a wonderful assortment of names that we could have appropriated. We could have had a Winnie the Pooh room and a Paddington Bear room and any number of other names—including Teddy, of course. But for reasons that probably can't be explained to this day, we decided just to make it simple and leave our rooms numbered.

But now the exception had arisen. There was no way that Room 5 could any longer be Room 5 after the months and years of torrid lovemaking scenes that had allegedly taken place there. From that time forward, the brass number on the door continued to read "5", just as every other room had a brass number of its own. No guest who ever stayed there ever knew of or heard that their room had a name. But to Joan, Dan and me, that room was known forever after as "The Loving Room".

*　　　　　　*　　　　　　*

October 28, 1991
Dear Chris and Tom,

Sorry that it's been quite a while since last I wrote but things have been just about as hectic during foliage season as they were during the summer. I have also come to the conclusion that we're developing a greater degree of confidence in what we're doing and the tight grip on the lifeline that you have provided us is not quite as vital. We were discussing this last night (when I realized that I haven't been in touch quite as regularly), and we came to the conclusion that my letters were, in a sense, our assurances to you that we were being good stewards of your investment. At the same time, my reports were a process of evaluating and reassuring ourselves as well. If that doesn't make a lot of sense to you, just skip it and go on. I never was much of a philosopher anyway.

Last month, we had a call from southern Virginia from a lady who oozed aristocratic southern charm. She wanted to come during the peak of foliage season, she wanted the very finest accommodations that we could offer, she wanted us to be prepared to refer them to the very best restaurants in the area, and on and on. Then she called back after she received her confirmation to say that maybe the very best accommodations cost a bit more than what she had in mind and she could probably settle for next best. And, as you can probably tell the way I'm writing this, she called back over and over with some little change or question. Among those changes, she revised her reservations from the peak season to the very end of the season, for no apparent reason. The aristocratic charm, which she had previously oozed, began to lose a bit of its luster.

Anyway, they booked for this past weekend in the name of Mr. and Ms. Henri Renot. The one change they hadn't made was to cancel their reservations.

Just as an aside, when I got off the phone with Madame Renot the first time, it occurred to me that, when I was small, my Father used to tell us kids that we weren't really Irish at all. Grandpa Toner's grandfather had supposedly come over to Ireland from France. His name had been Renot when he lived in France but to make it sound more authentic in his newly adopted land, he turned it around backwards and adopted Toner as the family name. Oh well, a bit of meaningless trivia, undoubtedly made up of whole cloth by my Father, but it struck me as rather funny that I was finally going to meet someone by that name.

Well, the Renots were the last to arrive on Friday afternoon. They pulled up to the entrance in a gigantic black Lincoln and shut the engine down right there. Madame Renot alighted from the passenger seat and was a stunning sight to see. She was probably in her mid—to late 40's, a very shapely blonde, dressed in an obviously expensive tailored Navy blue suit with a red collar and a white blouse. Most people arrive at the Inn in jeans and Nikes so I was struck by the fact that she was so stunningly attired. She was also wearing red spike-heeled shoes, and to complete the ensemble, she had on what, for lack of a better name, I will call a Greta Garbo red hat with a wide snap brim that extended down over her eyes, accented by huge dark sunglasses.

About the time that I was signaling to Joan to come over to the kitchen window to sneak a look at our arrivals, Henri was removing himself from the driver's side of the car. It took only a glance to recognize that he was a perfect match for Madame. He wore a perfectly tailored double-breasted blue blazer, a white silk shirt with a long, pointed collar that extended out over the blazer lapels—and a cravat. My gawd, I hadn't seen a cravat since I watched "The Great Gatsby", but here he was, looking for all the world as if he had stepped right out of the movie screen. To top off his appearance, he had a pencil thin mustache and wore a beret and sunglasses. Either I was going to get ill dealing with these people or this was going to be another weekend to remember.

After all the telephone calls, Joan wanted no part of checking them in, sensing that their might be some difficulty. So I was elected. When I met them at the desk, Madame instantly turned on the syrupy charm. Her smile was radiant and she said it was so-o-o nice to arrive at our gorgeous Inn and it was such a pleasure to meet me. She knew me instantly because I looked just as chahmin' in person as I had been over the phone. I always was a sucker for southern belles. This was going to be my pleasure after all.

When they were officially checked in, I began to take them on my tour of the public area, relating some of the historical facts about the Inn and pointing out the things that I always thought were of interest to new arrivals. When we reached the plaque signifying that the property was on the National Register, Madame Renot suddenly burst into a fit of uncontrollable giggling. I asked her if I had said something wrong. She regained her composure and said, "No suh, ahm so sorry. Ah was just thinkin' of somethin' funny that happened in the car on the way out here."

It seemed a reasonable explanation, but something just didn't quite ring true. Though I couldn't figure out what it was. When we continued through the den and into the dining room, she again started giggling and I began to feel myself getting irritated. It had to be directed against me. I wasn't trying to be the slightest bit humorous and here she was, evidently finding me to be quite the wag. Just at that instant, she moved and positioned herself at right angles to where I was standing. For the first time, I was in position to see her profile and get a good look at her face behind the enormous sunglasses.

Then it took just a moment for the wheels to turn and all the keys to drop into place. I reached over with one hand and lifted off her hat, and at the same time, plucked the sunglasses of the bridge of her nose with the other. Then I took her in my arms and gave her a huge hug and kiss. Mr. and Ms. Renot had completely hornswaggled me. In fact, it was Karen and Tom Gensler, two people who are very high on the short list of the best friends that we had ever made in the many years that we had served in the Air Force. And, as I had just found out, they were two superb impersonators and actors.

We had been stationed with Karen and Tom both in Germany and Japan and had some memorable adventures in both locations. He is a flight surgeon, had recently been promoted to brigadier general and is currently the command surgeon at Tactical Air Command. They were the last people on earth we ever expected to see at the Inn last weekend. The three of us were very excited to see one another and began making a lot of racket laughing and exclaiming about their masterful subterfuge. "But wait a minute," I said, "Joan doesn't know you're here. Put the hat and glasses back on. We're going to get her as well."

While I set off to the kitchen, Karen deftly set her disguise back in place. We thought things might be more convincing if Tom went up to their room briefly and came back down when he heard Joan's voice. Out in the kitchen, I just shook my head at Joan and declared that this couple was unreachable, a pair of nuts if ever we met one.

"Would you believe," I told her, "that after this lady changed her reservation from a luxury room to a standard room, she's now complaining that the room she has is not up to the standards that she anticipated? She's about to drive me crazy. You have a lot more patience than I do so you go out and talk with her."

Reluctantly, she headed out to the front desk to face the monsters. Karen picked up the cue perfectly and to Joan's offer to be of assistance, she began a whole litany of mild complaints that totaled up to her being very unhappy. Joan tried to tell her that the room that she had initially reserved would have been much nicer but, unfortunately, that was no longer available. About that time, Tom came around the corner and chimed in on the chorus of complaints. As I watched from the sidelines, I could tell that Joan was reaching the end of her tether and was either going to start crying or lash out at these chronic complainers with a fury that is rarely unleashed.

At that point, I walked over to Karen and said, "Lady, the problem with you is that this guy doesn't act like a Frenchman at all. What you need is more love and affection to bring out the real woman in you!" With that, I took her in my arms and practically bent her over backwards in an embrace. Joan looked on with horror and practically screamed, "Dick!! What in hell are you doing?"

As Karen and I were returning to the vertical, she took off her glasses while I removed her hat, and, simultaneously, Tom doffed the beret and the pencil thin mustache. Joan stared for an instant in utter disbelief and then half laughing and half crying, raced around the desk to enfold them both in her arms at the same time. That made it two-for-two for the Renots, the second charade being just as convincing as the first.

Needless to say, we had a weekend that was filled with laughter, nostalgia and wonderful company. But once again, we were reminded of the bane of the innkeepers' existence. Friends and family, no matter how close, always have to take second priority to the guests at the Inn, and no matter how hard we try, we can't help resenting that intrusion on our private time.

We hope circumstances will be better when you are able to visit us next spring.

All the best,
Dick

The "Renots" were to get one more shot, but a little bit of explanation is necessary before relating the tale of their next victim.

When we arrived in Germany in the early 1980's, we knew the Genslers as passing acquaintances but little more than that. However, Dan and their son, Courtney, were very good friends from high school and hung around with one another much of the time. Both had just turned 18 and Court was fortunate enough to have obtained his driver's license since he had lived in the States when he was 16. Dan, by contrast, had lived in Europe since he was 14 and was not eligible to get a license in Europe until after he had reached 18. To be honest, this requirement didn't displease us at all, particularly since Dan seemed just as willing to wait until we returned to the States to start driving.

As the story was related to us later, Courtney had run out of gas in his old clunker of a car somewhere on the opposite side of the base and he asked Dan to help him retrieve it back to the quarters area where we all lived. Dan agreed willingly and Courtney "borrowed" his Mother's new pride and joy, her little Fiat Spyder 2000 sports convertible that had barely a few thousand miles on it, to go get gas and get his own car running again. Probably Dan was too macho to admit he didn't have a license. The truth of the matter was that he really didn't even know how to drive, though he had occasionally been behind the wheel.

All went well as far as getting the clunker gassed up and started again, but then the next error in judgment took place. Courtney decided that he would drive his own car back home while Dan would drive the Spyder, stick shift and all. Dan wasn't going to pass up the chance to get behind the wheel of a nifty sports car and off they went, though hardly smoothly. He managed to get the car safely back to the house, a very large, multi-family building that the German government had built for the U.S. forces in the late '40s. It was of solid construction, concrete block with a stucco finish, that sat just a few feet across the sidewalk from the parking area.

As Dan pulled into the parking space, his foot slid off the brake pedal and back on to the gas. Right over the sidewalk he went and head on into the building with enough force that it was heard and felt by all those inside—and made the front end of the Spyder a foot or so shorter than it had previously been. Both boys were unhurt but badly shaken, for obvious reasons. They probably took just enough time to get their stories straight (which refreshingly was to tell the truth) and then Dan came home to where we lived in the building next door.

He had always been a very honest and responsible kid, and this time was no exception. After a bit of hemming and hawing, trying to find the right words, he blurted out the whole story to his Mother. Evidently, Court was doing the same thing next door but both mothers decided to choose the wiser course of action—wait 'til your father gets home.

Around dinner time, our phone rang and it was Colonel Gensler calling to ask me if I had heard what had happened. I had barely been in to door for a few moments and though Dan was roughly two-thirds of the way through his second recitation of the tale, I told Colonel Gensler that, yes, I knew what had happened. For lack of any better way to continue, Tom asked me what I planned to do about it.

I told him that we were a responsible family and believed in being accountable for our mistakes. But I went on to say that from what I had understood of the situation, there was at least equal culpability on the part of a young man who took his Mother's car without permission. And then allowed someone to drive it without even checking to see if he was a licensed driver.

"Based on those factors," I went on, "I'm willing to assume responsibility for half of the repair costs of the car, but under the circumstances I believe that equal culpability requires equal accountability and I believe you should pay the other half."

There was a brief silence on the other end of the line, and then Tom replied. "Well, I'll be damned. I forgot for a moment that I was dealing with honorable people and I think your offer is not only fair but very generous." And after another brief pause, he asked if Joan and I might come over after dinner and join them for a drink and to shake hands on the agreement.

The stage was set for a very special and enduring friendship that has lasted to this day. We have often laughed over the event that brought us together. It was also the perfect set up for the thespian Genslers to pull their Renot act one more time.

Dan and Seamus had been off all day, visiting a friend who lived in the southern part of the county. We were now feeling comfortable enough to permit each other to get away for a break and Dan would reciprocate for Joan and me later in the week. So he was unaware that the Genslers had arrived when he got home later that evening.

When Tom and Karen came down for breakfast the next morning, they had once again taken on the guise of the Renots, and they were ready. I had already mentioned to Dan in the kitchen that these people were just as odd as we expected them to be and told half of the stories, at least, of their arrival. Karen came to the Dutch door and I had seen her coming so I went out to bait the trap. After chatting with her briefly, I went back to the kitchen to ask him if he had been around to the guest area of the parking lot when he returned home. I then went on to mention that the lady at the door was claiming that some one had damaged her car and she thought it was his fault.

You could almost see the hairs bristle on the back of his neck as he told me that he never went near the guest parking area and had, instead, pulled directly into the family spaces when he returned home. So I suggested that he go out to talk to her.

Karen couldn't have given a more masterful performance. She began by telling him that she had been awake after they returned home from dinner. She heard what she thought was the sound of an accident at about 10:30 PM (which was the time Dan had returned home, as she had learned from me). She had looked out the window to see a red Honda Prelude (the car Dan had been driving) scooting out of the driveway. She went on in detail about checking her car this morning and finding a dent on the rear fender and a bit of red paint so she was sure that Dan had been the culprit.

Dan was making polite denials but he seemed stunned by the claim and between trying to remain polite but becoming increasingly angry at her insinuations he finally suggested that they go outside and look at both cars. As she stepped back to let him through the Dutch door, he asked her what kind of car she was driving. She replied that she had a Fiat Spyder that was almost brand new and she really adored that car, and as she spoke she dropped the southern accent and returned to her normal voice. Dan stopped dead in his tracks, took a closer look at Tom who had been standing in the background and then began to laugh. With a mild expletive, he quickly discovered that, like his parents before him, he too had been completely fooled and it was his turn for the hugs.

It was with great reluctance that we said farewell to them early on Monday morning but the seeds had clearly been planted for good-hearted revenge. Over the next six years, we made two tries at catching them off guard, only one of which was reasonably successful.

In that six year interim, Tom had retired from the Air Force and taken a medical administrative position in St. Louis. Using their daughter, Heidi, as a co-conspirator, we almost surprised them with an unexpected arrival at their home, but unforeseen circumstances caused a last minute cancellation of our trip. A few years later, they had moved on to Santa Fe and while our surprise arrival was hardly as elaborate as the charade they had set up for us, we still managed to catch them off guard. But, of course, the gotcha contest isn't over yet.

In the workaday existence of innkeeping, there are wonderful memories like these that will be talked of for years after and, of course, every time we renew our long-standing friendships. We were most grateful for the visits of friends to the Inn and particularly appreciative of everyone who came to visit— despite the advance knowledge that we wouldn't be completely free to entertain and spend time with them. That understanding is but one of the many tests of true friendship and like the Gensler's visit, we discovered that friends were more dear than ever when they visited us at the Birchwood.

*   *   *

November 26, 1991
Dear Chris & Tom,

The three of us are as excited tonight as we have been at any time since we've been here.
One of the serendipitous benefits of locating in Lenox is that we have over one hundred relatives living within a radius of 150 miles. Joan has only a handful of close relatives but her Father and Aunt Dorothy and Uncle George (the couple who brought her up after her Mother died when she was ten) are all still living in the Boston area though each is well along in years. My family, by contrast, is huge—good Irish Catholics, of course. I have six brothers and sisters; they have among them 19 children, including my two brothers with no

kids; and most of their children—our nephews and nieces—are married and have children of their own.

This is all by way of saying that we have decided to close the Inn for the Thanksgiving weekend. We have sent an open invitation to all in the family to come and stay with us for an old fashioned family celebration. I think Joan totaled up the potential acceptances at somewhere over 105 people if everyone comes. Needless to say, that would be a very tight squeeze in a 12 bedroom inn but no one seems put off by that at all. As of today, we have 48 confirmed acceptances, three more who will come for just one day, and another nine who are tentative but probable. Is that going to be a party or not!?!

We are still doing some last minute shuffling of the room assignments but we're quite sure that everyone is going to fit together and be reasonably comfortable. My oldest brother, Jim, has a recreational vehicle that sleeps six, and he's bringing that up to park just outside the front door. He and his wife, Imogene, say that they are going to sleep there but it might be better (and a lot more homey) for them to give up the RV to the younger kids and enjoy one of the guest rooms.

We've worked out a priority system for rooms that is built first on age, then on the size of the immediate families and finally on what the parents of the younger children would prefer to do. Most of the generation behind us are typical of the times in that they like to travel and they camp out from time to time, so sleeping bags will be in order for most of the youngsters. We're "assigning" the rooms based on what we think will best suit the needs of everyone—especially Joan's family and my siblings—but I' m sure that flexibility will be the order of the day after everyone arrives.

We will make pizzas for all who arrive on Wednesday evening, which will likely be a significant majority of the "guests". With the variety of made-to-order types that we'll be offering, perhaps we should have bought a Domino's franchise instead of an inn, but then there wouldn't be any place to sleep, would there. We will also prepare Thanksgiving dinner and, in traditional New England fashion, we will serve the dinner in the early afternoon. My sisters, bless 'em, protested long and loud over that decision because they think it's too much work for us to do. But we're set up for doing something that size and between hosting small multitudes for Thanksgiving during AF days and the added training we've had since coming to the Inn, I think we have enough experience to carry it off.

We have two 25 pound turkeys in the fridge already, the stuffing is already made and about a quarter ton of vegetables are waiting to be prepared for the occasion. I'm embarrassed to say that we are currently too strapped for funds to supply the beer, wine and other libations for other than the dinner. But once again, everyone thinks that it would be ridiculous for us to even try to provide for the whole weekend and are packing in all that they will need (and probably a little more for the hosts).

Not to be outdone by our efforts for the holiday, my sisters and sisters-in-law have organized the rest of the meals for the weekend. One family group will do the dinner on Friday night and another group will handle Saturday. While it will be "pot luck", in the loosest sense of the term for both nights. Knowing the ladies in charge, each meal will instead be a well coordinated feast. We're also blessed with a large number of good and adventurous cooks, especially within the younger generation, so it should be quite a show. Everyone will have their vehicles loaded down with breakfast and lunch items and lots of snack food when they arrive, so it has all the earmarks of a gastronomical orgy. From the many phone calls we've received in the past two days, I think our company is just as excited as we are.

We seem to have solved the seating problem as well. The regular tables in the dining room are going out on the front porch and we have rented banquet tables and folding chairs that are set up in the dining room and den. Based on the max numbers that have indicated they will or may come, we should all be able to sit down at the same time. We will serve buffet-style and we have adequate warmers and other serving pieces so that the food will be hot and fresh for everyone. We will probably even escape the invariable "little kids' table" that used to be the bane of my existence at large family gatherings back in the olden days. Truth be known, I probably wanted to sit with the big people because I was nosy and wanted hear the juicy gossip that wasn't available from cousins my age.

One of my nieces, I'd say she was a favorite if I weren't supposed to have preferences like that, has regretted but for the best possible reason. Paula is very close to 40 and has been married to a superb guy named Dick Waterman for well over ten years. They have always wanted children but never have been able to have them. Through a long and circuitous path, they became interested in adopting a Chinese child, a girl needless to say, and they will be in Szechuan region of China over this Thanksgiving to pick up their new daughter and bring her home. We're absolutely delighted for them but they will be especially missed this weekend. A toast to all three of them will certainly be in order.

The principal reason that I mention Paula is the note that she wrote to Joan and me telling about their trip. Mine is a very well organized family and we had instituted a reverse pyramid system for "making reservations", with each of my brothers and sisters responsible for the bookings for their own portion of the clan. Even though she had already been officially listed as a regret, Paula chose to write to us anyway to express her apology. I'd like to quote you just one sentence from her letter.

She said, "I can't think of anything more exciting than going around a corner and bumping into someone you've never seen before in your life, yet all the while knowing that person is, at the very least, a first cousin."

To tell you the truth, I can't either and it's one of the primary reasons we're walking on air right now. There have been a number of get-togethers in the past among fairly large segments of the families, primarily because they all live in relatively close proximity to one another. But this will be the biggest and most comprehensive of all. I'll send you a "hot wash-up" report when it's over.

Meanwhile, best holiday wishes to you both. You'll be well remembered in our reflections on what we're thankful for this year.

Fond regards,
Dick

To say that it was a success would be an understatement. In fact, it was so successful that it became a tradition that was repeated year after year, though a family reunion on Thanksgiving was to recur only one other time after that. We didn't set aside that first Thanksgiving for a reunion without a great deal of prior thought and extensive consultations with the more experienced innkeepers in town. We had an intuitive feeling that this particular holiday, especially in New England, was one that was traditionally celebrated at home. All of the other innkeepers seemed to agree with us. We were told that we could expect the odd guest for a night or two over that weekend, but a full house for even one night was probably out of the question.

But the fact of the matter was that, in that first year, we could have filled the Inn with paying guests almost twice over. We had one group alone that wanted to book eight rooms for the four-day weekend and we had to turn them away. We told each caller that we were already filled for the weekend—a bit of a psychological gimmick to indicate for future reference that we were very popular—but of course there was no mention of who it was that was filling the Inn. It would have been a bad message to send to say that we were closed, particularly to someone who might be thinking of calling again next year. As luck would have it, however, we never had a full house for any of the subsequent years that we remained open to the public. But back to that first Thanksgiving.

Our families have always had that Amish barn-raising spirit, if you will, of gladly donating their time and effort to help one another out. The old adage that many hands make light work was practically a family motto. Each time someone in the family moved into a new house or planned to redecorate, the clan turned out to clean, paint, plant, rake leaves or whatever else the new homeowners had to do. And the events usually turned into a celebration of sorts, as well. But even with that historic precedent, the Birchwood Inn was about to turn into the granddaddy of all barn-raisings over the next eight years.

Oldest brother, Jim, (who also happened to be a major investor) started the ball rolling by calling me right after the initial invitations went out. "You need to start putting together a list of things that need to be done," he began, "and let me know a few days in advance so that we can bring the right tools and supplies to do the work. I'll take care of letting everybody know what to expect while we're there and maybe we can get some things done and save you the effort". To be honest, they could have been staying for a month and probably would not have had enough time to complete the list we put together, but there was still a lot of fall clean-up that needed doing and that was the focus of the plan.

Mother Fortune and Mother Nature decided not to cooperate, however, and the first snow fell on the Berkshires in the days immediately prior to Thanksgiving. So the plan changed from outside to inside, and inside meant painting and patching. The dining room was most in need of a new paint job but it was followed closely by the woodwork in the hallways and entrances to the guest rooms on all three floors. So when the family cars and trucks began to arrive, bringing folks from all over New England, they were not just loaded with food supplies, they also had everything from drop cloths to paint brushes, ladders and all the other tools and equipment needed to do a professional paint job.

And we had a professional among us. Gerry Sullivan, the husband of another "favorite" niece, had been painting houses ever since he was a pre-teen, working summers for his father's business. And even after he graduated from college and became an English teacher in the Boston school system, he still spent his summers on the business end of a paint brush. He declared forever after that weekend that we had wasted his genius. He claims to be the best and fastest sash cutter within a six state radius and we had frittered away his talent doing flat painting on woodwork. But that was an issue that he needed to raise with the job foreman (Jim), who also happens to be his father-in-law. Gerry still likes to recall that the imperious "general" had decreed that there would be no drinking until the workday was over, but he still had his can of Budweiser "paint thinner" with him for use as needed.

Thursday was a day of rest for everyone, and an opportunity to tour the area for many who hadn't been to the Berkshires. But Friday and Saturday were work days. And by mid-afternoon on Saturday, the look of the dining room and hallways had been completely transformed. Every bit of woodwork had been washed and repainted and the ceilings throughout all had a fresh coat of paint. The work that was done would have taken Dan and me at least a month, putting every free minute we had into the task, but it was all completed, and as well as any professional contractor could have done it. The three of us were most inarticulate in expressing our appreciation, but the family waved even that off, saying it was their small contribution to thank us for what we had done for them. THEY even sent US thank-you notes after they returned home. Amazing!

Despite the work schedule, there was still plenty of time for enjoyment, and meal times were the best. We sat elbow to elbow in the dining room and once a reminiscence from our childhood was recounted, the stories began in earnest. They were mostly funny, probably more so at the time of telling than when they actually happened, and the laughter was infectious. The younger generations sat there enthralled. I would have expected them to quietly wander off to play games or to chat among themselves about things that were more interesting to them. But instead, they drank in every word and only ventured a comment when they needed clarification of some of the more preposterous events that had been recounted.

It was especially delightful to watch the looks on their faces as they gained insights into the reality that we had all been kids once, too. The look that asked, "my Mom (or Dad) did what?" was probably the most common expression of all. For some reason, we don't seem to tell our children the funny or foolish experiences that we had when we were young. Perhaps we're afraid of what that might do to our image in their minds. But just let a group of close siblings get together and all the rules change. The insights between generations that were gained through those evenings, that weekend and for every other family gathering, probably did more to bring individual and collective families closer than all the ardent parenting efforts that any of us have ever expended.

On a less obvious level, there were also the occasional healings that took place. Resentments or hurt feelings, though few in number, that had been harbored for years had a way of being aired and resolved in the warmest and most forgiving ways. It was not just the old folks of our generation who used this opportunity. Occasionally we would notice two people, usually sisters or brothers, but also parents and children, off in a corner talking earnestly and giving off the unmistakable aura that they were not to be interrupted. Those sessions usually ended with emotional embraces and a few tears, but they were always tears of happiness that clearly announced that a long-standing grudge had been forgiven or wound had been healed.

In family reunions, there is, supposedly, a greater likelihood that the opposite will take place, that hurt feelings or anger are common outcomes of such events, at least if we are to believe the social scientists who caution against the hazards of close family contacts over holiday periods. But these eventualities never came about. There was the occasional misunderstanding, or the pouty lip of a teenager who didn't like being reprimanded, even if it had been done privately. But every reunion was, in fact, a time of true celebration and happiness and, in my humble judgment, all of us, regardless of generation, are far richer today for the experience. Joan, Dan and I most certainly are.

*   *   *

December 3, 1991
Dear Chris & Tom,

What a time we had. I had forgotten what wonderful families we have and how much fun it could be when we get together. It was, in every respect, an overwhelming success as far as I was concerned. It was especially delightful to get to know so many of my nephews' and nieces' children (does that make them grandnephews and grandnieces?), some of whom are about to finish high school and get on with college or careers. The most enjoyable part of it was that there wasn't a single one—from ankle biter to high school senior—that disappointed me in any way. Marvelous youngsters, but then that's to be expected when their parents are all superb young men and women.

Perhaps my "overwhelming success" evaluation was made from a biased perspective. A few others might take issue with that conclusion. It seems that the only down side of the whole weekend was, more than anything, my own doing. Joan probably put it a little more succinctly when she told me that I was acting like a horse's ass for the first couple of days—and I have to admit that she couldn't have said it better. In looking back over the weekend, I'm a bit put out with myself for being overly protective of the property and wanting "everything in its place" at all times. Half a brain would tell me that's a sheer impossibility with 56 people running around most of the weekend. But it took one of the younger generation to put me in my place very firmly.

One of my nephews, Brian Vossmer (my sister Nancy's second youngest), is one of the nicest young men you could ever want to meet. Brian is in his early 20's and he and Dan share a remarkable family resemblance. They were often taken for brothers when they were out and about the town together. At any rate, Brian is one of those kids who never has to be asked to do anything; he always pitches right in whenever there is work to do. At one point after Thanksgiving dinner, the pans were piled up by the sink, just waiting for someone to scrub them. Seeing no one else with a hand up, Brian rolled up his sleeves and started in.

Apparently, he wasn't doing things quite the way I would have done them, and as the self-appointed kitchen supervisor, I was giving him more advice than he needed. First, the water wasn't hot enough. Then he wasn't rinsing the pans well enough. And after a few more of my timely comments, he didn't say a word but left things as they were, dried his hands and headed off into the den to join others watching the football game.

Moments later, my brother, Jim, came into the kitchen laughing so hard he had tears running down his cheeks. When he gained a little composure, he asked those remaining in the kitchen what had happened. Nobody seemed to have an answer for him, so he went on to say that Brian had come into the den, stood in the middle of the room, and speaking to no one in particular said, "Who said the goddam general's retired?" Needless to say, I didn't find that quite as funny as everyone else did, but it certainly opened my eyes to the realization that Joan wasn't alone in her observations. If I didn't get the message right away, I should have as the days went by. "Who said the goddam general's retired?" became the byword for the rest of the weekend and if I were even just tempted to become "supervisory" again, someone would repeat the *phrase for my benefit. And you think Rodney Dangerfield is the only one who doesn't get any respect.*

More seriously, my behavior was probably an extreme example of the pressure of having our fortunes and our lives totally wrapped up in this place. Even though they are all family and I would trust them with anything I own, the intensity of the protective attitude I've developed had evidently blinded me to the obvious. For the remainder of the time they were here, I tried to be more patient, a lot more appreciative of their team efforts and a little less critical about whatever was done. But it doesn't take a Cassandra to see that I'm going to have to watch myself carefully in the future.

And the worst part is that it truly was a magnificent team effort. It wasn't just doing dishes, sweeping floors and preparing meals. They all pitched in to make tremendous improvements in the longer term appearance of the house. They scraped, washed and repainted all the woodwork in the dining room and all of the corridors throughout the house. The place looks shiny and bright, better than I had ever hoped it could. But on top of that, most of them stayed on for the day on Sunday and decorated the whole house, inside and out, for the Christmas holidays. It looks like an updated version of a Currier & Ives print—absolutely gorgeous. We had loads of laughs and much good natured ribbing throughout the weekend, but putting up the Christmas tree had to take the cake.

On Saturday, Joan and Dan went out to the boonies to get a tree that they had selected at a tree farm two or three weeks ago. It had to be cut down and dragged out of the woods by tractor. Dan said that the family who owns the farm reminded him of stories he had read about the back woods of Appalachia. His recollections of the movie, "Deliverance", caused him some concern and he was quick to check over his shoulder any time one of them was behind him. Eventually, the tree was loaded on top of the car and they finally made it back to the house without any problems. Joan must have thought we had 25 foot ceilings in the library from the size of it. While I exaggerate slightly, it had to be at least 18 feet tall if it was an inch and our ceilings are only 10 feet high. Also, the trunk was about 10 inches in diameter at the base and it wouldn't come close to fitting into the largest tree stand we could find. So there was a tiny bit of trimming required.

You would have thought it was the Keystone Kops and the Three Stooges all together out in the parking lot trying to get the tree cut down to size. I think every male who hadn't yet left for home was there "helping"—and it was Joan's turn to supervise. There were enough saws, hatchets, pruners and other tools available to level Kennedy Park, but it still took half the morning to get the tree cut down to size. Then we had to carry it all the way around to the front porch entrance because it was still too broad to get through the entrance door. When we finally got the tree into the library, the real fun began.

We ended up putting the tree on a stand made of 2x4s, which was then inserted in an old galvanized wash tub that was then filled with a combination of big heavy rocks and sawdust. The rocks were supposed to weigh down the base and the sawdust would be dampened to keep the tree fresh. But the rocks weren't enough. The tree was so broad and heavy that we then had to brace it with pretty substantial guy wires that were attached to the heavier pieces of nearby furniture and concrete building blocks that had been tastefully covered with green cloth. In one extreme case, a wire was tied to a twenty penny nail that had been driven directly into the floor through the carpet.

The wags who allege that a giraffe or a camel resulted from a design by a committee have never seen what a similar group can do to a Christmas tree that is too heavy and too large for it's surroundings. But I must admit that the tree is a thing of beauty now that it has been fully decorated. I don't think I've ever seen a nicer looking tree than it is now, and the credit, as usual, goes to the ladies.

But the tree wasn't the only thing that the gang decorated. The entire house, inside and out, is now wearing full dress for the holidays. Every window in the house has a wreath, 20" across, with a huge red bow on it, hanging on the outside. Just below the wreath is an electric candle with a clear bulb mounted on the windowsill inside. At night, the Inn is absolutely breathtaking, particularly with the outside floodlights that accent the whole exterior. The huge porch that fronts toward the street has garlands wound around all the columns, with massive red bows at the head of each column. The white exterior and green shutters make a perfect backdrop for the decorations.

The inside of the house is equally gorgeous. Every guest room and all of the public areas have been treated to a holiday makeover. Joan has been making holiday wreaths and swags for the interior for most of the fall and at least one appears in every room. She also made a small swag for the exterior of each guest room door, plus larger ones that are hung all through the public areas. And each mantel is wearing a whole new set of decorations, ranging from antique German nutcrackers to teddy bears and other stuffed animals dressed for the holidays. We have been to Williamsburg, Virginia, during the Christmas season and I thought I'd never see anything to compare to the beauty of that historic sight. But I can honestly say that I have now seen the equal. The historic old Birchwood Inn is just dazzling. And I'm convinced that our family is missing its calling by not going into the decorating business.

I know this has been an extra long letter but one last item before I quit. The teen age girls, who outnumber the boys by about eight to one, elected to use the library as their huge bedroom for the weekend—about twelve of them in there, all in sleeping bags. They only needed to be told once by one of the "elders" that they were giggling too loudly in the wee hours. We discovered the reason for the giggling Monday after all had left. It seems that they looked through the games (like Monopoly and Scrabble) that we have for our guests in the bottom of a bookcase in the library and discovered one that I didn't even know was there: "Dr. Ruth's Good Sex Game". I guess they must have played the game every night and then hid it behind a large pillow each day (where our housekeeper, Paula, found it) so the old fuddy-duddies wouldn't take it away from them. In this day and age, it was probably no big deal to most of them, but even if it was the initial introduction to the birds and the bees for the younger ones, it surely was a lot better way to learn about sex than I had at their age.

We really wish you could see the house. We will, of course, send pictures. Meanwhile, in case I don't get around to writing before the Christmas holidays arrive, Joan, Dan and I send our love and best holiday wishes to you both. May the season be one of the best ever for you and may we be fortunate enough to see you during the new year ahead.

Dick

That initial family decorating effort for the holidays was just one of the many traditions that was established that first year. Every year thereafter, Thanksgiving weekend marked the time that the family came to do the decorating—sometimes on Friday or Saturday, depending on our guest load, or on Sunday and Monday if we were full for the weekend. If anything, the Inn became more beautiful as each year passed. It is always injudicious to select out individuals for the lion's share of the credit for any achievement. But in addition to Joan, I will have to say that my sister, Nancy, and her husband, Art Vossmer, (Brian's parents) along with my sister, Paula Lee, are the principal artists who made the Birchwood the most glorious holiday site in the Berkshires, year after year.

There is no doubt that the beauty was the result of a very substantial team effort that first year and many of the younger generation contributed wonderful ideas and the talent to carry them off, especially another "favorite" niece, Cheryl Vossmer. But my sisters, Nancy and Paula (we refer to her as "**our** Paula" to distinguish her from our housekeeper and one of our grandnieces who also shares the same name), were clearly the sparkplugs behind the whole effort. Both are tireless workers, exceptionally talented in a variety of craft work and wonderfully creative. Without them, the effort would have taken a week or ten days and the results wouldn't have been anywhere near as spectacular.

As if to prove my point, they decided after the decorating was completed the second year that the skirt that we had used to cover the tree stand and the surrounding floor was just not up to the standards of the rest of the decorations. So they went back home to suburban Boston, mobilized their quilting group and put together a round Christmas quilt that would rival anything in the Neiman-Marcus holiday catalogue. It is a stunning patchwork of red and green pieces, interspersed with squares of poinsettia blooms and trimmed with red and green bands. It opens along one radius to a center circle that is exactly the right diameter to fit around the tree trunk. And they designed and sewed it in just two days. The following Thursday, the UPS driver brought the package—again with a thank-you note tucked into the folds of the quilt they had made. Most of the holiday decorations stayed behind when we sold the Inn, but that quilt will remain one of our most prized possessions as long as there is a Christmas.

That first holiday season, the Berkshire Visitors Bureau, a state-supported tourist bureau for the entire county, selected the Birchwood as the most beautifully decorated business establishment in the region. Personal bias aside, it probably could have been selected every year thereafter for that honor because it just became more beautiful year after year, thanks to our extended family. Dozens of people stopped in front of the house to take pictures each year, day and night. And there were enough other homes and businesses in the area who adopted a slight variation of our exterior decor that we were forced to conclude that imitation is, indeed, a most sincere form of flattery.

Having mentioned Nancy, I must also admit that her son, Brian, was not the only one to put me in my place that first family weekend. As they were leaving on Monday morning to go home, Nan asked me if everything looked OK or if there was anything else that they could do before they left. With my head still firmly planted in my nether regions, I replied that it would probably take me another two weeks to get everything back where it belonged, but that was OK, we had the time.

She pulled herself up to her full five feet in height, put her hands on her hips and said, "Well, tough shit!" Never having heard her say any more than damn once or twice before in our lives, I found that hilariously funny and reacted accordingly. Two days later, Joan asked me if it wasn't time for me to call Nancy and apologize. Stunned, I asked her what for, and she informed me that Nan was dead serious and very angry when she had made her parting comment. She went on to say that she, Joan, was none too happy with my tactlessness either. With tail tightly tucked between my legs, I made the call, but by that time, Nan found the whole thing to be pretty funny as well. Needless to say, loving sister that she's always been, I was forgiven. But you'll have to ask her if I ever did anything again that was worthy of her wrath.

We never quite achieved that same level of participation for family reunions in the years ahead. The teens grew older, their horizons expanded and while they still recall that first Thanksgiving together and a few other occasions with great fondness, the demands of college and the priorities that are generated by love interests, usually seemed to win out. Other large reunions took place, sometimes in connection with a holiday or other times just when slowness of business would permit, but there never was the same turnout that we had that first year.

In all the years we spent at the Inn, nothing was anticipated more excitedly or made our lives more pleasant than a family reunion, no matter the size or the attendance. More often than not, attendance was limited to just the senior generation. Most were retired and could come any time that they chose, so we often got together on the less busy weekdays. Along with my two sisters and their husbands, the small group of family who were able to come most often were my brother, Jim, and his wife, Im, and my younger brother, Charlie, and his soul mate, another Joan. My Joan's Father, Eddie, her Aunt Dorothy and Uncle George, and her cousin (George and Dorothy's son), Bill and his wife, Jeanne, would most often constitute the delegation from her side of the family.

I would have been happy if those times came at least once a month or even more frequently. Within my own family, we had always been close as youngsters, and got along amazingly well for a large family living in the relatively tight quarters of our youth. But our friendship, appreciation for one another and mutual love grew many times over and fairly flourished during those years at the Inn. Each time they came, the routine was pretty much the same. They came loaded down with food for the occasion and fully prepared to work. And the old Birchwood invariably looked better when they left. Whether it was winter, spring or fall, Jim always led it off with a reminder to put together a list of things to be done, and just as regularly as the seasons, they were always looking for more to do before the end of the second day.

But the evenings, to borrow a term from the television industry, were always prime time. Most everyone stood around the massive kitchen and chatted while some of us prepared the meal and all shared a cocktail or a glass of wine along with laughter and wonderful conversation. When the meal was served the venue changed to the dining room, but the spirit never wavered. And it was an unusual evening if the animated discourse, laughter, nostalgia and camaraderie lasted for less than four hours. Late in our innkeeping career, after we announced that it was time for us put the Inn on the market and retire, brother Jim would get very philosophical late in the evenings and recall the wonderment of those days. And then he'd ask rhetorically what we were ever going to do to replace such priceless togetherness. We are all still pondering that question today.

*   *   *

December 18, 1991
Dear Chris & Tom,

As long as the last letter was, this one will be short. Just wanted to tell you how disappointed that I was that we didn't overlap at Swiss Ski School. From what Carol Anderson told me before I left for Switzerland, I was sure that we were going to have at least one evening together, but I guess it was not to be.

Can't say that I was all that impressed with Saas Fee, but then the weather wasn't particularly cooperative with so much snowfall and fog. My first trip there clearly wasn't at an optimum time. You were probably better off being there the second week, from what I hear, but that's the risk we take when skiing in the Alps in early December. The hotel where we stayed was superb. It had just opened and the facilities, staff and the food were exactly what you expect in a four-star Swiss hotel. And it was very conveniently located both to the village and the lifts. As always, it was a treat being with the Andersons and MacMillans again, but must admit that it would have been even more enjoyable if you had been there too. Of course, my being the fifth wheel with Joan back at the Inn wasn't all that pleasant either. All told, however, I'm glad I went, even though it wasn't quite what I hoped it would be.

On the final day, I went through the usual drill of taking the cog train down to Brig, manhandling the skis and baggage over to the Zurich express train (which I just barely made) and then relaxing for the long train ride to Zurich. I met another American and two Brits on the train, all of whom had been at ski school, so our reflections back on the week there helped the time pass. It was just about dark when we arrived in Zurich and we took the shuttle to the Holiday Inn that is close to the airport. No place in Switzerland is cheap these days but it sort of frosted me to pay $200 a night in a Holiday Inn. Especially when I can remember, not too many years ago, staying in many of them with the whole family for around $20 per night here in the States.

When I got to my room, I turned on CNN just in time to get the Stateside weather report and was a bit dismayed to hear, right off the top, that, "The Berkshire Mountains in western Massachusetts are in their second day of an early season blizzard, or nor'easter. Over 30 inches of snow have already fallen, trees and power lines are down and there is no let-up in the storm forecast for at least another twelve hours." At that point, I was very grateful that it had been Joan who talked me into going to Switzerland, rather my insisting that I go, against her wishes. But it still made it all the more imperative to get back home—if the roads were open when I got there.

The flight connections were perfect the next day and I arrived in Hartford just about on time. Joan was there to meet me, driving her Maxima, so I figured the driving and the snow accumulation couldn't be too bad if she didn't drive our newly leased 4WD Nissan Pathfinder. The answer was relatively simple. The storm was every bit as bad as I had heard—something that became more readily apparent the closer we came to the Berkshires—but she didn't drive the Pathfinder because she couldn't.

Dan had taken a young lovely who was staying alone at the Inn out in the storm to demonstrate the superb handling capability of a 4WD vehicle in snow. Unfortunately, it wasn't a very impressive demo because he bottomed out in a drift and became totally mired up over the axles. Not so bad if the drift had been on the town roads but he had chosen to go up to the reservoir area which is desolate in the middle of summer, let alone in the middle of a nor'easter. They tried for an hour or so to free the vehicle but by then it had turned dark and was *getting much colder. Good sense prevailed and they (including Seamus) hiked the five or six miles out of the woods and back to the Inn.*

Seamus thought it was great fun and porpoised through the six foot drifts all the way back home. The two humans didn't find it enjoyable at all, however, and for a while they apparently harbored the fear that they might not make it. But they did and the fire in the den and the hot toddies were very popular that evening. Needless to say, the first chore that I faced the morning after I returned was to hike back in with Dan and rescue the vehicle—no small task since the damp snow that had been holding the truck was now frozen solid. We finally managed after a couple of hours, and ever since we returned to the Inn with the Pathfinder (undamaged I might add), we have been shoveling snow, snow and more snow. I think I'm paying for my solo vacation. Our immediate area topped out at about 40 inches, and while other locales nearby had more, I didn't feel the least bit cheated with our lesser amount.

One last note. If I thought the house looked beautiful before, decorated for the holidays with just a dusting of snow on the ground for accent, it looks magnificent with the huge snowfall. We have definitely taken the pictures a second time.

Again, all the best for the holidays,
Dick

On my return, the Inn did, indeed, look smashing but if it took snowfalls like that one to make it look that way, I'd just as soon settle for a little less. That one snowfall in early December had more than doubled the snowfall for the entire previous winter (admittedly a rarely dry winter). And though none of the storms that occurred later in the winter were ever its equal, there was great joy in the Berkshire ski industry that year because we had natural snow on the ground, and plenty of it, from mid-November through the following Easter. The common saying that the Berkshires are beautiful at any time of year (except early spring, it says in small print) was borne out in spades that winter and we were to benefit from the number of skiers who came to enjoy the ski season. No one chose to challenge Mother Nature's ability to close roads and strand vehicles again, however, at least not in our household.

Each year, the Chamber of Commerce requests one of the member inns to host an annual Christmas party for the rest of the membership. As the new guys in the town and in the Chamber, we volunteered to host the affair our first Christmas in Lenox—and we did so for the following three Christmases as well.

While there are over 100 business memberships in the organization, and that number represents at least double the number of people who are potential attendees, considering families and employees. But we were assured that a turnout of 50 to 60 people is unusually large, based on past history. The Chamber offered to purchase soft drinks, the makings for punch and some light snacks for the guests, but that wasn't going to be anywhere near enough for Joan.

Instead, we put out some rather more substantial hors d'oeuvres, such as deviled eggs, shrimp with cocktail sauce, Swedish meatballs, cheese logs and crackers and the like. We also provided red and white wine and beer for those who preferred more potent holiday spirits to soft drinks. Just in case the estimates were wrong, we planned for closer to 100 people—and we still fell short by quite a considerable number. It seemed like the whole town had turned out and we couldn't have been more delighted. The food ran out too quickly but there was still enough wine and beer as well as some cheese and crackers for the late comers, right up to the end.

As a courtesy, the town officials were always invited, Chamber members or not, and we were pleased that most of them came. Just as I had always found in my military life, it was always better to establish a rapport socially before trying to do business with someone. Each of the officials that I met that evening, of having already met them, got to know a bit better than before, seemed quite affable and it was clearly going to be a pleasure to work with and hopefully socialize with them in the future. Everyone in the Chamber with whom I spoke seemed very nice as well and, in fact, there were a few new friendships forged that evening that were to last for our entire time in Lenox.

Late in the evening, at least from the standpoint that it was about two hours beyond the time that the affair had been scheduled to end, the Lenox fire chief came over to me to exchange holiday greetings and thank us for inviting him and his wife. After a few moments chat, he leaned over to me in a very confidential tone and said, "Nice tree!" I thanked him for noticing and he leaned back again and said, "Unfortunately, it's illegal. You're not supposed to have a live tree in a public place, especially a lodging establishment. It's against the fire code."

I looked at him dumbstruck. It had never even entered the realm of possibility in my mind that we shouldn't have a live Christmas tree in the library and none of us had even given a moments thought to the fact that it might be against the fire code. But come to think of it, we had been pouring gallons of water into the wash tub every day (mixed with a table spoon of bleach and a half cup of Karo corn syrup, just as Heloise had advised) and still the needles were drying out and starting to drop off.

"Do I need to take it down?" was the only thing that I could think to say, fully expecting him to say that he'd be back to inspect by noon the next day. Instead, the chief smiled and said that he might look like a mean and ugly Scrooge, but he certainly wasn't going to act that way. "No just keep it watered real good," he said, "and take it down right after the holidays. But I'd start looking for a fire-resistant artificial tree for next year in the after-Christmas sales if I were you. Damn shame, though," he concluded, "That really is an awful nice tree," and with a final wish for a happy holiday season, he and his wife were out the door into the chill night.

As we had heard from the chief, the compliments from all the guests were most effusive. We had clearly been successful in our first venture into the social life of Lenox and the holiday season had taken on a very bright glow. All was right with the world.

*   *   *

December 28, 1991
Dear Chris & Tom,

When we first bought the Inn last summer, Tony McPeak, the new Air Force Chief of Staff, was kind enough to send us a letter of congratulations and best wishes. Tony and I have known one another since we were majors, and we became friendly, as couples, when we were stationed together at Air Force headquarters in Europe back in the early '80s. After we received the note, I called Tony's office and asked for a picture to go with it, which we now have proudly framed and hung near the entrance to the Inn. You need to know this by way of introduction to two special guests who spent most of the Christmas week with us.

All of the people we had for Christmas were very pleasant and seemed to appreciate being with a family for the holiday, even if it wasn't theirs. But the most appreciative were a young Army couple, stationed at Fort Devens in eastern Massachusetts. It didn't seem to start out all that well when these youngsters arrived, however.

We saw them coming and as Joan started out to check them in, they were just coming through the entrance door, right near where Tony's picture and letter were hung. That apparently caught their eyes as soon as they entered because Joan heard the young man say, "Oh shit, we come a hundred miles to get away from the military for the holidays and, of all places to pick, we end up in a place owned by a general. Incredible."

Joan had all she could do to keep from laughing out loud but instead ignored the comment and got them checked in. Well, they couldn't have been nicer. Their names were Autumn and Glenn Aguinaldo. Dan met them at a Travel Expo that he went to earlier this month. The personnel services folks at Fort Devens put on the Expo each year in order to introduce the soldiers and their families stationed there to the tourist attractions of the region. As a "cost" of setting up a booth at the Expo they ask that every establishment offer at least a 10% discount to the all soldiers and their families that visit with them. It is obviously a fair exchange if there ever was one and, in fact, something that we had already decided to do for all military guests.

Both Autumn and Glenn are active duty soldiers. She has been in the Army just a short time but he has been around quite a while, a relatively senior NCO. I think they met and married at Fort Devens that is the home of a Green Beret brigade. I suspect that Glenn is somehow associated with that organization, though he talked very little about his job when we got to know them. Autumn is currently in a clerical assignment but awaiting a move to Chinese language school, out near you in Monterey, and she's slated to become a linguist, probably in intelligence.

Their "unfortunate choice" in coming to a military-owned inn didn't seem to phase them after they got to know us because we invited them to share Christmas dinner with us and they accepted eagerly. Dan had suggested that we have a real old fashioned Christmas dinner with roast goose instead of turkey. His idea was inspired by a Christmas dinner menu in "Bon Appetit" magazine and it was superb, even if I do say so myself. Along with the goose and all the trimmings, we had thinly sliced potatoes that were baked with wild mushrooms and chicken broth and a bit of goose fat drippings. That was accompanied by a variety of oven roasted root vegetables (e.g., parsnips, carrots, shallots, etc.). Of course there was an excellent Bordeaux to go with it and a choice of homemade pies for dessert. We felt just like we were normal people and the day turned out to be quite pleasant, despite caring for the few guests that we had.

Our own personal Christmas was celebrated late on Christmas Eve when all of the guests were either out or in their rooms. We closed off the library and, with our traditional family eggnog (recipe enclosed in case you're interested), we opened our gifts which Joan had earlier placed under the tree. It was not quite the same as a normal family Christmas—probably because we were constantly checking over our shoulder expecting a guest to need something—but it was enjoyable nonetheless. The hit of the night was Seamus. He was like a little kid and seemed to love opening the presents. It was amazing to watch how carefully he could unwrap things with his mouth and front paws, never damaging the contents. He would then parade around the library with his new toy and bring it to each of us so we could congratulate him. It got so that he wasn't satisfied with opening his own gifts—he wanted to help everyone. As I said, just like a little kid.

We decided later that this would have been the better holiday to invite the family because we had relatively few guests in the days surrounding Christmas. However, I doubt that we would have had the family turnout that we did at Thanksgiving. Too many prefer being home so it probably wouldn't have worked out as well. Trying to second-guess when to do these family affairs will clearly be a losing proposition to begin with, so we'll just give it our best shot in the future.

New Years Eve doesn't look a heck of a lot better. Potential guests seem to want a complete package where they can go somewhere, enjoy the ambience of an old-fashioned New England inn and not worry about going out or driving anywhere. At least that's what we've concluded from the calls we've been *receiving—with very few bookings being made. Oh well, it's too late to do anything about that now but it is certainly something we will keep in mind for next year.*

Hope you all had a merry one. We'll drink a toast to you on New Years Eve— probably sometime between 9:00 and 10:00 PM, because that definitely will be bedtime for these pooped puppies unless the guests have any late evening needs. Have a great 1992.

Fond regards,
Dick

HOLIDAY EGGNOG

1 dozen eggs
1 cup brandy or cognac

2 cups white or golden rum
1 cup sugar (more or less, to taste)
1 quart whipping cream

Put the rum and brandy into a punch bowl with a minimum one gallon capacity. Add the sugar and completely dissolve it in the liquor. The sweetness of the final product can usually be judged from taking a small taste of the combination. Separate the eggs into two separate bowls that can be used with an electric mixer. Beat the yolks until they are as frothy as possible and then blend the beaten yolks into the sugar/liquor mixture. Then beat the egg whites until they are very stiff and fold into the punch bowl contents. This will take considerable time as the beaten whites will tend to stay together. Finally, whip the cream until it is stiff enough to peak in the mixer, and fold all of it into the punch bowl. Use a spatula or paddle to blend the ingredients together because a whisk will tend to flatten the texture. Serve with a sprinkle of nutmeg according to taste.

HINT 1—Canadian whiskey or bourbon may be substituted for the rum if those flavors are preferred. Quantities, of course, may also be varied according to taste, but this ratio provides for a very smooth blend and flavor.

HINT 2—Keep the punch bowl tightly covered in the refrigerator and the eggnog will last for two weeks to a month without spoiling. The alcohol "cooks" the eggs and cream and greatly reduces the chance of spoilage. It also kills any bacteria that might be in the eggs for those who may be apprehensive about eating "raw" eggs.

For obvious reasons, we had a special soft spot for military people, especially the ones who were young, relatively new to the service and still trying to adjust to a new way of life, often times, in a strange part of the country. Glenn and Autumn Aguinaldo were the first military guests that we knew of and they were to come back quite a few more times while they were stationed at Fort Devens. Even after they left, we kept in contact with them at Christmas time and they never failed to mention how they often speak of that first Christmas with us and how we made them feel like part of our family.

In addition to Fort Devens, Hanscom Air Force Base is also in eastern Massachusetts. Hanscom has long been the primary electronics research and development center for the Air Force and there are significant and long standing linkages between the Air Force and the university community around Boston, particularly with the Massachusetts Institute of Technology. And while the mission at Hanscom, by it's nature, requires a relatively permanent scientific and engineering civilian work force, there are still a few thousand military personnel stationed there and we were always delighted to welcome Hanscom-based guests, as well.

Our gut instinct was to let all our military guests stay with us for no charge, since we were acutely aware of the relatively low pay of military people, especially the young enlisted kids who were too often eligible for food stamps in high cost of living areas like Boston. But we were also aware of the fact that we might end up on food stamps ourselves if we didn't break even at the Inn, so we charged them a nominal fee, depending on their rank, primarily. The very young junior enlisted people were charged very little; the more senior officers were given a token discount of about ten percent; and those in the middle were charged accordingly.

Most of the younger kids had basically the same reaction that the Aguinaldos did when they discovered that an old general, out to pasture, was going to be their host. We're pleased to say that it took just a short time for the realization to wear off and they become comfortable and apparently felt at ease.

A young lieutenant from Hanscom had been married in his hometown in North Dakota but they couldn't afford a real honeymoon right after the ceremony. So as next best choice, he brought his new bride directly back to the base but was able to spend the first weekend following their wedding with us at the Inn. I probably dominated far too much of his time trying to get back "up to speed" on the thinking and attitudes of today's young officers, but he didn't seem at all reluctant to share his views with me. When they checked out on Sunday noon, he shook my hand and said, "Gee, you were really great to us, sir, and you more than made up for the honeymoon we missed. If I didn't know it, I would never have guessed that you were a general." I still haven't figured out to this day whether that was a compliment or not.

But chatting with the military guests sometimes had its drawbacks. A lieutenant colonel and his wife came from Hanscom to stay with us and in a very brief introductory discussion, I discovered that he was heavily involved in an area in which I was keenly interested. It seems that we spent hours after breakfast on Saturday talking about his area of expertise, my previous experiences in the same area and the current status of affairs. Finally, his wife came into the library with a very plaintive look on her face and apologized for interrupting. But, she went on, if she wanted her husband to "talk shop" all weekend, they could have stayed at home and he could spend all day talking shop with his next door neighbor the way they always do. I was, in no small way, embarrassed by the situation, especially when I clearly remember Joan making similar plaints in the past. Apparently, and in spite of the fact that I left the colonel alone for the remainder of their stay with us, I didn't manage to engender much trust in his wife. They never made a return visit.

During the Christmas holidays, it never failed but what some guest, military or civilian, would bring up the old movie, "Holiday Inn", starring Danny Kaye and Bing Crosby. The plot of the movie revolved around two hoofers who had recently served in World War II together under the division command of a general for whom all of the troops would go to the ends of the earth. It seemed that after retirement, the general and his wife had bought a small New England inn and the word was out among his old troops that things were not going very well. By now, Kaye and Crosby had become big musical comedy stars on Broadway and they were determined to help the "old man" out by doing a special performance of their Broadway hit show at the inn.

In the most memorable scene in the movie—to me, at least—Kaye and Crosby arrived at the inn just in time to see the old man carrying a load of wood into the huge parlor in order to lay a fire for the guests. Kaye was chagrined to see this and said, "Jeez, the general is doing private's work. This is terrible!" And with that, he went over to his former commander, took the wood and mildly chastised him for doing work that was "beneath his dignity".

At least once every Christmas season when I was carrying a load of wood into the den to lay a fire, some guest—usually an older one, but sometimes someone who had just recently seen a reprise of the movie—would ask me, "Have you ever seen 'Holiday Inn'? There's a scene in there where the general is carrying…."

"Yeah, yeah, I've seen it," I'd tell them. But the funny thing about it is that Danny Kaye, Bing Crosby nor anyone else ever even suggested that it was beneath this old man's dignity to be laying the fire. And of course it wasn't. But they sure enjoyed the seasonal glow that those efforts brought to the holidays and all winter long.

*　　　　*　　　　*

January 3, 1992
Dear Chris and Tom,

Just a quick update on the holiday season. As it turned out, New Year's Eve was pretty much as we had feared. We filled about seven or eight rooms—which isn't all that bad—but with the prospect of the dark ages just around the corner, we need all the revenue that we can get. Missed opportunities, like missed buses, seldom come back to give you another chance. But like the buses, another comes along eventually and we are determined to be on board when next New Years arrives.

Actually just one other inn that we know of did a New Years package deal that included dinner on the big night. They had it catered by one of the better catering outfits in the area—but I suspect they had to book almost a year in advance in order to get them. The caterers brought the meal almost ready to serve and did the final preparation just about time for people to sit down. They provided all the linens, dishes and flatware and they brought along a serving staff that was reportedly well trained and genial. To add frosting to the cake, they even cleaned up, leaving both the kitchen and the dining room as clean as they found it. Only trouble was that, according to the innkeepers, they merely broke even on the dinner. I guess that can happen when you price the package as an inducement for bringing guests in, rather than attempting to make a profit on the whole package. Their rationale for doing this? "We were completely booked up, weren't we?" Can't argue with that logic.

The guests that we had were all very nice, and while we were a bit concerned about over indulgence, we were pleasantly surprised to find that not only was it a very sober bunch, many of them had called it a night well before 11:00 PM. And we called it a night just about the same time. Perhaps there are other ways that people have to celebrate the arrival of the new year.

Up 'til now, we have had the Tanglewood season and the foliage season to keep our bookings up. But the time has come when our marketing talents are going to be challenged to the max. And even though we have five ski areas within a half hours drive of the Inn, we have to be realistic and recognize that most skiers are not "inn types". They'd rather stay closer to the slopes—preferably ski-in and ski-out accommodations. They'd probably be put off by the relative elegance of the Inn—only the worst kind of slob wants to tromp into a place in ski boots and wander across oriental carpets. And they'd much prefer the beer and pub food ambiance of an apres-ski *lodge as opposed to the fine dining restaurants for which Lenox is known.*

I guess I'm really trying to reconcile myself to the fact that the patronage of downhill skiers, at least, is not going to be as abundant as the inn brokers implied. We do have an excellent cross-country ski area in Kennedy Park, right across the street—and it's free to the public. The sport seems to be gaining in popularity so that certainly can be one hook in our marketing appeal. But we've got to do better than that.

We're looking hard for a solution and I'm sure we'll come up with more good ideas. Sure would be nice to be like the innkeepers across the street. They're shutting down next Sunday and are taking off to Africa where they'll stay until early to mid-April. As Dan noted earlier, this business wouldn't be half bad if it weren't for the guests.

As sort of a year end appraisal, we sat down and tried to figure out the things we've been doing right so that we could concentrate on them. One thing we came up with is that the guests really like our large breakfasts. One particular breakfast is the favorite, based on the fact that the recipe has been the most requested, by far. It is a breakfast casserole dish that we conjured up by combining two recipes that we had found in two separate cookbooks. We named it Huevos Albuquerque, and I'm attaching a copy of the recipe in case you'd like to try it some day for brunch guests.

Meantime, hope your holidays went well. We'll keep you posted. And Happy '92.

Dick

HUEVOS ALBUQUERQUE

1 4.5 oz can chopped green chilies
6 oz shredded Monterrey Jack cheese
6 eggs, beaten
1 c. milk

24 oz small curd cottage cheese
6 oz shredded sharp cheddar cheese
1 c. Bisquick or equivalent
1/4 c. liquid (or melted) margarine
Cayenne pepper and salt to taste

Whisk all the ingredients together in a large bowl until everything is smoothly blended. Lightly spray a 9" x 13" Pyrex dish with Pam (or equivalent) and pour the mixture into the dish. Cover tightly with food wrap and place in the refrigerator over night. When you are ready to cook, uncover and sprinkle with bacon bits or commercial soy based substitute (e.g., Bacos). Place in a pre-heated 375° oven for one hour or until the edges are browned and the top is golden.

Cut into 12 equal pieces and serve immediately topped with a dollop of warm salsa or taco sauce. Corn bread or corn muffins make a tasty accompaniment.

HINT: For variety, sliced mushrooms or canned French fried onion rings may be substituted for the green chilies.

HINT: All or a portion of the casserole can be frozen after it is cooked. To serve later, let the saved portions thaw in the refrigerator over night, cover with aluminum foil and put into a preheated 400° oven about one hour before serving. Immediately turn down the temperature to 200° until serving time.

With the slow season following directly after the year-end holidays, we became very focused on ways that we could bring in more guests over the next few months. In general terms, advertising is the key, at least until word of mouth becomes the most important source of potential guests finding out about the Inn. The challenge, of course, was to find out where the advertising dollar could be spent most profitably.

Most of the innkeepers in Lenox believed that it was impossible to survive the dark ages without advertising in the *New York Times*. That made a lot of sense to us since the majority of our clientele, thus far at least, seemed to come from the New York metro area. Those same innkeepers also agreed that it was a waste of money to advertise in Boston because Bostonians "don't know the Berkshires exist and aren't interested in finding out". That seemed to have merit as well because many of our own Boston area family members who came for Thanksgiving had never made the two-hour trip west of Boston before. In general, most people from eastern Massachusetts seemed to prefer going to the mountains in Maine and New Hampshire for winter sports and were drawn to Cape Cod or the north shore around Gloucester and Rockport in the summer.

But even if the *Times* provided the best return on advertising investment, we also needed a hook—something that would convince the reader to choose our Inn over all the others in the area. We had to come up with something that made us sound more attractive than any place else—and explain our offering all within the six lines of tiny print which was the maximum that we could afford to buy.

After much thought and consideration, we decided that our "hook" would be food, or international gourmet dinners, to be more precise. Many of the telephone inquiries that we had received in the late fall were looking for "packages", an inclusive arrangement that offered bed and breakfast and something else—and at a discount or at least an apparent one. We had lived in various parts of the world, we knew regional specialties and we weren't afraid to try to do international dinners for up to 25 people. Gourmet dinner packages on weekends, we decided, was the secret to our out-bidding the other inns for winter business. Even though our first attempt had been a near disaster.

Leo Mahoney was the first friend that we made in Lenox and not just because he was an acquaintance of my brother, Jim, or that he was our insurance agent. He had gone out of his way to give us good advice, both on business matters as well as getting to know the power structure of the town. He was a native of Lenox and happened to have been the Town Moderator for the previous 20 years, the individual who presided over the town meetings and appointed most of the non-elected town officials. So he knew well from whence he spoke.

His interest in our success went well beyond our client relationship with his company and he genuinely wished to see us succeed. What better way than to throw a little business our way. Could we and did we want to do his office Christmas party at the Inn, to include a sit-down dinner for 40 to 45 people? Even though we had never tackled anything on this scale—the recent Thanksgiving didn't count because it was a family affair with everyone pitching in to help—we jumped at the chance to do it.

Leo's idea of an office dinner party ran to basic fare, a turkey or roast chicken dinner—something along that line. But if we were going to do international gourmet weekends throughout the winter and early spring for our weekend guests, we should certainly be able to do something better than that. It would be great practice. And even if we had never done anything quite that large, we had done some pretty fancy dinners for twelve. All we had to do was enlarge the quantities a bit. What better holiday meal to have than to replicate a wonderful French "peasant" meal that we had experienced in a delightful bistro on Île St. Louis in Paris.

As we described it to Leo, following cocktails and light snacks in the library, the guests would come to the dining room and find baskets of salad and baskets of sausages on each table along with bottles of red and white wine and plenty of crusty French baguettes. The salad basket was filled with whole vegetables—red and green peppers that had been seeded and the stems reattached, cucumbers, carrots with the greens still attached, Bermuda onions that had been skinned, large white mushrooms caps, whole celery stalks complete with leaves, hard boiled eggs and a few other things. The sausage baskets would be stuffed with whole rolls of pepperoni, summer sausage, hard salami, liverwurst and Lebanese balogna, with a ramekin of country paté in the center of each basket. And all the baskets contained sharp knives so that each individual, in turn, could cut off what he or she wanted and then select the condiments of choice from the table.

This first course would be followed by the main or hot course, which for this meal we proposed coq au vin, pieces of chicken marinated and cooked in red wine and Spanish onions and served with steamed wild rice. The meal would be completed with a large cheese board for each table, laden with wedges of Swiss, Roquefort, Brie, cheddar, and whatever other good cheeses were available. Again, cheese knives would be on the board for the guest to make the selection and serving size he or she chose. More crusty French bread would accompany this course.

Leo hadn't heard of anything quite like this before and his facial expressions became more and more skeptical as we gave him the details. But when we assured him that it was a real crowd pleaser, that people became increasingly animated as the meal progressed, then he finally agreed. He would provide the wine and cocktail mixes, since we didn't have a liquor license, and we would take care of the rest including a licensed bartender, Dan. All for ten percent over the cost of food—with no charge for labor.

When the big evening came a week before that first Christmas, we were primed to make a smashing success out of the dinner. The salad ingredients, sausages and cheeses had been carefully selected at Guido's, the best local market; the coq au vin had been prepared in advance and only needed to be heated before serving. All was in readiness and we were going to wow them. And things went beautifully through cocktails and then getting the diners to the table.

Our predictions to Leo had been right. He happily winked his acknowledgment to Joan as he prepared to make a few remarks before eating, and the crowd became even more animated and in high spirits as they began the first course. The jubilant mood was probably helped by the fact that they were a bit squeezed into the dining room, as we used the same table and seating arrangement that had proved successful during the family Thanksgiving celebration.

As we served the main course, we began patting ourselves on the back with elation as guest after guest remarked, as they were served, on what a great idea this was. But "plating up" and then serving the hot course between the closely spaced tables didn't go anywhere near as smoothly as we had hoped. With only Joan and Dan serving in these tight quarters, it seemed to take forever to get the plates on the table. And I was just barely keeping up with them as they dashed back and forth between kitchen and dining room. People were still in an ebullient mood, however, and there was little notice made of the slow service.

But as we began to clear the table for the cheese course, we were overcome by a sense of disaster. Much of the chicken wasn't completely cooked and plate after plate was coming back with most of the chicken uneaten and blood red meat staring us in the face. Probably the worst case was the plate given to Bill Sabin, our lawyer and Leo's good friend whom he had invited as sort of a guest of honor.

The major hazard in making coq au vin is to avoid overcooking it because the chicken shreds, falls off the bones and becomes, essentially, a bony chicken stew. Even though it tastes fine, the appearance is hardly appetizing. And I certainly succeeded in avoiding that pitfall. The meat was so underdone in some of the servings that it couldn't come off the bone—and who wants to eat rare chicken to begin with. I was mortified and Joan and Dan were equally embarrassed and upset.

But despite this near disaster, the guests were very kind in their departing comments about the evening—including Bill Sabin and Leo. We apologized profusely for the chicken but Leo brushed it off as "one of those things". He was sure that everyone got plenty to eat and far more importantly, they all had a grand time. But he never booked his Christmas party with us again. And we learned some unforgettable lessons for our coming venture into gourmet dining on which we were about to embark, not the least of which was to have an adequate number of servers for the size of the crowd.

*   *   *

Part III

Getting Confident

There's a story that way back at the end of the 19th century, the director of the U.S. Patent Office proposed to the sitting president that his office be closed down permanently. He was absolutely convinced in his own mind that everything that was ever going to be invented already had been. The fact that the family automobile, the airplane, radio, television, the microchip, and the personal computer, as just a few examples, were yet to come shows how desperately wrong that misguided chap turned out to be.

So knowing that factoid, it is with a great deal of hesitation that I suggest that by the time we began our second calendar year at the Inn, we had "seen just about everything". We had run the gamut of interpersonal relations within the family and recovered from those difficulties. We had faced some very tight financial times, and learned that there were ways to forestall those sorts of problems. We had had enough unpleasant guests to last a lifetime, but we had come to know that others like them would be back on rare occasions. But we also knew that they would be rare and our visitors, in the overwhelming majority, would be a delight to have with us.

And we had discovered that we were doing enough right to assure that special guests would return time and again.

The learning process was not over, any more than it ever is in life itself, but we had climbed the learning curve very rapidly. So although we had clearly not seen everything yet, chances were that we would be able to take any eventuality in stride that might come along in the future. It was with this in mind, therefore, that we set off into the next phase of our career with a far more positive attitude, a commitment to better our offerings and an experience base that was sure to improve our confidence and abilities.

January 22, 1992
Dear Chris & Tom,

Well I'm tremendously pleased to tell you that Joan's operation is over and Dr. Jupiter is totally confident that it was a success. It's not very nice to blaspheme the hero of the tale, but he is so self-assured that it is eerie—it almost borders on arrogance. But while I say that, I also have to admit that he's made a believer out of me, and more importantly, Joan. We're nearly as convinced as he is that his assertion that "the leg is fixed" will turn out to be true. But we've also been disappointed too many times over the past five years to be absolutely sure.

I won't bore you (or upset your tummies) with the details of the procedure other than to say that it was a technique that he had worked out in collaboration with a group of Soviet orthopedic surgeons—apparently with State and Defense Department blessings for cooperative non-military technology. It took well over four hours to get her back in the recovery room and I sat with her— and a lot of other poor souls who had just had major surgery—while she came around. She was still rather heavily sedated, but lucid, when they brought her back to the surgical ward. Fortunately, she was not in terribly bad pain, or at least that's what she told me.

But we are most certainly going to miss her help this weekend. We started the international dinners two weeks ago, and while it was fairly hectic with Joan's help, it's going to be a madhouse next Saturday with her on the sideline. Even though we have hired a couple of waitresses who normally work in local restaurants for the occasion, Joan is such a steadying influence when things get hectic, and that certainly will be missed. It will not be the same without her. By the way, she absolutely refused to practice holding a tray while on crutches, so that's out. Hopefully she'll feel well enough to sit up at her "command post" in the kitchen to boost our morale.

We're tremendously thankful that it's over, she's doing pretty well, and all signs point to the prospect of a full recovery. What a great day that will be, if it is.

All the best,
Dick

The international dinners turned out to be a big success, at least from the standpoint of the reaction from the guests. Each was a four-course meal—appetizer, salad, entree and dessert—usually with two choices of entree since the number vegetarians and those who eschew red meat seemed to be growing.

Our first dinner after Joan "left us" was something that we felt very confident in doing—a wise way to get started. It was advertised as an Asian dinner, but it was primarily Thai in origin. The first course was a lemon grass soup, which sounds far less appealing than it actually is. We followed that with a green salad with sesame dressing and a few other Asian goodies thrown in to make it seem authentic. The third course was giant prawns cooked in a delicious Thai brown sauce, served with asparagus that had been sautéed in peanut oil with a variety of Thai seasonings, and served along with aromatic steamed rice. The dessert was a fairly exotic fruit cup with papaya, lichees and other tropical fruits.

Unfortunately, there were only five couples who chose the dinner option and only seven rooms that were filled for that first weekend. One of the guests who chose the dinner package we could probably have just as well done without.

When Dan and I were cleaning off the tables from the main course, one of the diners grabbed my arm as I was passing his table and said, "Hey waiter, how about giving me another helping of the shrimp. That was really good!"

Dan said that he expected me to haul off and punch him, but to both of our surprise, I managed to keep my composure and not let my irritation show. I told him that I wasn't sure whether there was any more but I would try to find him another shrimp in the kitchen. Joan was more irritated than either of us when Dan went into the kitchen and told her what had happened. "You should have asked him if he was accustomed to doing that in every restaurant that he went to, or else tell him he would be charged for it," she advised me. But I went ahead and gave him another prawn with some sauce and rice—on a clean plate even.

The next morning at breakfast, he walked over to me and with his hand partially covering his mouth he said softly, "Gee, I'm terribly embarrassed. I owe you an apology. I didn't know you were a general."

Without acknowledging his apology, I replied, "Well perhaps if you were civil to all waiters every place you went, you wouldn't have to worry about apologizing after the fact." I didn't wait for a response, but instead, went about my chores preparing and serving the breakfast. Later, when he was checking out, he told me that he not only had a very nice weekend, an excellent dinner, but he also learned a very important lesson that he'd remember in the future. His wife looked very skeptical.

Unfortunately, the international gourmet dinners did not achieve what we had hoped, despite the fact that we offered (and advertised) such tantalizing weekend productions as French Provincial, German Gasthaus, South Asian, French Haute Cuisine and a Visit to the Caribbean. While most of our guests chose the package offerings over the next three months—and clearly seemed to enjoy them—we never did seem to attract any more guests than we might have otherwise, though that is impossible to tell, of course. We never filled the inn with those offerings except on holiday weekends, and then, ironically, we didn't offer dinner because we were quite sure that we would have a full house anyway.

There were certainly many down sides to the effort, the first being that we didn't make any profit for all the effort expended. While it's probably a terrible business practice, we intentionally priced the dinners at, or slightly above, the break-even point, without even costing our own labor. The objective, after all, was to draw more guests to the Inn where we would make a profit on the rooms and it also made our occupancy rates look much better. Unfortunately, we probably managed to alienate a few of the local restaurant owners in the bargain.

But even more negative was the time that was involved. While one of us was cleaning up from breakfast on Saturday morning, the other was out shopping for the fresh ingredients that would be served that evening. The rest of the day was spent preparing for the meal, doing as much pre-cooking as we could, and then with time out only for serving wine and cheese, final preparations began. By the time that we finished cleaning up from the dinner in the evening, it was usually after midnight, which meant about four or five hours sleep before getting up to begin all over again. So, despite having a big success from the culinary standpoint, about mid-April we decided that our restaurant days were over and we ceased offering dinner packages except on special occasions. There were no protests from the Lenox restauranteurs.

Was it enjoyable? Actually it was, and it was a particular pleasure when we received positive feedback from the guests who clearly had enjoyed the meals. We even had later requests to start up our "restaurant" again, even if it were only for the winter months.

Did we miss it after we stopped? Not one single bit. The task of running the Inn was time consuming enough for the three of us without adding the additional burden of a restaurant. And as noted earlier, we gained a tremendous amount of respect for the small, full-service inn owners who have both an inn and a restaurant to care for, with minimal help. It's not an easy or glamorous life, by any means.

*   *   *

February 25, 1992
Dear Chris & Tom,

Things are going rather well, I'm pleased to say. The biggest news is that Joan had her six-week check and, just as Jesse Jupiter had predicted—no, asserted is a better word—the leg is healed. Last week, Joan went into the hospital on crutches, for security reasons more than anything, because she had already managed to put a lot of weight on the bad leg. But she proudly and happily walked out with just a little help from a cane. Needless to say, there was a major celebration when we arrived back in Lenox. Also, needless to say, she's back to full duty, a week later, though she's not yet as swift as she used to be.

But an event over the weekend probably made her wish that she were still out of commission, at least for an hour or so.

We had a full house over the weekend—Presidents Day—and most of the guests checked in fairly early on Friday. Two couples, who booked together and were also traveling together, showed up real early, at 10:00 AM, looking to get into their rooms. Check-in time is normally at 2:00 PM—a fact that is clearly pointed out on the confirmation cards that we send out—but we will usually let people check in at any time as long as the rooms are ready. In this case, one of the rooms had been occupied the night before, hadn't yet been made up, so we suggested that they go downtown, look around and have a bite of lunch and come back around 2:00.

One of the ladies (they were all about our vintage) started making a bit of a fuss about not being able to check in immediately. So I went on to explain the obvious—that the guests in one of their rooms had still not checked out yet (checkout time is 11:30) and the room still had to be made up after that. My explanation didn't seem to pacify her at all so I asked to see her confirmation card. And of course, right there in plain English, it said what the check-in time was. "Well, I never read those things anyway," she claimed and with a snort and a huff, she turned on her heels and they all headed out the door.

Instead of coming back at 2:00 on the dot, as we expected, they obviously found something else to do because they finally showed up around 3:30 or 4:00. I was in the kitchen doing something or other when I heard a woman's voice scream, "You're a goddam liar and you have a goddam nerve to look me in the eye and tell me that."

Knowing that Joan was out at the desk, I quickly hurried out there to find out what on earth was going on. As we recreated the picture later, it seems that the four of them had gone up to the two rooms and instantly came back down again to say that one room was unsatisfactory. Joan asked them why and was told that they "weren't accustomed to staying anywhere that had shared, public bathrooms". Joan, of course, told them that the bathroom for Room 2 was in fact across the hall, but it was private, the key to their room locked the door and that we provided terry robes for them to use to cross the corridor.

When their voices began to rise in contradiction, Joan went on to mention that when their reservations were made, she had taken them herself. She had very explicitly told the person who made the reservations that the only available room that had twin beds, as they had requested, was a room with private, detached bath, and she went on to explain in detail what she meant by the term. In fact she had remembered the reservation distinctly because the woman she spoke to rather snidely pointed out that she and her husband still slept together, but their friends must be getting old because they had to have twin beds.

Joan's assertion that she had told them in advance about the detached bath was what prompted the screams of "goddam liar", and when I arrived on the scene, all four of them were in a chorus of shouts—all of which was derogatory and profane and all directed at Joan. As soon as I entered the desk area, I got a vague glance or two but the venom directed at Joan continued unabated. I stepped in front of Joan, held up both hands and asked for quiet, and then asked that one person calmly tell me what their problem was. The woman who had made the reservations began, in a loud, fishwife's voice, to tell me a tale that I knew to be patently false. When she finished, I asked her who had made the reservations and on whose credit card the deposit had been made.

"I did, and it's my credit card. Why?" she responded.

"May I please have your card again," I asked, and once again she fairly screamed at me, "Why?"

"Because I'm giving you your deposit back and you're going to leave here right now!" I told her. "No one speaks to me in that tone of voice and with gutter language, let alone screaming at my wife the way you did, and there's no way we want you under our roof tonight or any other night."

"You can't do that," she shouted, "We have reservations and we've paid for the first night in advance."

I didn't even give them the chance to go through Dan's favorite routine—if you're not happy, we're not going to be happy, etc. "Not anymore, you don't," I said, "and if you won't give me your credit card, I can simply run a refund using your deposit slip. In any case, you're getting your money back, you're going to get out of here right now, and if I get any more trouble from you, I will call the police and have you escorted out of here and all the way out of our town, if necessary."

The four of them were stunned. They stood there slack-jawed, and in complete silence, while I ran their refund through our credit card processor. I asked Madam Big Mouth to sign the ticket, which she did without making a sound, and finally said, "Now get out of here and don't ever darken our doorway again!" A bit melodramatic, I admit, but it seemed the thing to say at the time.

They mumbled audibly as they made their way to the door and then stood in the parking lot for some time, apparently assessing their options. But we never heard from them again and nothing could have made us happier.

After they had left, I noticed that a nice couple in their 30s, along with their daughter who was about 12, had been sitting in the library throughout the whole episode. I went in to apologize for the ruckus, especially because the youngster had to be exposed to such horrible behavior and language. The man smiled at me, "No apology necessary," he said, "It's probably good for her at her age to see just how rude and despicable some adults can be. And also how calm and patience—and quick thinking—can defuse a potentially explosive situation. Matter of fact," he went on, "If I had been you and it was my wife they were yelling at, I'm afraid I would have punched those loud-mouths right in the jaw. We were cheering you on in here."

Be that as it may, it was great to see their backsides heading out the front door. But in all honesty, I hope I never have to do that again, at least not right away.

Fond regards,
Dick

Though we never did hear from them again, we heard about them for a while. In assessing their options, they evidently decided to try Whistler's Inn, directly across Main Street from us. Apparently, they inundated Joan Mears, the owner, with all manner of tales about how rude we were, how terrible the Inn was, and so on. Joan told us later that she listened for a few moments and then told them that certainly they had to be wrong, "…because we've known the Toners for quite some time and they're the nicest people in town." She also said that she had heard enough to know that she didn't want them staying at their Inn either, so she told them that she didn't have rooms for them.

We were to receive a bit more feedback from others as the next few weeks went by and one incident in particular must have really taken the wind out of their sails. Reportedly, they made a point to go by the Chamber of Commerce office to register a formal complaint. The executive director, Beverle Reiman-Marcus, listened patiently to their tale of woe, as was her custom, and then sweetly informed them that just couldn't have happened the way they said. She knew the people who owned the Birchwood well and was sure that they must have been at some other place.

We certainly got their attention, however, because somewhere in the conversation they asked Beverle if the police really would escort them out of town if one of the innkeepers asked them to. Beverle assured them that they would and, in fact, had done so "just last week". "This is a very quiet and peaceful village," she told them, "and we're not very tolerant of those who try to upset that tranquility". It was an out and out prevarication, of course, but she is an elegant lady and had obviously sized up the folks she was dealing with in very short order.

It's a shame that 99% of the guests we entertained over the time we owned the Inn were as nice as they could be, yet we remember most vividly the remarkably small handful of trouble makers that we came in contact with. But then, that simply emphasizes the point that the bad ones were few and far between, thus making them all the more memorable.

Perhaps an even more interesting example of the bad apples came as part of a very well rehearsed and effective con job. Dan had been out doing the shopping one morning and when he arrived back at the Inn, he mentioned two young men that he had met outside the supermarket where they were collecting donations for "prevention of teenage drug abuse". In this day and age, that's a sure-fire way of getting the attention of the area parents if ever there was one. They had told Dan that they were Boston police officers, on a leave of absence, and they had come out to Berkshire County to help with collections for DARE, a joint police and parental anti-drug program.

In the course of conversation with them, they asked Dan if he knew any place where they might get lodging for the next week or so. It would be as a contribution in kind for their campaign, of course, and Dan told them to come by the Birchwood later to see what we might do for them. It was to be a team decision, but the cause certainly seemed worthwhile as Dan explained it to Joan and me. And sure enough, they showed up at the door late that afternoon saying that Dan had told them to come by.

Perhaps it was my military background extending itself to paramilitary forces, but when I laid eyes on them, my first reaction was that they were the scruffiest looking cops I had ever seen. They had long hair and beards and were wearing dirty jeans with tears at the knees. They looked like they hadn't had a bath in weeks, and their overall appearance was totally unlike what you might expect of police officers seeking charitable donations. So I asked them about it, right off the top.

"We're undercover narcs," they told me, "and this is the way we look on the job. Matter of fact, looking like this lends authenticity to our message, especially when we go into classrooms and teen assemblies. The kids really dig the way we look and they know we're on the up and up," one of them explained. And then, as if on cue, he took out a picture of himself, clean-cut, in a policeman's dress blue uniform. He also handed me a photocopy of a letter from the Boston Police Commissioner, authorizing the time to do this and certifying their credentials. They also had badges, ID cards and all the other identifying data that a cautious person might ask for.

So they convinced me. Not just convinced, they impressed me. While they clearly looked like scags, they were well spoken, personable, and they were doing something very positive for our community. Sure we had room for them. One of the carriage house suites was vacant for the next week, and allowing them to stay there was the least we could do to prevent teen drug abuse in our newly adopted community.

The next morning after the lads had "gone out to work", Paula came over to the kitchen and asked who the slobs were that were staying in suite # 1. She went on to say that they had cooked a steak the night before, but instead of using a broiler pan, they had just plopped the steak on the oven rack and let the juices run all over the place. In addition, there were dozens of empty beer bottles scattered all over the suite, their few clothes were strewn everywhere, water had been spilled all over the bathroom, and the place was in a general mess that would take hours to clean. Clearly, I was going to have to have a long chat with these lads when they returned in the evening.

Then I started to think a bit more clearly. All of the credentialing material that they had shown me was from Boston, over 120 miles to the east. None of their papers said a single word about Berkshire County and none of their credentials had been locally authenticated. Maybe, just maybe, they weren't such nice guys after all.

I called the Lenox Police chief to ask him if he knew anything about this pair or if they had checked in with him before beginning their charitable campaign. The chief told me that he had never heard of them, but cautioned that they might have checked in with the Pittsfield department since Pittsfield is also the County seat. He offered to make a check when he was up there later in the afternoon, but I told him no, I would call and would let him know the results.

When I spoke to the Pittsfield desk sergeant, he told me that they had, indeed, heard about these lads, but not in they way I might expect. In fact, there was a warrant out for their arrest in nearby New York state where they were wanted for larceny, fraud, conspiracy to defraud, impersonating a police officer and a few other felonies. He went on to question whether I knew their plans for the day, which I didn't, but I identified the shopping center where they had first come to light the day before.

Apparently our phony narcs must have found the pickings pretty good in that same shopping center. According to the call I received back about an hour later, they had just been picked up there and were behind bars awaiting the local magistrate's decision whether to charge them locally or extradite them back to New York where they had a bigger book on them. The sergeant also asked me if they had left anything behind. When I told him it was just a handful of dirty clothes, he responded, "Then I wouldn't expect them to be back to check out."

It seems ironic that these seemingly intelligent young hoods who were clearly glib, well-prepared and rehearsed, were so dumb as to trash the free rooms they were being given as a base for their operations. More than likely, they would have been caught eventually, but there's no telling how far into the future that might have been if they hadn't disgusted Paula with the way they left their room. Perhaps, the old motto—crime doesn't pay— needs to be expanded to include—and neither does being a slob.

But things have a way of balancing themselves out. It wasn't but a few months later when a good looking, well dressed, middle-aged man came to the Inn looking to rent one of the carriage house suites for at least a month. He was writing a book, he said, and needed a place of peace and quiet to do the final chapters and complete the editing of it so he could make his publisher's deadline. It happened that the same suite was available for the month—cleaned up by now of course—and we agreed on a rental price that he generously offered to pay in full, in advance.

We had told Paula what he was doing and suggested that she look for his car before going into the suite to make up the room because he was really anxious to have quiet and privacy. The following morning, after making up the room, Paula came over to announce that she didn't know what the book that he was writing was about, but it must have been one of those steamy romance novels because he was certainly working at getting some inspiration the night before. In reality, the book, according to our guest, was a highly technical treatise, thus demanding his full and concentrated attention to be sure that every statement was correct and could be verified. But it didn't matter to us that he had sought out a muse for inspiration that night before. We had no restrictions on entertaining as long as it was done within the bounds of civility.

But the odd thing was, that was the only day or night that he ever set foot in the suite from then on. We kept waiting for him to come back and labor over his manuscript, or barring that, to ask for the balance of his money back. We kept the occupied sign in our guest book for the full month that he had booked the room but we neither saw hide nor hair of him again.

Naturally, that prompted our speculation about why he wanted the room, or why we saw him only once. One theory was that he had the greatest assignation in history planned and it was worth a month's rent to keep his rendezvous. But that didn't make sense because we would have gladly rented him a room for one night for considerably less.

Another thought was that he had just been overwhelmed by the book and a bad case of writer's block and had decided to chuck the whole thing. But that didn't make sense either, because he surely would have told us and asked for a part of his money back, if that were the case.

Perhaps it was a case of reading too many trash novels, but the idea that made the most sense in the long run was that he was a local guy, married, who had met up with "the love of his life". This was going to be their trysting spot for the next many weeks, far away from the prying eyes of co-workers, friends and especially his wife. But apparently he wasn't very slick at this sort of thing because, bingo, his wife caught him at it on the very first night. But truth or imagination, we'll never know. A month later, his rent pocketed, we put the suite back on the market and never, ever heard from him again.

*   *   *

March 25, 1992
Dear Chris & Tom,

As I was preparing to write this note, I thought that you two must be getting pretty tired reading my complaints about the lack of money, or the misdeeds of a tiny handful of guests. So I decided this one wasn't going to be that way. Instead, I want to tell you about one of the more touching and moving experiences that we've had.

Occasionally, when people make reservations, they will inform us of certain special requirements that they might have, and almost invariably, they politely and almost beseechingly ask if we can handle their needs. They might range from the need for special milk for lactose intolerance to the refrigerated storage of special medications, such as insulin. On rare occasions we can't accommodate some of these requirements, such as an elevator to the second floor, but we are always able to steer them to a place that will be just right for them—one of the nice things about the cooperation among innkeepers in Lenox.

Last weekend, we had a couple here who fell into the former category—the simple need to refrigerate some special foods and medications and to provide them 24-hour access to the storage area. Of course, we told them that we would gladly take care of that need and we suggested that we could probably handle most anything else that might come up.

When Arlene and Roger Wilson arrived about mid-afternoon, it was immediately obvious that something was seriously wrong with the man. He was shockingly gaunt, looked as though he couldn't take another step and leaned noticeably and heavily on his wife for support. The lady seemed to be in a surprisingly buoyant mood for someone whose husband was clearly in serious physical condition. And after we checked them in, she said that they would get comfortable in their room (one of our nicest of the fireplace rooms) and then she would be back down with the items that needed to be refrigerated.

When she returned, she had a fairly large quantity of food products, such as soymilk and other health food items, along with a variety of medications. We invited her out to the kitchen to show her precisely where the items would be stored and asked her if there was anything else that we might help her with. She drew herself up with great dignity and grace—an obviously refined and cultured woman—and with a vague hint of a sad smile on her face, she went on to explain their circumstances. Apparently, her husband, Roger, had been suffering from pancreatic cancer for quite some time and though they thought it was in remission after extensive radiation therapy, it had recently returned and had virulently metastasized throughout his internal organs. He had been given only a month to live and their stay with us was to be their last "celebration" together.

As we listened to Arlene tell of the situation, with almost a surreal calm and serenity, we had all we could do to hold back the tears ourselves and put our arms around her for comfort—whether that was hers or ours, I'm not certain. But in her nobility, she wanted no part of this. This weekend was not to be sad or in any way maudlin. It was truly meant to be a celebration of their great love for one another and a time to enjoy. There would be time for sadness and tears later.

The food products that she had given us were items for a macrobiotic diet that his physicians had placed him on. It was supposedly the only type of food he could manage to hold down without terrible pain and thereby provide him with the nutrition that he so desperately needed. She explained that the medications were all to dull the pain that he was experiencing. It was too late to take any therapeutic medications. She noted that the foods were unappetizing to look at, at best and, with our permission, she would be happy to come out in the kitchen to prepare them at breakfast time. I insisted that they were our guests and we wanted them to feel that way. If she would show me what needed to be done, I would be proud to make Roger's breakfast along with all the others. That seemed to please her greatly.

She and Joan then went out into the library, where they worked out a schedule of sites and events that the two of them might enjoy, while not being overly taxing on her husband. By chance, a macrobiotic restaurant, operated by a fairly young Japanese couple, had recently opened in the nearby town of Stockbridge. Our elegant guest reacted to this news just as she might have a few years before when told of a five-star French restaurant that was just waiting for them, personally, to help them celebrate this special occasion. When she and Joan were finished mapping out their itinerary for the weekend, she said that she needed to go back up to the room to see how Roger was doing. But just before heading out of the library, she briefly hugged Joan and said, "I knew this was exactly the place that we wanted to come to when I spoke to you on the telephone. You were so sweet. I can't thank all of you enough for your kindness."

We saw them frequently over the course of the next two days, and each time we did, they looked more like young kids on their honeymoon than a middle aged couple facing an imminent personal disaster. Despite his pain and frailty, Roger was animated and friendly. He joked with all of us, especially about the most unappetizing food that he had to eat—and even apologized to Joan because she had to serve it. When wine and cheese was served, he laughed about his bottled spring water and claimed that it was good that his doctor had put him "on the wagon" because, in his better days, he probably would have handled one of those carafes of red wine all by himself. We were constantly amazed to see the joy that radiated between them and lit up the whole house.

When it was time for them to check out, Joan and Dan looked at me and said that this one was going to be mine—they just didn't feel up to saying goodbye to such extraordinary people. Neither did I, but one of us had to do it and I was certainly the one who had had the most experience with this type of situation.

Both of them came to the desk, smiling brightly and holding hands. I was probably overly formal in explaining their bill to them and then processing the credit card payment, but I was afraid that I would lose my composure if I let down my guard. But with the formalities finally taken care of, I took both of their hands in mine at the same time and managed to blurt out something like, "Thank you very much for being with us this weekend. You taught us all a great deal about love and life, and we all wish you the very best."

This lovely, gracious woman, still holding my hand, drew me out from behind the counter, put her arms around me and said, "Thank you dear man. Everything's going to be just fine." And then pausing only long enough to slip by the Dutch door to the kitchen and blow a kiss to Joan and Dan, the Wilsons were gone.

As I look back on them four days later, I am convinced that they were two of the most remarkable people that I've ever met. If ever faced with a similar situation, we can only hope that we would show the same amount of courage, dignity and patience. We will never forget them.

Looking forward to your visit,
Dick

While the Wilsons were, indeed, two of the most memorable people that we met in our career as innkeepers, they certainly were not the only ones to display courage in the face of adversity and to make us feel very special in the process. Not very long after this experience, a lovely lady in her sixties came to stay with us. As we came to know her, she explained that she had just lost her husband of nearly 45 years. She had been spending all of her time in the home that they had shared for most of their married life and she found herself becoming increasingly lonely and depressed.

To try to relieve that depression, she thought it would be good to get away and, consequently, had come to spend a weekend with us in the Berkshires—a place that both of them had enjoyed together many times before. Unfortunately, she spent most of the time in her room, which was one of the smaller ones in the Inn. She rarely went out other than for an evening meal by herself, and we were concerned when she was leaving that she had failed to accomplish her goal of starting her return to a more normal life. Joan had even admonished her, kindly and gently, that she could have done a little bit more while she had been with us. But she then went on to express the hope that at least these two days might be her first step toward finding herself and taking a new path in life.

That evening, we received a call from the dear lady, her voice almost frantic with concern. She told Dan that her diary was missing—the most precious thing that she had in the world because it was a day by day account of her husband's last days. And as she described it, at least, it sounded like a period of time that was the equal in difficulty to the ones that the Wilsons had experienced, yet punctuated with that very special love that only older people have the privilege of experiencing. Dan told her that we would scour the room and the places in the Inn where she had been and we'd call her back one way or the other.

Fortunately, the diary was found. For some reason she had tucked it in one of the tiny drawers of the antique sewing machine that was a decorative piece in her room. She was delighted to receive the call and of course we sent it off by priority mail the following morning.

It was just over a week later that a small package arrived from one of the better-known gift shops in Boston. In it was a small Hummel figurine— she had obviously seen Joan's collection from our early married life that was on display in the den—and along with it was a lovely letter expressing her gratitude. The final paragraph was directed to Joan and it is worth quoting in its entirety.

"Your thoughtful little lecture to me just before I left has not gone unheeded. I thought about what you said most of the way home, and I knew, without question, that you were right. So as soon as I learned that my diary was safe, I sat down and made out a list of all the things that I used to enjoy doing, and I have set a schedule for myself to do every one of them. And in just a few days, I've discovered that I can still find as much enjoyment out of life as I once did. I have you to thank for that, my dear. So you see, my trip to Lenox wasn't a waste of time after all. I will always remember and be grateful to you for opening my eyes again to the joys of life —just as my husband would have wanted me to do. Thank you."

And it was not just women who shouldered the burden of loneliness with courage and dignity. Toward the end of our time at the Inn, we received a reservation from an older gentleman who had lost his wife and dreaded the thought of spending the first Christmas without her in their home. He thought it would be good for him to get out with other people during the holidays and he had heard that we were very nice people and our Inn was more like a home than a hotel.

As was the usual case, Joan's heart went out to him even before we met him and when he had checked in, she invited him to share our private, family Christmas dinner with us—just as she had invited the young Army couple during our first Christmas at the Inn. It was clearly the right thing to do because he obviously enjoyed himself and was in a very positive frame of mind when he left two days before New Years.

A month later, we received a package from him that contained a very brief note. He said that he had decided from talking to us that he needed a new challenge in life, something to occupy his time and his mind, so he had taken up oil painting. Contained in the package was the very first piece he had done. The painting was somewhat abstract in style and, to be quite honest, it really wasn't very good. But the sincerity with which it had been sent, and the gratitude that accompanied it, more than offset any lack of artistic genius.

But this tale would not be complete without mentioning Arlene Wilson's return to the Birchwood Inn. Exactly one year later, to the weekend, she made reservations to come back to the Inn—alone—and occupy the same room that she and Roger had shared the year before.

We sat with her for hours that weekend, listening to the story of how he passed away only three weeks after they had come to stay with us. He had talked about that weekend every day before he died, she told us, and even in his worst pain and in that gray netherworld of high morphine doses, he still smiled each time he mentioned their "celebration". He had passed gently in the night, at home in their own bed, and she was convinced that he died a very happy and contented man. She, too, was certain that there couldn't have been a better way to say farewell to one another. And despite the residual grief that still lingered around the edges of her consciousness, she told the story to us with the same sad smile and elegant demeanor that she had shown the year before.

She said she felt compelled to come back even though it might seem strange to someone that didn't know the two of them very well. This was her way to put an end to her period of mourning, and though we were likely never to hear from her again, she would always remember us for the joy that we brought to her and her beloved Roger just one year previously. And we never did hear from her again but somehow we are confident that everything is still fine.

*   *   *

April 28, 1992
Dear Chris & Tom,

I can't remember whether or not I told you—and I'm too lazy to go back and check—but our personal accommodations have changed drastically, and for the better I might add. We decided around Thanksgiving time that the lower demand on rooms did not any longer justify three adults and three animals sharing 288 square feet of living space each night. So Dan and Seamus have moved into Room 6, which is right over the kitchen and immediately adjacent to the back stairs leading from the kitchen to the second floor.

It's been marvelous, for all of us. And while we still live in "the hovel", it has magically transformed from the crowded, messy grotto that we once lived in to a relatively palatial place of escape for Joan, me and the kitties. I guess "relatively" is certainly a relative expression in this case, but I can't tell you how much the change has improved our collective outlook on life.

Along with the living arrangements, we also changed the work routine, at long last. It was silly for all of us to get up at 5:30 AM, work all day, and then all go to our room after nine in the evening—only to continue answering the phone well into the wee hours of the morning. Joan and I are now getting up early to do breakfast, etc., and in exchange, Dan stays up until closing time in the evening while we steal away to the hovel right after dinner. We are also putting the telephone answering system on at night telling the callers that the reservation desk is open from 7:00 AM to 9:00 PM, and please call back then. That should put an end to the curious from "the City that never sleeps" calling on the 800 number at 3:00 AM to ask if "ya guddany snow up dere".

I'm going into this detail to set the stage for a rather memorable experience that we had this week. When Joan and I arrived in the kitchen shortly after six last Monday morning, there was an almost overwhelming smell of SKUNK that greeted us. Now we know that we're in the country and that skunks are rather common denizens of the area, but the kitchen? All the windows and doors had been closed over night, of course, so my first thought was that the skunk had sprayed right outside the kitchen window. No luck there. There was a nice fresh smell of spring outside the house, so that couldn't be it.

My next target was the basement, and as I opened the door in the butler's pantry to what the New Englanders call "the cellah", the stench was overwhelming. Oh my god, I thought, we have a skunk in the basement. But how could that be? There's only one access directly from the outside and that's the big steel bulkhead door (that Joan can't even lift, let alone a skunk), and another heavy wooden door at the foot of the bulkhead stairs. No way a skunk could get in that way. Nor had one come through the house, certainly. But someone was going to have to go downstairs to check, and I didn't see Joan volunteering. Oh well, if I were to be sprayed, it would wash off eventually, and I didn't have any place special to go for the next week. So off I went.

Much to my surprise, I wasn't met by an upraised tail at the foot of the stairs, nor did I get any sense of a skunk being present in the laundry room. So I continued on, by the wood room and into the shop area, and still no sign of Brer Skunk—or any convincing evidence that he had ever been there. So I continued on to the west end of the basement, toward the china vault and furnace room. As I entered the small room that connects to the other two, the smell became almost overwhelming—nauseating, certainly, and I wasn't above gagging a bit. No smell in either the vault or the furnace room, whose doors had been closed, so it appeared that I had tracked down the source, if not the culprit, and I was just going to have to get to the bottom of this later. Meanwhile there was a breakfast to cook. Ugh!

With the help of a very effective room deodorant spray, we tried to make the dining room free of skunk odor and managed to mask most of the smell. The reactions of most of the guests were a bit puzzled. The room smelled just fine to them, they told us, and no, they didn't get the slightest odor of skunk. But one young fellow said that he did, indeed, get the hint of a skunk, and he loved it. It reminded him of growing up in the country in Pennsylvania and had nothing but happy memories from those days. Whatever makes you happy, I guess.

Well, I won't stretch out the tale any longer than I have to. After Dan got up, we began the hunt in earnest and would end up devoting the next two days to the "search and destroy" mission. As it turned out, there was no skunk in the basement or anywhere else in the house for that matter. The skunk, or what was left of him, was in a window well under the front porch and that subterranean window just happened to face into the basement room where the smell was most pronounced. I had tracked it down to the right place, but our odor-causing varmint was outside the window, not inside.

As we were to discover later, the skunk had probably fallen or jumped into the window well the previous fall—perhaps searching for a nest for the winter. He had obviously tried to get back out but the well was six feet deep with vertical concrete sides, and he had died and frozen over the winter. The coming of spring and the warm weather thawed out the carcass and, eventually, the odor that was generated was not just the noxious skunk defense mechanism, but also the additional pungent bouquet of his rotting flesh.

The basement windows had long been sealed up with a plastic sheeting and then covered with plywood from the inside. The poor creature, in his panic, had broken the glass of the window, torn the plastic sheeting to shreds and darn near scratched and chewed his way through the half inch sheet of plywood before the cold got to him. And in addition to his freshly thawed corpse, we also found the skeletons of two possums and some other smaller rodent that we couldn't identify—perhaps a rabbit.

But taking the carcasses out to the back woods and burying them wasn't enough to rid the area of the smell. And I was convinced that I had it embedded in my nostrils for life. We tried every backwoods or over-the-counter remedy for skunk odor that we could find. Tomato juice, the instant solution according to a neighbor, didn't even touch it. "Odor Mate" from the local pet store was equally ineffective. One of Dan's friends swore by Massengale Douche, a feminine product that I'm sure the manufacturer is not likely to

*advertise for these purposes. And I refuse to even think of any other connection
between the two. But that didn't work either. Even the local U.S. Department
of Agriculture field office had a solution—a fifty-fifty mixture of dish detergent
and household bleach diluted in a little baking soda and water. I'm sure the
smell of that concoction probably helped if only to mask the other aroma. But
Dan and I still smelled skunk and we had to press on.*

*The only practical remedy that we came up with was to dig out another six
inches of dirt at the base of the window well, and take that out in the woods
and bury it as well. And it worked pretty well, but by that time the smell had
permeated everything in that part of the basement and it was just going to take
time to go away. And it also became apparent that to avoid any recurrence of
this calamity, we had to slither under the porch on our bellies—the clearance
was about 12" around the infamous window well—and cover the well with
heavy boards. All in a day's work, it says under our job description.*

*And as they might say in tales of the macabre, "Still, on cold, foggy and damp
nights, the window well, to this day, gives up its malodorous reminder of the
morbid events of that April day." Yuck!*

Take time to smell the roses,
Dick

Though the circumstances never got that bad again, this was not the last
time that we would have an encounter with the ubiquitous New England
polecat. We knew they nested right out in the woods behind the house
because we would frequently get a whiff of their pungent aroma the first
thing in the morning. But from a distance, it's very tolerable—almost a
part of the pastoral ambience, if you can stretch your imagination that far.

One particular evening after dinner, as we were turning over the night
shift to Dan, Joan started out the door to the back porch with the intent

of proceeding on to the entrance to the hovel. As she started to take the single step down to the porch level, she looked down and in a matter-of-fact voice said, "Well how in the world did you get out here, Big Kitty? You're supposed to be in the house."

In fact, Big Kitty was in the house, standing right behind her in the kitchen. Suddenly, she realized that the big kitty that she was addressing had a big bushy tail and two white stripes down his back. She pulled back into the kitchen and slammed the door with amazing speed and alacrity and stammered, "My god, I almost stepped on a skunk."

But apparently—and fortunately—the skunk was a lot more startled than she, because as Dan looked out the door, he could see the telltale waddle scooting across the driveway just as fast as the little varmint could move. Things happened so fast that Brer Skunk never got a chance to lift his tail and leave a distinctive reminder of his presence, and he was probably just as happy about that as we were.

As time went by, we changed our innkeeper housing situation quite a few times. During the summers, Room 6 would be needed for guest revenue purposes and so we had to find Dan a new place to stay, and we were especially interested in a more permanent solution so that he wasn't bouncing around every few months. He didn't want to move back into the hovel and, as much as we love him, we didn't want him there either.

By this time, Dan had made many friends his own age in the village and he put the word out that he was looking for a place to live. And it wasn't long before he was asked to share the rent on a very nice house that was about five miles from the Inn. It was fully furnished except for a bed in the guest room and some place to store his belongings. And those items were quickly available from the storeroom in the attic. So in the late spring of 1992, Dan "left home" and it was an even better situation for him than Room 6 had been.

Whenever Dan took an occasional evening off for a little social life with his friends, Seamus stayed with his "grandparents" while his buddy was away. And it was on one of these occasions that Seamus learned a very up close and personal lesson about skunks.

It was just about time for me to leave the kitchen area and head over to the hovel, and the last thing we did when Seamus was with us was to take him out one last time. There's no pet that I've ever seen who loves to go out as much as he does, so he rouses himself from near stupor to a prancing, jaunty *bon vivant* as soon as he steps outside the door. That night was no different and he assumed his normal rakish trot as we headed around the driveway toward the guest entrance.

Just as he reached the entrance area, he stopped dead in his tracks, his ears went up and his tail began to wag most enthusiastically. You could almost hear him think to himself (I thought later since I couldn't see what he was looking at), "Oh boy, a kitty, and I sure do love playing with kitties."

Only, as it turned out, this was one of those black ones with a big bushy tail and two white stripes down the back. Unfortunately, the skunk was in the corner of the ell, right under the kitchen window, and there was no escaping Seamus' enthusiastic scamper across the 20' separating them. In a flash, the skunk's tail came up and his aim and timing couldn't have been better. He caught Seamus directly in the face from no more than three feet away and, of course, stopped him dead in his tracks. And as the poor startled pup wheeled on his heels to run back toward me, Brer Skunk neatly slipped away and headed off to the more friendly confines of the back woods.

Seamus was temporarily blinded by the spray, and stumbled his way through the small garden, crushing a drain pipe extension into a twisted mess in his haste to retreat. He was clearly in pain, his eyes were shut tight and he was whimpering just a little bit—a rare thing for the pooch that has an incredibly high threshold of pain. As luck would have it, the garden hose had still not been drained and put away for the winter, even though it was well into November at the time. I rushed him to the hose and, as gently as I could, I began to wash out his eyes and his face where the brunt of the attack had occurred. He clearly knew that I was helping him, because he sat, good as gold, while I cleaned his eyes until he was able finally to hold them open.

But that wasn't to be the end of our evening's effort. Joan had come out to see what the racket was, and I asked her to get a coat on and go to the nearby pharmacy to get a package of Massengale Douche. After all, Dan's friend, Roy, had told us some time before that his prescription for skunk spray was for dogs, not for window wells, and he had convinced me that it would work. While Joan was gone, I called the vet to see if there was anything else I should do for his eyes—there wasn't—and then I mixed up a batch of the USDA special formula and started to wash the poor guy off. Once again, I had all I could do to swallow down my gagging from the odor, but the look of utter dismay in Seamus' eyes impelled me onward to help him.

We spent most of the next hour and a half out in the driveway, first scrubbing him with the USDA formula, rinsing him off, and then applying the douche and rinsing him. After about five cycles of this, we were getting chilled to the bone. And Seamus, the pup who is impervious to cold and swims happily in an icy pond or would lie all day in a snow bank if you let him, was finally beginning to shiver himself. Apparently, in the process of scrubbing him deep down to his skin, I had bypassed his insulating layer of fur and he was getting just as cold as we were. Residual smell or not, it was time to dry him off for the night and get all of us inside where we could warm up.

As had been the case earlier when we had the problem in the basement, the scent molecules had firmly attached themselves to the moist insides of my nostrils. So I wasn't sure whether Seamus still smelled badly or it was greatly magnified beyond what someone would find with a fresh nose. We would find out when Dan got back to pick up his buddy shortly before midnight. I stayed up in the kitchen with the pup and as Dan walked in the door, he first asked me what I was doing, still up. And then he said something to the effect that, wow, there must be a skunk real close by.

When he had heard the story of the encounter three hours before, he hugged Seamus so the aroma couldn't have been all that bad. But he still decided that this might be that rare night that Seamus was going to be restricted to sleeping on the floor. And like the basement after that earlier encounter, whenever the pup was out in the rain for at least a year after, the distinctive aroma of skunk would emerge from his pores and he wasn't quite as pleasant to be near as he usually was.

I'm not sure whether Seamus has ever seen a skunk close up since that day. But he's a smart old guy and I suspect that if he did, his jaunty prance would halt in place and rather than charging ahead to greet his new playmate, he more than likely would wisely retreat to a tactically safe place. And I would certainly do the same thing.

*   *   *

April 28, 1992
Dear Chris and Tom,

Can't tell you how much we appreciated your visit. Just wish it could have been longer. Chris, the tiny lamp shades that you bought to reduce the glare of the sconces in the dining room just arrived via UPS and they are perfect. They not only achieve the intended purpose, but they also dress up the room and put the ideal finishing touch on it. I can recall my grandmother had shades just like these on the sconces in what she called her "sunroom". I guess Nana's old house and furnishings qualify to be genuine antiques by now, so the shades lend an air of authenticity as well. Thanks very much for your thoughtfulness—and also your perfect choice of just what the dining room needed.

While offering thanks, I can't overlook the tremendous help that you were, Tom, in tracing all the electrical circuits in the house. Having the old knife-switch and fuse style of circuits is one thing, but trying to find the proper circuit to shut down when there were minor electrical problems or new additions to be made was a pain. As I mentioned to you, it took me almost as long to find the right circuits as it did to install the new Casablanca-style overhead fans and lights in the small rooms on the third floor. I hope to get these same fans in all the rooms before the summer season, and your efforts will make that considerably easier. One of my pet peeves is that electricians never seem to mark the circuits on the breaker/fuse panel box when a house is built. Looks like this has been a chronic problem ever since electricity was adapted for household use.

Some day I'll get around to putting a Plexiglas cover on the panel to show it off, as you suggested. While it is clearly a show piece of days gone by, I have a nagging concern that some character is going to find the panel, even though it's hidden behind the Dutch door, and promptly fry himself over that 100 amp input to the panel. Unfortunately, curious humans don't have the same benefit of nine lives that cats seem to have, and we would end up being liable, of course. An added incentive to get it done.

I think we're as excited as you two are over the new mountain home that you've bought at Mammoth Mountain [CA]. The videos were stunning, especially the snow tunnels that have to be dug to get into the house or see out the windows in the dead of winter. Your plans for all the improvements sound exceptionally ambitious and I hope your contractors are more dependable than the ones we've hired here. We'll look forward to seeing the place one of these days, as well as your gorgeous home in Carmel Valley.

Speaking of visiting you, we won't hold you to your proposal that we have an annual reunion of the WWWG each winter. That sounds like a very large undertaking to us, but I must admit, it also sounds like a tremendous time would be had by all. We will certainly be delighted to take you up on your invitation some day, but only after you have had time to think it over and be sure that you really want to take this on. Maybe it's our experience with entertaining a number of guests that prompts the caution, but at least you can be sure that your guests will pitch in and help.

Our discussion on improved financial management has also been very helpful. We have already done away with the use of petty cash for our day to day purchases. Each one of us now has a corporate American Express and Visa card, and of course this will provide a much better record of what we spend and what we spend it on. Trying to assemble all the receipts and notes to detail our expenses for the tax accountant was an absolute bear of a chore and I'm certain that things will be a lot easier in the years ahead.

As I said, your visit was much too short, but you certainly reinforced our efforts—and our choice of property—in the short time you were here. We pretty well thought we were on the right track but it always helps to have your own judgment bolstered by someone whose opinions and insight you trust. Thanks again for the lamp shades and all your other contributions. It's on to year two with considerably more confidence and advanced preparation.

Our love to you both,
Dick

While it was intended as more of a social visit than anything else, Chris and Tom's visit got us started on a lot of things that we might not have done otherwise. Chris was an art major in college and her taste, ability to visualize and her practical background in craft work are considerable. I have often told her that she could have out-Martha'd Martha Stewart if she had set her mind to it earlier and undertaken the initiative. She's that good.

Both she and Tom offered ideas for sprucing up the place—at a relatively small cost, an important consideration at the time—and for making our daily efforts a little easier. Though many of the changes may seem minor, they made a real difference in the quality of our offerings when the suggestions were implemented.

I think I'll always remember Chris's reaction to her cup of tea at breakfast their first morning with us. She is an inveterate tea drinker—perhaps from all the years they had lived in England—and she knows good tea and bad. She mentioned that her tea had a slight hint of coffee flavor to it, which led us to realize that we used the basket which held the coffee grounds to heat pots of water for tea. Naturally, it gave a taste of coffee to the water that a tea drinker wouldn't appreciate, but we rarely drink tea and it never occurred to us. We probably had tea-drinking guests who had the same reaction that Chris did but hesitated to tell us. A new basket for our Bunn coffee maker, to be used for tea water only, was purchased the next day and we never had the same problem again.

It turned out that the Houses initial idea to host a WWWG reunion had already been well thought out and it did, indeed, become an annual affair. But first an explanation of the meaning of WWWG.

In the mid '70s, a small group of us—most all Air Force couples except for one Navy officer and his wife—became close friends and social buddies when we were all assigned to the Supreme Headquarters, Allied Powers in Europe (SHAPE), NATO's military headquarters in Mons, Belgium. Coincidentally, each of the men was assigned to a key position in the headquarters and had a decided influence on the policy and programming decisions affecting the allied military forces in Europe.

We worked long hours, often well into the night to meet important deadlines. But when we partied, we did that with equal vigor and enthusiasm. We developed the habit, over time, of meeting for lunch at the Officers' Club each Friday, primarily to review our efforts of the past week and to try to forecast the directions that we would propose for upcoming issues. It so happened that the special offering at Club each Friday was the national dish of Belgium, *moules marinères avec pommes frites* (mussels steamed in white wine with crispy French fries). To be authentic, the dish also had to be accompanied by chilled Muscadet wine, and we were never averse to doing things properly.

As time went by, our luncheon meetings lasted longer and longer, our wives were often asked to join us and our custom began to be noticed by other diners at the Club. Rumors began to get back to us that we were becoming known as The Rat Pack (a pejorative prompted by jealousy?) because we also socialized on weekends and went on at least one ski trip together each winter. Not only did we discount the name because it had already been adopted by Frank Sinatra, Dean Martin, et al., we also thought that we should have the prerogative to chose our own name, if we were to be lumped together as an infamous band of brigands. And what could be a better descriptive than the White Wine Working Group, or WWWG. And the name has stuck to this day.

And so it was that the WWWG has had an annual ski reunion each winter at the House's beautiful mountain chalet at Mammoth Lakes, California, every year since 1993. Their Mammoth home is known as The Far Side as opposed to their Carmel Valley home which they have named Casa Casa (the House House). At times, the full membership doesn't make it, but Joan and I have had perfect attendance. Joan, of course, can no longer ski because of the damage done earlier to her leg, but she always found vital rest and enjoyment nonetheless. She reads, takes an afternoon nap if she feels like it, goes shopping with Chris or visits the local spa for relaxation. We are all skilled cooks (a modest way of saying gourmet chefs), and have a grand time taking turns preparing lavish dinners most every night that we are there. Each evening continues to be just as much fun as they were when we regularly got together 25 years ago.

Tom and Chris would very kindly ask us each December to select the dates for the following year's reunion, knowing that we were the most slavishly restricted by time. We are also convinced that they were prompted to hold the affairs, in large part, to give us a break from the routine of innkeeping. They not only succeeded marvelously in doing this, I think the annual ski vacation at Mammoth also helped us to maintain our positive attitude, let alone our sanity. And we have always been deeply grateful for their affectionate consideration and generosity.

The "circuit mapping" which Tom did made future electrical improvements much easier. As I had hoped, we installed Casablanca-style ceiling fans in all the rooms on the third floor before that second summer and it made a huge difference, especially on the rare hot and muggy days that we sometimes encountered in July. The new fans even made for a pleasant breeze on nights when the outside air was cool but still. Our nephew, Brian Vossmer (of the "goddam general" fame) is a master electrician and he kindly installed the fans in some of the rooms on the second floor where the switching arrangement and circuitry was a bit more complicated than I was willing to tackle. The luxury rooms were appropriately air-conditioned, though the guests rarely turned it on.

Another improvement that we made was to add commercial dead bolt locks on each of the bedroom doors. This change was prompted by an event, both humorous and embarrassing, that occurred during our second summer. It seemed that during that summer, particularly, we had a number of friends of Seiji Ozawa, the BSO music director, stay with us while they were in town for the concerts and a reunion with their old friend. One of these was the executive director of one of the major symphony orchestras in America, and he arrived with a beautiful lady who was considerably younger than he.

Near ten o'clock one morning during their stay, one of our young high school girls knocked twice on their bedroom door, pausing between knocks as she had been trained to do. When she received no answer, she used the master key to open the door so that she could begin making up the room. To her shock and great dismay, she found the gentleman and lady totally involved in the act of love-making and closed the door as quickly as she could. Obviously, our guest was more alerted by the presence of someone in the room than he had been when the housekeeper had knocked earlier because, right after she rushed downstairs to tell us what had happened, he came rushing after, not quite fully clothed and with fire in his eyes.

He denied that the young lady had knocked, but of course we knew differently, and we also knew why he hadn't heard her. To ameliorate his concern, I promised him that there would be a dead bolt lock on his door before that evening, and that was the beginning of the installation of the dead bolts on all the guest room doors in the Inn. I think by the end of the weekend, probably after retelling the tale many times to all his BSO friends, he actually found the intrusion to be much more humorous than embarrassing, but I'm not sure that our innocent young high schooler has recovered from the experience to this day.

*   *   *

May 26, 1992
Dear Chris & Tom,

As you no doubt recall, when we first began this business nearly a year ago, we were so strapped for revenue that we would accept virtually anyone as a guest as long as they could pay their way. As a result, we had ignored the frequent suggestions of our fellow innkeepers to develop and publish our policies. They advised us to include them as an insert in our brochures so that we would have some basis from which we could selectively choose our future guests—and be sure that they, in turn, wouldn't cancel on us at their whim. Looks like we're going to have to do that now.

Probably the most controversial policy that we need to develop pertains to children. Everyone's child is an angel, of course. However, only three of the 17 country inns in Lenox will permit children under teenage to stay there. So there must be a reason, particularly since the owners of each of these three inns have little children of their own, living in the inn, and they probably believe they would be a bit hypocritical to deny lodging to other little ones. We never followed that policy—until now, at least—but we are going to implement it after a recent experience.

People with young children tend to be very rare visitors to Lenox, particularly during the Tanglewood season because classical music lovers tend to be a bit older than pop music groupies so they very rarely have young ones with them. Last summer, we took a few couples with young children but were assured by each in advance that the children were well behaved and serious—which I guess is fitting for little ones being included at the BSO's debut performance of Gustav Holtz's "The Planets".

The reason that most inns don't accept children has far more to do with the preferences of their guests than it does with the personal preferences of the innkeepers. An older couple reading in the library doesn't like to be assaulted by little ones yelling and racing back and forth in front of them. Nor does a younger couple who have hired a nanny to care for their own children so they could get away for a weekend want to be awakened at 3:00 AM by a hungry infant in the next room or down the hall. So despite what might appear to be an insensitive policy at first glance, if you want repeat customers, it's good to cater to what they want. And knowing this, and in full appreciation for the cautions from our well-meaning friends, we occasionally accepted young children, fortunately without any bad experiences. At least until now.

Last weekend, we had a couple in their mid-thirties walk in without reservations and they had two young children, a boy about seven and a girl about five. We cautioned them that we don't normally take children because ours is a getaway location. As to be expected, we were assured that their children were "quiet, very mature, perfectly behaved" and that they would fully respect the privacy of the other guests. The family went out for dinner shortly after they were settled in their rooms, so for all we knew, the youngsters were living up to their parents' advanced billing. It wasn't until the next morning that they showed their true colors.

As Joan and I came over from the hovel at 6:00 to begin breakfast preparations, we heard the little girl, screaming her loudest, and the sound of racing feet coming from the library. I quickly headed to the source of the disturbance and found our "angelic, mature" young man chasing his sister around the couches with a very real, unsheathed samurai sword in both hands. It was poised above his head, in perfect kendo *fashion that he probably learned on children's TV programming or video game, and he was just waiting to get within range to expertly bring it down and slice his sister in half.*

It wasn't quite as dramatic as that. The sword was one that had been presented to me as a departing gift when we left our assignment in Japan, and though it was hand made of high grade steel with very authentic workmanship and detail, it had intentionally not been sharpened. But nonetheless, it would have done considerable damage had he succeeded in striking her. And he could easily "run her through" with the point.

As I became aware of what was going on, I went toward him and said in my most authoritative voice, "Stop right where you are and give me that sword—now!"

He heard the first part because he screeched on the brakes immediately. But instead of handing me the sword, he turned toward me with the sword still in striking position and a look on his face that indicated that his quarry had changed from his sister to me. We were about ten feet apart at this point, so I took another step toward him with my hand out as if to accept the sword that I expected him to hand over. Instead of doing so, he moved both his hands and the sword higher and farther behind his head as if to cock it and get more power into his swing.

That was all I needed. As I stepped toward him again, I glowered at him and growled, "You little son of a bitch, you hand that sword to me, handle first, or I'm going to break you in half with my bare hands." And with that I went into a karate position, which was actually a bit ludicrous because I haven't practiced unarmed combat for about 25 years. But it sure fooled him. He meekly lowered the sword, handed it to me and then, with his eyes flooding with tears, he begged me not to tell his parents.

Obviously, I did tell the parents and as you might expect from parents of angelic children, they didn't believe that their child would ever do such a thing. And the little girl refused to back me up, probably because she knew that the little bully would beat the crap out of her the first chance he got. Apparently, I had insulted them because, right after breakfast, they checked out a day earlier than planned. As for us, right after breakfast, we started drafting our policy statement card, with one of the leading items being, "Sorry, but we cannot accept any children younger than teen age." We don't need any other experiences like that.

All the best,
Dick

Despite the fact that we had very adequate liability insurance, Joan has harbored a fear—perhaps concern might be a more accurate term—that we might be sued for any one of a thousand reasons in this litigious society of ours. As a firm subscriber to John Locke's theories of property ownership on which our democracy was built, I was determined that we should have the right to choose to accept or reject certain guests—within the law—so that the character of our Inn would be maintained. As a result, many extra hours were spent in drafting our policies. In addition to our policy on children, of course, other topics, such as, a prohibition of smoking anywhere in the Inn, the exclusion of pets (Seamus and the kitties decided that one), and a minimum stay during Tanglewood, foliage season and holidays are also included. And then there's the final catchall phrase, "We reserve the right to change our prices and terms without notice".

The rate card, which contained our statement of policies, went on to specify, in detail, our deposit and cancellation policy.

> To guarantee your reservation, a one-night advance deposit is required. You may send a check that we must receive at least seven days prior to your arrival date. Deposits may also be made by providing us with a credit card number and authorization to collect the deposit. If you should have to cancel your reservation, we will require notice ten days prior to your arrival date. Your deposit, less 10%, will be refunded to you. If cancellation occurs less than ten days prior to your arrival, we regret that we will not be able to issue a refund. When making guaranteed reservations, please remember that you are making a commitment to us, just as we are making one to you.

To no one's surprise, the only policies that caused problems were those regarding children and the advance deposits. Money and children seem to be very sensitive subjects to some people, or at least our approach to them. The people who would vehemently insist on bringing their children to the Inn "because they have just as many rights as an adult does" were the same people, probably, whose children cry loudly or run around wildly during a Boston Symphony concert. The volunteer ushers who request that the parents control their children are often subject to the same verbal abuse that we occasionally received when we declined reservations that included young children. We clearly were violating the children's First Amendment rights to free expression.

It took a while, trying to explain why we did not accept young children to those who were adamantly unwilling to listen to any explanation, before we realized the proper solution. We no longer offered a rational clarification for the policy whenever someone indicated that they would have young children in their party. Instead, we would respond by saying, "I'm sorry, but we can't accept children under teen age but I'll be very happy to give you the names and phone numbers of the inns that do." Almost without exception, this was adequate. In defense of many young parents, they were simply looking for a place to stay. For the majority, some reasonable relief from their frustration and dilemma of finding accommodations for the whole family seemed to be their primary objective.

We quickly learned that we needed to recite the whole litany of the deposit and cancellation policy to everyone who made a reservation. We also asked if they agreed to that policy in advance and, therefore, authorized us to take the deposit on their credit card. When we mailed out written confirmations, we enclosed a copy of the rate schedule, including the policy statement— just to be sure. But occasionally there were those who claimed they never heard of the policies, even as they held the card in their hand while talking to us. But fortunately those occasions were fairly rare.

The character of some people comes through very clearly when they get aroused over what they perceive to be an injustice. One woman who claimed to be a junior partner in a very prestigious law firm in Boston cancelled her reservation well outside the ten-day limit. When I told her that I would return $81 of her $90 deposit, she became apoplectic. She claimed that she had never heard anything so "crude and blatantly dishonest in her life" and went on to say that she had "traveled the world over" and never been charged a processing fee for cancellations—even though she acknowledged being told of our policy in advance. She went on to threaten a suit, which is what lawyers do, I guess, but we never heard from her again.

Even worse was a state senator from New York whose secretary had made reservations for him and later called within the ten-day period to cancel. She politely explained that he had a last minute commitment, so I said that we would waive the forfeiture of the entire deposit of $120 but would hold back the 10% processing fee as if the cancellation had been with sufficient notice. She asked me to hold and I expect that she was just passing this message on to her boss. Instead, he came on the phone himself and immediately started screaming at the top of his lungs at me, beginning with the ever popular, "Do you know who I am?"

My frank and honest admission that I didn't, in fact, set off the worst tirade of shouted profanity that I had heard since my days aboard ship with young sailors. He then changed his tack to threats. He knew the attorney general of Massachusetts and he knew this person and that person, and he was going to put me out of business so fast that it would make my head spin. And all this over $12. I was so taken back by his behavior and language that I couldn't do anything but laugh—which, I'm sure, irritated him even further. Finally, I just told him that I hoped that he could make it another time and hung up the phone. Naturally, we never heard from him again—nor the attorney general.

But we often made exceptions to policy, depending upon the nature of the cancellation and the manner in which the guest spoke to us. A young man from Brazil told us that he had neither a credit card nor an American bank account but asked that we accept reservations for him, his mother and sister. He was so earnest that we had no doubt that he would show up on schedule—without making a deposit—and of course he did. And the three of them couldn't have been more delightful.

We also had a lady call, in tears, the day before she was due to arrive to tell us that her husband had suddenly died that morning. She went on to say that she knew that her deposit was forfeited but asked that if we were able to rebook the room if we might consider refunding her money. Times were going to be tough, financially, she said. Well, we didn't resell the room but her story was so touching, and she sounded so sincere, that we refunded the entire amount anyway. A most gracious thank you note followed within a few weeks.

But two of our most interesting guests didn't pay for their room at all. One Monday night in early spring, while there was still some snow on the ground and a definite chill in the air, we decided to turn out all the outside lights and close for the night. We had just finished dinner and were about to settle down to a relaxing evening of reading, when there was a knock on the kitchen door. Joan went to the door and standing there were two nuns, carrying what looked like small black Gladstone bags and dressed in full black habit down to their ankles, a style of dress that we thought had become passé many years before.

One of the nuns said that she knew that we were closed but that "the Lord had led them" to our house as a place where they knew that they could find refuge for the night. Joan invited them in, and though we should probably have been suspicious in this day and age, they both looked almost saintly in their robes, their demeanor and the expressions that they wore on their faces. We offered them two of our small rooms on the third floor and asked them what time they would like to have breakfast in the morning. Our offer seemed to embarrass them and they made some minor protestations that such luxury would be too much to ask. But we insisted and they went quietly to their rooms.

The next morning they came down to breakfast, carrying all the linens they had used and they asked if they could use the laundry to wash the linens and remake the beds. While we declined their offer, it was a most unusual suggestion and we were grateful for it. We were to learn that they were from a convent in Apache Junction, Arizona, but what they were doing in Massachusetts, and why, remains a mystery to this day, just as what brought them to us in the dark of night when we were closed. After breakfast, they disappeared with grateful thanks just as silently as they had come—and with a promise that we would be remembered in their prayers for our kindness. I hope they still do pray for us. Such saintly women certainly must have a direct line to the Good Lord, and we need all the help we can get.

*   *   *

June 22, 1992
Dear Chris & Tom,

Have you ever had the occasion when you were a good guy, did what you thought was right, with every good intention, and then paid a price for it afterward? Well, that's sort of the situation in which we find ourselves just now. You recall I told you about Paula, our housekeeper, and what promise she showed when we hired her. Well, our expectations were way too low. She wasn't good. She was superb. And because I opened my big mouth, she's now leaving us.

No, it's not what you expect. She's leaving to go back to the local community college and make use of the God-given talents that she has, and we are the ones who put the idea in her mind and have prodded her to do it.

When I mentioned Paula the first time, I told you that she was painfully shy, lacked a sense of self-worth and to make things worse, she was on the verge of a divorce. Well, the latter has come to pass, or at least the wheels are in motion. She has reached a fair settlement with her husband and it will probably be as amicable as divorce can be these days, once the lawyers get involved. But Paula needed someone to stick up for her because she could have been dumped on pretty badly without help. And I guess we contributed to that.

Not long after the divorce became imminent, Joan and I sat her down and tried to get her to realize that she was not going to make ends meet on what we were paying her. They had agreed on some measure of child support and education payments for her two teenagers but Paula would have been hurting personally. And that's where we jumped in and convinced her that there should be education support for her as well. We told her that she needed to get all her household expenses covered while she completed her training course as well as having her tuition and books paid for her.

It was not an easy sell. She insisted that she was a terrible student when she was in high school, and besides, she didn't even know what she would want to do—not to mention her insistence that she probably would flunk out. Well for the last three weeks we've been getting brochures, exploring the various opportunities and, most importantly, trying to talk her into a positive attitude and the confidence that she can succeed. Very reluctantly, she has chosen the medical assistant/receptionist course. Her soon-to-be ex-husband has paid the deposit on the tuition, and she begins classes in September.

It will be terrible to lose her, not just because she is an immaculate housekeeper, but because all of us in the family have become exceptionally fond of her. She seems very attached to us as well—all, I should say, except Seamus. Despite the fact that they have a family dog of their own, she's very much afraid of our pup, and he's not yet full grown. And, of course, every morning when she arrives, Seamus has to go running right toward her with a huge grin on his face, his tail wagging wildly, and offering his warmest greeting. She has taken to entering by the front door, instead of the kitchen, to avoid his reception.

But the good news is that she'll be with us through the upcoming Tanglewood season and will keep us on track until school starts. I know right now that the summer will be a constant process of daily reinforcement and encouragement to assure her that she's made the right decision, but, in the long run, it's the only reasonable thing to do and she's going to be an unqualified success—despite herself.

And speaking of Seamus, we had a most eerie experience with him last weekend. As a final gasp before the summer onslaught, Dan went back to Arlington, Virginia, to visit his old buddies for a long weekend. And since they're inseparable, Seamus also went along. Early on Saturday evening we received a call from a lady who asked if we owned a dog named Seamus. Thinking it was a local call, I told her that we did. She replied that she didn't know how it came to be, but she lived in Virginia and Seamus had just followed her and her husband home when they were out for a walk.

I asked her to please hold on to him, told her that our son was there visiting with the dog, and I would do my best to contact him by telephone so that he could come to pick him up. Dan had left us the phone numbers of all his friends, thankfully, and I got hold of him on the second call. I asked him if he knew where Seamus was and he answered, yes, he was out in his friend's back yard playing. It was not without a little panic on his part that he learned about our recent call. I gave him the lady's address, of course, and also asked him to call us back after he had picked up the pup. Just to make sure, I called the lady back to tell her that Dan was on the way.

When Dan called back, he was a bit breathless. It seems that the house at the address that I had given him was in total darkness when he arrived, and he was fearful that he had copied the address wrong. But he went to the door and rang the bell anyway. In a moment, both a man and a woman came to the door, and immediately revealed the reason for the darkness. Both of them were completely blind.

As it turned out, Dan had carefully closed the gate in the fence at his friend's house when he put Seamus in the back yard for a romp, unaware that there was a gate on the other side of the house that was, unfortunately, open at the time. Seamus, being Seamus, quickly found the opening and decided that he was going to take a bit of a tour of the town. Apparently he had seen the couple from the opposite side of Lee Highway, a very busy six-lane, divided road that was near where Dan's friend lived. The couple was walking with their seeing-eye dog and if there's anything Seamus loves better than people, it's other dogs. Fortunately, the guardian angel of innocent puppies was with him, because he made it across Lee Highway unscathed and teamed up with the seeing eye dog for the walk home.

The blind couple seemed to recognize that he was a puppy so they took him in. They had evidently asked a neighbor to come over to read his dog tags for them, and finding that his name, address and phone number were on the tag, they kindly called us in Lenox. No wonder they were surprised to find a Lenox dog in Arlington, but how remarkably kind they were to assure that he got back in the proper hands again. It would have been a devastating loss for all of us— Dan in particular—and we will never be able to express our gratitude to this couple adequately.

Well, that's both the good news and the bad news from here, but it'll all turn out to be good news in the long run. Paula is an intelligent, capable and lovely woman and we'll be very proud of her when she makes this important transition in her life. And Seamus is coming home with Dan tomorrow, never again to roam—we hope.

Our love to you both,
Dick

Paula left, as scheduled, the following September with a great deal of trepidation and not a few tears when she said goodbye. I think she had found a sense of security with us, particularly as she had used us as a sounding board throughout the divorce proceedings, and looked to us for understanding and advice. We had initially urged her to try to reconcile and forgive her husband's wanderings, but it soon became obvious that he had no intention of giving the other woman up, making reconciliation impossible.

I had even met with him over lunch to try to get him to see all he was forfeiting, but these efforts were fruitless. Joan and I concluded that, though he had never been physically abusive to Paula, he had stripped her of all her self-esteem and sense of personal worth over the 18 years of their marriage and then decided to throw her over because she was so timid and indecisive. He seemed like a nice guy, but I don't think I can ever forgive him for what he did to that fine woman.

Paula left with a promise to keep in touch and to report on her progress from time to time. And to no one's surprise, she was true to her word. At the end of each phase of her studies and training, she came to us with the news that she had received high grades in the portion of the course just completed. An amazing accomplishment to her mind, but not to ours. And despite this positive feedback loop, she always predicted failure and expressed dread when entering each upcoming phase. I particularly recall when she entered the laboratory phase of the course telling us that she could never in her life stick a needle into someone and draw blood. Even if she got the needle in, she was positive that she would either faint or vomit when she saw the blood entering into the syringe.

Needless to say, all her fears were gracefully overcome and she graduated very high in her class at the end of the 12 months of study. She and her classmates all interned at various physicians' offices during the year. All three of the doctors' offices where Paula had served competed with one another to hire her after graduation, along with two or three others that had read the superb evaluations that had been rendered by her various professors. She expressed some small amount of insecurity when she told us of the position that she had accepted, but it was with a great deal more self-confidence and optimism than we had seen from her previously. Family and friends, some new and some old, had done a very fine job of bolstering both her spirits and confidence during the finalization of the divorce and her completion of the course of study. As the years went by, she became the self-assured, successful woman that we had hoped she would. She updated her hair style, gradually amassed a wardrobe that was suited to her professional status, and assumed an attitude that I had only hoped would one day be possible.

About a year before we sold the Inn, she came by one day accompanied by a nice-appearing man about her age. She said that she hoped that we didn't think she was silly, but they had decided to get married and because we had changed her life once, she wanted our approval before she changed her life once again. It was easy to see that he was very supportive of her and they were very much in love. And though it wasn't really our place to do so, they left with our blessing. And to make the fairytale complete, according to all we have heard both from the newlyweds and from friends who know them, they have lived happily ever after. And we couldn't be more delighted.

As for Seamus, his roaming days didn't end with his adventures in Arlington, Virginia, but fortunately he never again has challenged the fates by crossing major highways on his own.

*   *   *

November 19, 1992
Dear Chris & Tom,

Things have been pretty quiet here lately. We're still waiting for enough snow and cold weather for the ski season to get underway along with the arrival of the holidays and a much improved business outlook. But that doesn't mean that we haven't been busy.

As you may recall, we developed a special affection for the Japanese people when we lived there and still feel that we owe them a debt of gratitude for their kindness and generosity to us. It appears that an opportunity to repay that debt, at least partially, has suddenly presented itself.

We received a call from Japan for reservations in late August or early September through an international telephone operator/translator. The lady who made the reservations arrived last week, by limo, and though she spoke just a tiny bit of English (and we, even less Japanese) we soon discovered that she had come for Parents' Weekend at one of the very exclusive, private girls' schools in the Berkshires.

Mrs. Misawa (or more correctly, Misawa-san) had done a remarkable job of arranging a schedule of pick-ups and drop-offs with the limousine company, despite the language barrier. After the first day of running around to all the planned functions, she asked us, in typically polite Japanese fashion, if it was alright if she brought her daughter to the Inn for an afternoon and possibly to stay over night with her. Of course, we were delighted to have her do so.

Late the next afternoon—a Friday—Joan was bringing wine and cheese into the library when she found mother and daughter off in a corner where the child was noticeably sobbing and in a very unhappy state of mind. She went to them without drawing attention and asked Hisako, the young girl whom we had just met, if there was anything that we could do to help. Apparently, she had learned from American teenagers very quickly because her immediate response was, "I hate it here!" meaning, we were to find out in short order, the school she had entered just two weeks previously, not the Birchwood Inn.

Since there was nothing we could immediately do to correct that situation, we decided that we'd try to cheer her up by diversion. A nearby commercial apple orchard was ripe for picking, so to speak, so the next afternoon, Dan kindly took both of the Misawas out to experience apple picking with the intent of making an apple pie when they returned. Now what could be more American than that?

They returned with a large bag of beautiful tart and crisp apples, and I got down to the business of demonstrating to them how the classic American apple pie is made. I chatted away as I was making the pie, and though we were to find that Hisako's language skills were also very limited, she translated what I was saying. Or at least we assumed that's what she was doing. When I had finished and put an egg wash on the top crust, I proudly put the pie into the oven and said that we would soon have a treat for afternoon tea.

Mrs. Misawa then asked, through Hisako, if she could try to make one and since there was plenty of pastry left over, we naturally asked her to proceed.

To begin with, she peeled and cored the apples as if she had been doing so all her life and her fingers fairly flew as she cut them into small identical pieces that were as uniform as if they had been stamped out of a press. Then she proceeded to lay out the individual pieces on a bottom crust on which she had molded and shaped the edge in a most artistic and decorative way. I stood there watching her with a bit of egg on my own face as she asked if we had any peach or apricot jam so she could prepare a glaze for the apples. The end result was a magnificent European-style apple tart that was as beautiful, both in looks and taste, as anything that we had ever seen in France or Germany. As American as apple pie, indeed.

Our laughs over their "introduction" to apple pie making broke the ice considerably, and the remainder of the weekend had put Hisako into a much more personable and happy mood. We discovered that her primary problem with the school that she was attending was not with the school at all; it was with the other students. There were about 20 other Japanese girls who made up part of the resident student body. And, because of the social class system (based on wealth and position) that is still very much a fact in Japan, Hisako found herself to be on the low end of the totem pole.

After all, her father was merely a "salaryman", one of the millions of faceless technocrats that had exploded Japan into its prominent economic ranking in the world. Hisako's mother had been trained as a nurse, but had recently taken a position as a salesperson in an exclusive Tokyo shop that was owned by Mikimoto, the luxury purveyor of what are generally regarded to be the finest pearls in the world. The other girls in the school came from families of diplomats and corporate executives. Unlike Hisako, who had stated that she wanted to learn English and American ways to prepare her for a career in international business, the other girls were attending the school for much less purposive reasons. And they obviously had time for the traditional old school Japanese childhood sport of bullying.

When Mrs. Misawa left to return to Japan, we promised her that we would be a point of contact for her daughter and would have her over to the Inn on weekends when we weren't too busy to give her some attention. In turn, Mrs. Misawa thanked us most graciously and asked if we might, if we had time, help Hisako find another school where she would still get a quality education but, at the same time, feel more comfortable in her surroundings. We agreed and said that we would send her periodic first-hand reports on our progress—through a Japanese-American woman living in Tokyo with whom we had become close friends—and we would also let her know how Hisako was getting along.

With the foliage season (which was excellent, by the way) coming on, we didn't have much time for touring other schools. But in her typically meticulous fashion, Joan requested brochures from every private school within 150 miles of us (and there are a load of them) as well as profiles on their student body, special programs for non-Americans, etc. We also managed to take an overnight trip to Boston with Hisako, where we showed her around (she loved it) and visited two very exclusive private schools in the exurbs (she didn't like either of them). Somehow, I get the feeling that Hisako is not going to be merely a passing acquaintance. Methinks that with our own children grown, we may have just adopted another daughter.

Just one final political comment: We were shocked by the election of an anti-military draft dodger as our new commander-in-chief. That, plus his womanizing and lack of compunction about blatantly lying makes me fear for the future of our culture. The Baby Boomers have really done it to us this time.

More later. Meanwhile, have a great Thanksgiving.
Dick

And indeed Hisako did, for all intents and purposes, become an adopted daughter, temporarily at least. The following spring, we took a number of weekdays off and brought Hisako to at least 12–15 private schools in Massachusetts, Connecticut and New Hampshire. We had to get her out of school to do this, of course, and with our practiced inability to be devious, we explained to her current headmistress precisely what we were doing and why. She, in turn, was not particularly pleased by the impending loss of a student, and probably the $25,000 tuition that it represented, but to her credit she was primarily motivated by the welfare of the child and both she and her staff were highly cooperative.

At each school that we visited, Hisako was given deluxe treatment, probably for the same reason that I just noted—the hefty tuition. The annual fees for boarding students at all of these schools was very comparable—to one another as well as to the highly regarded universities in the area, such as Harvard and Yale. It was also an eye-opening experience for Joan and me, having both attended public schools and never having previously been exposed to the rarified atmosphere of the "privates".

But Hisako wasn't impressed. While the reasons varied, she rejected the thought of attending any one of them. After talking to her at length, and explaining that these schools were the very best of their type that America had to offer, we discovered a common thread in her objections. They weren't "homey" enough; she wanted to feel like she was living with an American family, not at an institution. And her logic was very sound. If she was going to absorb American culture and gain any proficiency in the language, that could better be done in a home not in an institutional environment—particularly one that had a large percentage of non-Americans in the student body.

Well, we didn't need to be hit over the head to see the light. And after a great deal of soul-searching as well as investigation into the possibilities and legalities, we asked her if she would like to live with us the following year and attend Lenox Memorial High School. As an aside, there is a law in Massachusetts that anyone living within a given school district, regardless of status, is eligible for a public education at no cost to the individual. And of course, Hisako brightened instantly at the thought and immediately said yes.

She was due to return home to Japan for the summer, so there would be time to work out the details—and we would not surrender the important room revenue during the Tanglewood season. But before she left for her trip back across the Pacific, she was registered to begin the next school year as a full-fledged member of the Class of 1996 at Lenox Memorial High School. The guidance counselors at both her former school and the local high school expressed serious reservations about her ability to succeed—primarily because her English language skills had not improved very much over the previous ten months—but Hisako had no such doubts. And she left for Japan a very happy young lady.

When she returned, our challenge was easy and difficult at the same time. We put her into one of the small rooms on the third floor and she seemed comfortable in every respect. She was remarkably neat and well behaved and never gave us a moment of concern for the entire time she lived with us. She had given her word to her father that she would never even so much as try cigarettes or alcohol until she was 21 and she honored that oath to the letter—to the extent that she even refused a small glass of wine at holiday dinners.

We shared the breakfast and evening meals with her and urged her to converse with us during each. Joan tutored her in English (both the language and her course work in American literature) and I gave her nightly instruction in the math and science courses that she was taking, along with more language instruction. She was a remarkably apt pupil, particularly in the technical subjects, and she studied intensely for hours each night after the tutoring sessions. Her labor and intensity paid off handsomely, because she was on the honor roll every marking period throughout her time in high school.

But there was a serious down side to that as well. Her facility in English did not progress at anywhere near the rate that we thought it should. It was not long before we concluded that, despite her longer term goals, either she was simply not motivated or she was too shy to use and therefore learn our language. She had no social life to speak of, at least of the type that one might expect of an attractive, modern high school girl. She increasingly expressed her preference for things Japanese, such as clothing, entertainment, sports and other things of interest to a girl her age. And while she had a handful of girl friends with whom she socialized on occasion—and assumedly hung out with in school—she wanted no part of anything to do with boys, including her refusal to attend either junior or senior prom, despite numerous invitations.

And lest anyone conclude that Joan and I were too far removed from modern reality and things hip to realize that the child was a lesbian, nothing could have been farther from the truth. She wrote many times per week to her boyfriend back in Japan and the only truly personalized additions that she added to her room were a number of pictures of him. She simply wanted nothing to do with things American, a strange outlook for one who reportedly had come to America to learn the language and the culture.

As her language skills continued to remain relatively stagnant and her remoteness from American teenage culture increased, we asked Dan to talk to her to try to discover the problem. Despite her obvious respect and fondness for us, she seemed to have a "big brother" attachment to Dan and often confided things to him that she'd be reluctant to discuss with us. While Dan didn't make any definitive discovery, he learned that whole idea of schooling in the United States had probably been a big mistake. She really would have preferred to be back in Japan in her own schools and with the friends that she had grown up with since early childhood. However, if she were to give it up and return to Japan, she would be a year behind her friends in school because of lost time studying in the U.S. That would result in a serious "loss of face", a shame that she couldn't possibly live with. So she had no other recourse than to continue to plug away at her studies and make the best of the situation. But that didn't mean she had to like it.

Despite the terrible dilemma in which she found herself, albeit self-made, she continued to do very well in school, her personal behavior was always above reproach and her relationship with the three of us was as warm and friendly as her Japanese cultural heritage would allow. We traveled around New England with her as much as our schedule would permit. She stayed, on a few occasions, with our relatives in Boston and seemed to enjoy herself with our nephews and nieces each time that happened. I particularly enjoyed helping her to pick out her equipment and teaching her to ski, and we had many enjoyable days together on the slopes each winter that she was there.

We were therefore quite shocked when, at the end of her junior year in high school we received a call from the parents of one of her friends. They asked our opinion of the two girls' collective decision for her to live with them for the final year at Lenox Memorial High School. Apparently, she was still obsessed with the idea that she'd gain more from living with a family that had children of her own age than with us (or at a private school). In a manner that I had previously found typical of the Japanese culture, the two girls had planned the details and received her friend's parental approval before announcing her decision to us.

And so it was that when she returned from Japan at the end of the next summer, she got her stored belonging out of our basement and made her way to her new home. We regarded the change, very frankly, with mixed emotions. She was no where near the burden or trouble she might have been during her laborious and emotional passage through teenage, even by comparison to the passage of our own three children. But there was a responsibility of having her as a member of our household that weighed on us seriously. Like all good parents of children that age, we had PTA meetings and teacher conferences to attend, SAT tests to schedule, plus as a non-English speaker, she needed to take a language proficiency test for entrance into any American university—which she did four times before she passed it.

We also took seriously our responsibility for seeing to her moral and spiritual guidance and all the other incidentals of assisting a child through adolescence. And we'd be dishonest not to admit that having her with us served as a minor distraction from our business responsibilities, another burden with which we were still not totally confident or secure.

After she moved, Hisako came to visit us frequently and we called one another on the phone from time to time. We also tried to continue our former habit of taking her on an occasional outing. The entire family with whom she lived for that last year in high school couldn't have been nicer to her or better qualified to inspire her to do her best. Hisako's girlfriend (and fellow conspirator) finished her high school career as a National Merit Scholar and the recipient of full academic scholarship to Stanford University. Hisako, as I previously mentioned, maintained her honor roll standing throughout, to the amazement of many in the staff and faculty because no concessions for her language deficiency were ever offered to her. But whether she ever achieved that elusive goal of absorbing American culture from living with her definition of a family remains in serious doubt.

But it was with great pride on the part of all of us that Hisako's mother and brother joined her other two "families" for the graduation ceremonies in the shed at Tanglewood. Sadly, her father had become stricken with cancer during her years in the United States and he was too ill to attend. Sadder still, he was to suffer an agonizing death shortly after her return to Japan, but at least she was able to spend his last days by his side. Undoubtedly, this was a factor in convincing her to attend college in her homeland rather than the U.S.

Mrs. Misawa and her son stayed with us at the Inn for graduation, as she did whenever she came to visit her daughter each academic year. She very proudly presented each of the three of us with our "graduation gift", as she put it. Joan received a gorgeous earring and necklace set of Mikimoto pearls, and Dan and I were each presented with a stunning Mikimoto wristwatch with a pearl inlay face. We will all treasure these remembrances not just for the intrinsic value in each, but because they will always remind us of the sweet little enigma of a teenage girl whom we came to love deeply.

We still hear from Hisako regularly. She has since graduated from a fine college in Tokyo and has begun her long sought career in international business. In a gesture that touches us deeply, we both receive at least a card and often a telephone call every Mothers and Fathers Day. She calls us on the telephone occasionally for no other reason than to say hello. And she has become a regular pen pal since she purchased her own computer and has joined the email net. So in spite of our sense of disappointment that Hisako did not return to Japan looking, acting and talking like a young American woman, apparently some of the best of our culture has clearly rubbed off on her.

*   *   *

January 5, 1993
Dear Chris & Tom,

Another year is gone and another holiday season is over. We had a very good season this time around and garnered a few successes to hang on the wall as well.

We made sure not to violate the fire code and had a proper artificial tree this year. It actually was far more beautiful than the live (dying?) tree that we had last year and it could not have been decorated any nicer. I told Joan early last year that since she is the one with the passion for Christmas, especially the tree—and we had no choice about live versus artificial—she should look for a tree that would meet all her expectations. She was an excellent shopper and found a full, thick Douglas fir that is ten feet tall. Like so much artificial flora these days, you have to touch it to realize that it's not real—except for the lack of pine aroma, as Joan was quick to point out. It took me about two hours to assemble it, but that beats the socks off ten people for half a day, as was the case last year.

We pretty much had a full house from before Christmas all the way through New Year's Day. All of the guests were as nice as they could be—the Army couple from Fort Devens came back again—but I need to tell you about one family, in particular.

We received a telephone call from Stockholm in mid-November requesting reservations for a family of seven. From the description of things, the carriage house seemed best for them and that's where they stayed. On some impulse, I asked the lady (who spoke unaccented American English) why they were coming to the Berkshires from Sweden for Christmas and I was quite surprised by the answer. She was an American, by birth, married to a Swede and they have lived in Sweden for most of their married lives. They had two daughters, both married to Americans, and a son who was in his plebe (first) year at the Naval Academy. Despite the fact that the boy had never lived in the States, he is a U.S. citizen through his mother and, therefore, qualified for an appointment. And New England turned out to be the most convenient place for their family reunion.

I had told the lady that I was a USNA graduate back in the dark ages and that I looked forward to meeting her son. I was also quite excited about their arrival and intended to give him a little encouragement at every opportunity while they were here. He needs all the help available getting through that most difficult first year. Unfortunately, when they arrived, the mood was far from upbeat and pep talks were no longer appropriate. The last thing that the kid did before his

Christmas leave began in Annapolis was to resign his appointment. And he had avoided telling his parents until they were on the way to the Birchwood.

The lad arrived in uniform, since having civilian clothing is not permitted at the Academy, and the look on his parents' faces was one of sadness mixed with severe disappointment—hardly fitting for such a joyful reunion. I shook the young man's hand warmly and asked him how he was doing. Instead of answering, he glanced at his mother with a look on his face that would break your heart. His mother turned to me and with tears in her eyes but a very stiff upper lip and she said, "We'll go in here (the library) for a few moments because Lars has something he wants to tell you."

What can you say to a kid in that circumstance? If my guess is right, he was probably wishing with everything in him that he had delayed his decision until after the holidays. And he may even have wished at that point that he could have recanted the whole thing. I told him that I was sorry, but that he certainly wasn't the first or would he be the last to decide that the Academy and he were not made for each other. Lacking anything better to say I put my arm around his shoulder and led him back to his family. I told them all that it was nothing to be ashamed of and that a military career wasn't for everyone. Then I suggested that they all put this unfortunate turn of events behind them and make up their minds to enjoy the holidays.

That was the ticket, apparently, because their moods changed visibly. I actually think that the lad's mother was somewhat expecting an angry response from me and was less upset by Lars' action than she was anticipating my reaction. For the week that they were here, they all seemed to enjoy themselves, including the young lad. Sadly, from my perspective, he avoided me completely all the time that they were with us, and he never came to the desk with the rest of the family when they checked out. Too bad.

New Year's Eve went exceptionally well. We hired a very good caterer to come in and do an excellent four-course dinner for the guests. We served champagne and hors d'oeuvres (that we had prepared) before dinner, had all the silly hats, noise makers and confetti for the revelers, and then served champagne again at midnight. Everyone was in a happy mood and seemed to enjoy the evening, but by 1:00 AM, all had headed off to bed. Three couples made reservations to return next year, so it must have gone over well. However, we'll have to do something a bit differently next year. Once the caterers and servers were paid, the dinner actually ended up costing us more than we charged for it. And we were up until after 3:00 AM cleaning up. Well at least we had a full house for those three days.

The slow season is now with us, but in addition to catching up on room maintenance and upgrades, it appears that I have another challenge ahead. I'm about to begin my second year as the president of the Chamber of Commerce and I'm faced with a minor civil war. I've seen it coming for quite some time, but the time is ripe to do something about it. More than anything, it's going to take time and patience, and while I'm not possessed of an overabundance of either, I'm sure I'll get things resolved one way or the other. It's a bit like coaching Little League baseball. You volunteer your time and effort. You have the best interests of the youngsters at heart, but generally the only rewards are parental complaints, second-guessing and criticism. Oh well, it's not the first time I've had a challenge like this and I'm sure we'll live through it.

Hope you enjoyed your holidays at the new ski lodge. We're really looking forward to seeing it when we visit you in two months. Can't wait.

All the best,
Dick

The future New Year's Eves went equally well, but they did not end up costing us money. After all, we had developed a certain level of expertise when were doing the international dinners, and there was no reason why we had to hire a caterer. We could do a dinner that was equally professional and we could do it for far less. We were particularly convinced it was the right decision after having had the clean up chores that first time around.

The menus over the following years were very good, some bordering on the spectacular. For example, for that first year we offered crab bisque, a green salad with Thai dressing, a choice of grilled salmon or beef tenderloin for the entree and profiteroles with chocolate sauce for dessert. Other years, the entrees included stuffed Cornish game hen with Cumberland sauce and trout almondine. Everyone seemed delighted with that first menu as they did each succeeding year.

We learned from Leo Mahoney's office party of the year before and hired servers each year. They managed to garner some huge tips in addition to what we were paying them, so they happily gave up the early part of their holiday evening to work for us. Things got a little hectic during serving time, but every one of the guests received a hot meal that was every bit as attractive in appearance as one would find in a fine dining establishment. We were so successful that we continued doing a New Year's Eve dinner successive year except the last that we owned the Inn. But that's getting ahead of the story.

The Chamber of Commerce was hardly a success story from start to finish. During the discussion of the Chamber at that first Labor Day party, one lady introduced an argument that, in retrospect, I should have listened to more carefully. She said she didn't care whether I had been President of the United States before coming to Lenox. It would be unfair of the Chamber members to throw me into the miasma of petty town politics and grievances without being around long enough to know the contentious issues and who the players were. Within a year or so I was up to my neck in controversy.

Whenever I had changed assignments in the Air Force, especially when I moved into command positions, I made a habit of keeping my head down, my ears open and my mouth shut—at least for the first couple of months. By following this same habit after my Soviet-style election as the new president, I learned a lot, most of which I didn't like. I use the term Soviet-style election because there was only one candidate for each position on the ballot and the only way someone else could win the election was to conduct an aggressive write-in campaign. There was no way that was going to happen; not when they had to search high and low to find someone willing to be nominated. But back to what I had discovered.

My first impressions confirmed the perception that the Chamber was little more than a referral service for the inns. That, in reality, seemed to be its only mission, despite the fact that the bylaws of the organization stated that we were supposed to be doing far more. In addition, we should have been promoting all the member businesses, working in conjunction with the town government for the orderly development of Lenox and promoting the establishment of or the relocation of new businesses in the town. A good chamber should also serve as active promoters and advocates for the cultural, civic and social betterment of the community. As I looked around, these other seemingly worthwhile objectives were being given short shrift, at best, and for the most part, overlooked entirely.

And as the veneer of Chamber operation was gradually peeled away, it became clear that there were a lot of unhappy campers in town and the membership was plummeting. All of the small shopkeepers, restaurateurs and the other businesses that had little or nothing to do with the inns, were dropping out of the Chamber because they saw no benefit in belonging. Why pay substantial dues only to find that the primary effort of the organization was geared to keeping the inns full? And while the argument could be made—and I frequently made it myself—that full inns meant people in town and therefore customers for their businesses, these folks weren't having any of it. Instead, a mass defection was underway and the non-innkeeper members of the Chamber formed their own organization, the Lenox Village Association.

The gauntlet had been cast down, and I was faced with pursuing one of two basic choices. I could take the easy route which would be to thumb my nose at the noble objectives stated in the Chamber bylaws and officially change the organization into what it actually was, an inn referral service. Or I could try to mend fences, build bridges and attempt to recreate a harmonious relationship among all the businesses, as well as with the town government. This latter connection had essentially been destroyed two years previously when the town wished to increase the room tax by 4%. The Chamber (read innkeepers) had bitterly and vociferously opposed it on the grounds that it would drive business away—which it never did. The resultant schism between the town government and the Chamber over that bitter battle still persisted.

Why didn't I listen to the lady who advised that I become familiar with the petty politics and grievances of the community before accepting the nomination?

Without going into the whys and wherefores, my choice was to attempt to create teamwork and a harmonious working relationship within the community at large. That decision created outspoken opposition and personal antagonism from a small minority of the members, all of whom were old, established innkeepers, unfortunately. But it was still the correct course of action, in my judgment, and I would do the same thing today if again faced with the choices. As time went by, I discovered certain evidence that would suggest that some of the innkeepers were getting favorable consideration in referrals from the Chamber, so it's probably no wonder that the animosity of those few ran so deep and was so bitterly expressed.

The first step in this "new beginning" was to modify the Chamber bylaws to make the decision-making process less cumbersome and to create some standing committees. These included an innkeepers association and a retailers association, both of which would look after the special interests of these business segments, yet still have the strength and connections of a united Chamber behind them.

The future of the Chamber would properly be determined by a vote by the general membership. Most of the "defectors" who had formed the Village Association recognized that my efforts were on behalf of the business community as a whole, and they returned to Chamber membership in large numbers even before the vote on my proposals. As I ran for an unplanned and unwanted re-election—no way I could propose all the changes and then not follow up—I made it clear that the bylaw changes and the new committees were inseparable from my candidacy. If the bylaw changes weren't approved and yet I happened to be re-elected president anyway, I would immediately resign and let the will of the membership prevail with respect to the future of the Chamber.

Some last minute efforts were made to challenge my restructuring efforts on procedural grounds and to promote a genuine opposition candidate for president. There were even anonymous phone calls to our Inn, suggesting in very crude terms that I should drop what I was doing, get out of the race, and better yet, get out of town.

The general membership meeting overflowed the Grange Room in the Lenox Town Hall and the debate was heated and personal. One woman, whom I had considered a friend up to that time, accused me of "misappropriating $20,000 in Chamber funds"—an act for which she profoundly apologized about a year later, saying that she had been convincingly mislead by the opposition leader.

But after all the rancor, the election wasn't even close. The vote ran about 85 percent in favor of the revisions. The members clearly demonstrated that they were at least equally committed to a harmonious Chamber and town as they were to the success of there own businesses. However, the opposition forces never did come around to the majority way of thinking, nor did they cease a not so subtle campaign of personal harassment and subversion of the Chamber during our remaining years in Lenox. But as one member of the Board of Selectmen told me, as we were moving out of town, "Few people appreciate all you did for this community, but they are certainly going to realize your impact after you leave. There will be no one as committed to making this Town a better place to live as you have been." Apparently, some people still appreciate the efforts of Little League coaches and other community volunteers after all.

*   *   *

Part IV

Getting Comfortable

Time fairly flew by over the next few years and, with experience and a more established clientele of regular returnees, we did indeed become more comfortable. We knew what we were doing and we became more confident, based on results, that we were doing things well and properly. It was not that we weren't conscious of the fact that there still was a fine enough line between success and failure or that we were no longer highly motivated. We still had to take money out of savings and put it into the business during the slow season of late winter and early spring. And we all still awoke occasionally in the wee hours of the morning, worrying about this opportunity missed or that risk that we knew we should take but were too conservative to do so.

But with the confidence in what we were doing, as well as in our decisions to make some fairly radical changes in the way we did things, we were certainly more at ease with running the Inn and less apprehensive that some disaster might strike. And the result was that our moods were more upbeat and there was far less friction lying just below the surface. It no longer was part of her routine for Joan—or any of us for that matter—to "wear one face" in the kitchen and have to change to a more congenial demeanor when dealing with guests. It's wonderful what a little confidence and a reduction in fear can do for one's outlook on life. Even though I still hadn't change my view that fear can be a most powerful and compelling motivator.

Though 1993 was not an uneventful year, it was essentially more of the same. Our guests were interesting and agreeable and most of the unpleasant incidents of the early years were a thing of the past. I became more heavily involved in work associated with the Chamber of Commerce and, as a spin-off, was invited to participate in more civic activities—to the extent that I was actually taking too much time away from the business. We had become comfortable not just with our business but also as active members of the community.

All this reinforcing sense of assurance prompted a gradual change in the frequency of our contacts with Tom and Chris as well. A lot of that change consisted of our greater willingness to use the telephone for other than strictly business and, as a result, my limited time was less consumed in the late night hours writing "reports" to them on our adventure. We had also begun our annual reunion at Mammoth Mountain and the discussions that took place there also decreased the need for detailed explanations. The letters to our principal benefactors, consequently, decreased in numbers and with the later addition of a new computer system, and access to the Internet and email, they disappeared altogether.

But for purposes of continuity, in the following chapters I have recreated many of those phone calls and emails from our log book with the resultant appearance, for the purposes of this narrative, at least, that our letters to Chris and Tom continued in a less frequent but unbroken string.

February 25, 1994
Dear Chris & Tom,

Joan has recently entered the final year of her fifties, and though I'm not sure that this has anything to do with the situation, she has begun to change—at least as far as the business is concerned. Up until recently, there was nothing that a guest might do, no matter how contemptible, that she wasn't willing to overlook. She has always been as sweet as she could be with the guests. She also seems overly concerned that our reputation might suffer if we reacted angrily or showed other than the greatest respect for the guests. She didn't even wholeheartedly agree with my throwing the four people out of the Inn a couple of years ago, even though they were cruelly hateful to her. I guess she was afraid that they would put a full-page ad in the New York Times suggesting that everyone avoid the Birchwood Inn because we were lousy innkeepers. Well, all that seems to have changed over the past number of months.

Over Valentine's weekend, two couples arrived, one of whom was typical of a number of couples, friends of our parents, that we both met as kids growing up in the Boston suburbs. These couples seem to be unique to the Boston area, or at least are more common there than anywhere else we've lived in the past. The women are generally very sweet and thoughtful but their husbands are the sort that, if we were to meet them elsewhere, we would probably refer to them as insufferable smart-asses. They can't seem to say anything straight-forwardly. Every remark is "cute" or tinged with sarcasm, and while they probably mean well—and think they have a great sense of humor—I often wonder how their wives put up with that all the time. Just ignore them, I guess.

Well, Joe was one of these guys, and he started in on his routine as soon as Joan met them at the desk. She asked them if they had reservations and instead of simply saying yes, Joe promptly asked her if she really thought they'd be here on this busy weekend unless they did. And the "humorous" interruptions went on like that all the time they were checking in. Joan was clearly getting irritated at his nonsense. When she brought them into the dining room and showed them the chalk board menu for the weekend, he interrupted once again to ask if we cater to special dietary requirements. She told him that we did, within reason, and even though we usually like to learn of those special needs when the reservations are made, she would do her best to accommodate his requirements.

With a grin on his face that clearly said the he was up to his same old mischief, he revealed his special dietary needs. For breakfast, he said, he always had baloney sandwiches on whole wheat with mayo and Dijon mustard. Joan didn't even blink when she told him, with an equally facetious expression on her face, that she would do her best to take care of that requirement.

The following morning we had Belgian Pancakes for breakfast. This is probably the most attractive of all our presentations, and if you like strawberries, it's one of the tastiest as well. You probably know the recipe, since we both lived in Belgium, but I'll enclose ours anyway. We always serve it with a huge daub of freshly whipped cream, which in turn is topped with a large fresh strawberry that has been cut in half and nestled into the daub of cream with a sprig of mint. People usually are very impressed when they first see their order come out of the kitchen.

When our two couples from Boston took their seats at a table in the dining room, Joan was ready for them. First, she brought out the two plates for the ladies and they, of course, made the usual gushing expressions of pleasure at the presentation. When she returned the next time, she had Belgian Pancakes in one hand and, you guessed it, a baloney sandwich on whole wheat with mayo and Dijon mustard in the other. She set both plates down, wished them all an enjoyable meal and calmly walked away.

The whooping and hollering and the cries of "serves you right" could all be heard clearly in the kitchen. And soon Joe's table mates were telling everyone in the dining room what he had done and how he had been badly beaten by Joan in a game of one-upsmanship. Meanwhile she just stood smugly in the kitchen, waiting for the next guests to arrive in the dining room.

When next she went into the dining room, she ignored Joe completely and went directly to the table where the new diners had seated themselves. Joe could stand it no longer and he finally said to her that he was really kidding when he told her of his special dietary needs. She looked directly at him with a completely straight face and said, "Oh, does that mean that you'd like the regular breakfast tomorrow?" giving no indication that he was going to get anything but what he had on his plate. The howls of laughter erupted once again, only this time the whole dining room joined in.

It was Dan and I who turned soft on this occasion. When the others at his table were just about finished, I did a plate of Belgian Pancakes for Joe and Dan brought it in to him. He placed it down in front of him, while taking away the partially eaten baloney sandwich. He said that he was probably going to get in a heap of trouble with Joan for doing this, but he thought he might like to have this breakfast instead of what she had served to him.

Joe peered up at him with a sheepish look of embarrassment mixed with gratitude on his face and very quietly thanked him. For the rest of the weekend, someone—his friends, a guest or one of us—would make a deadpan comment about a baloney sandwich each time Joe was around. He took it good-naturedly, but he must have learned a bit of a lesson because we never heard another smart-ass remark out of him after that. I love it!!

Hope all goes well,
Dick

BELGIAN PANCAKES

1 carton, fresh ripe strawberries
pancake mix

1 pkg whole frozen strawberries
whipped cream
mint leaves

The amount of fresh strawberries needed depends on the number being served, but one package of whole frozen strawberries is adequate. Thaw the frozen strawberries and cut the fresh strawberries in half (or in quarters if they are very large). Place them in a heavy pan over low heat while you prepare the pancakes. The fresh strawberries will release their juices as they heat. When the mixture begins to form a pink foam on the top, turn the heat down to low, just enough to maintain the temperature.

Using your favorite pancake recipe or mix (I prefer Bisquick), make according to instructions, but use about ten percent less milk or liquid than called for in the recipe. The batter will be very thick and almost pasty. Place a large spoon of batter on a medium-low heat griddle and flatten out the batter with the bowl of the spoon. Cooking time will be at least double and you need to be watchful that the pancake doesn't burn. When it is turned, it should be golden on the bottom and it will rise considerably to roughly one inch thickness. Pancakes may be saved until you are ready to serve, covered with aluminum foil in a very lightly sprayed cookie sheet in a 200° F. oven.

Place a pancake in the middle of the plate. With a large ladle, spoon a mixture of berries and juice over the pancake. Be sure that the pancake is completely covered with berries and that plenty of juice surrounds the pancake on the plate. Place a large dollop of whipped cream in the center, slice a reserved fresh strawberry in half, leaving the green attached, and place with the green up on either side of the dollop. Garnish with a sprig of mint and serve.

HINT—Be sure that the berries aren't too warm or they will melt the cream.

Perhaps instead of having a late-in-life personality change, Joan was being infected with a little bit of "the devil made me do it". Because each time she did something like that in the future, and there were quite a few times that her playfulness erupted, she would always say afterward that she couldn't believe that she had done such a thing.

Probably the most memorable of those events came during the following summer. We had a pair of delightful youngsters staying with us who were the image of the all-American young couple. He was tall, athletic looking and quite handsome while she had a look about her that would suggest that she was probably the head cheerleader when she was in high school and surely must have been voted "most likely to succeed". Both had bubbly personalities, were very warm and friendly and were highly complimentary about the Inn and our offerings.

A while after they had checked in, the young man came down to the Dutch door and asked if there were some trick to locking their bedroom door; he was unable to do so. To us, this was not terribly unusual because we had the old-fashioned skeleton key type of lock sets in the door and few young people had ever been exposed to them before. We told him that he had to fiddle around with the key a little bit but eventually he would get the feel of it and would be able to turn the key in the lock.

Late that afternoon, during wine and cheese, I saw him and asked if he was able to get the door locked. He seemed totally unconcerned when he said, "No not yet, but that's OK. I'll get it later."

About 7:30 that evening, we were in the dining room, which we always closed off for privacy during dinner, and we heard someone come to the Dutch door and ring the bell. We all had a special dislike of being interrupted during our evening meal and tried to take turns answering the bell. Tonight it was Joan's turn and, in spite of the interruption, she put on her friendly face and headed out to the Dutch door to see what was needed. From the dining room, we could hear that it was the young man again and it quickly became clear that he was still having problems with the lock.

To our shock, instead of telling him that she'd ask Dan or me to take a look at it, she very calmly said, "Well, if you're concerned about security, just push your bureau in front of the door while you sleep." He seemed to mumble something in response that we could not hear, but Joan just gave him her most winning smile, wished him and his wife a pleasant evening and returned to the table.

Dan and I were just about rolling on the floor trying to choke back the incredulous laughter, and she just looked at us and said, "What?"

Apparently, she answered her own question because, after a moment, she too began to laugh and said, "I can't believe I told him that. What's come over me?"

We honestly didn't give it much further thought and the young man never mentioned it again that weekend, even when he was checking out on Sunday morning. But seeing him again reminded me of his problem, so after they left, I took the key that he had turned in and went up to their room to try the lock. To my astonishment, the previous occupants had evidently broken off another key in the lock, and there was no way that anyone was going to get a key into the slot, let alone lock or unlock that door.

A flush of embarrassment passed through me as I looked at the inoperable lock set. Here we had treated this very nice young man like a dummy, and it was we who were, in fact, the dummies. It took me nearly an hour to get the lock set apart and retrieve the broken key. And then in a gesture of good will, Joan sat down and wrote the couple a brief letter of apology—and enclosed the broken part of the key for good measure.

On other occasions, not as humorous as these, Joan continued to show that no one was going to push her around any longer. Our local banker, with only our best interests at heart, reserved half of the Inn for a group of Federal bank examiners from Dallas who were coming for their annual inspection at his bank. The reservations were made almost a month in advance and overlapped into a popular weekend, so we had the unpleasant experience of having to turn a great many guests away.

On the day of their arrival, all six of them came to the door and rang the bell. Joan went to the entrance and invited them in. But instead of entering—or even saying hello—the man who appeared to be their spokesman asked her if we had TV in every room. When Joan told him we had a large screen TV in the den but none in the rooms, he asked if we had Internet access in all of the guest rooms. When she again responded in the negative, he said, "Oh, we didn't realize that this was just a boarding house. We can't stay here," and with that the whole bunch turned on their heels and headed back to the two rental cars in the parking lot.

When she burst into the kitchen, there was fire in her eyes and steam, figuratively at least, coming out her ears. She kept parading around the center island in the kitchen and repeating over and over, "The nerve of that SOB. He didn't know this was a boarding house!!! The nerve of him!"

Finally, she grabbed for the phone, and as soothingly as I could, I asked her whom she was going to call. "I'm calling Bill at the bank and I'm going to give him a piece of my mind. He's cost us half of our bookings for a busy weekend and the bank should pay for them after those ignorant clowns walked out on us."

While I tried to explain to her that Bill didn't do it intentionally and never would have booked them if had known what they were going to do, she calmed down and decided to let the situation drop. But it was great to see her reaction. No one was going to push my girl around any more. And no one ever did.

*   *   *

June 12, 1994
Dear Chris & Tom,

To misquote Charles Dickens just slightly in his opening lines of A Tale of Two Cities, *"They are the best of times. They are the worst of times." But instead of referring to the period surrounding the French Revolution and the overthrow of the monarchy, I'm referring, in this case, to weddings.*

We had a group here this past weekend that were enough to make one vow never to do another wedding again. Quite some time ago we learned—the hard way once again—that we needed to require all wedding parties to book the entire Inn for Saturday night if they were going to hold any of the official wedding functions on the property. In this case, the mother of the bride was going to do all the arrangements and she was to be the sole point of contact on the plans. That arrangement is essential if events are to run smoothly.

We wrote up a contract that had all the necessary details very clearly specified. She assured us that she would personally assign the rooms (because of the variance of quality) and she would tell us the room assignments, by name, at least two weeks in advance. And if there were to be any changes or additions to other activities, they would be settled at least six weeks in advance. A freeze on major activities would be mutually agreed upon and stated in writing. At that time, we would separately negotiate the cost of all ancillary arrangements (dinner, cocktails, etc.)

When the six week mark arrived, we agreed, in writing, that there was to be no one staying at the Inn on any other day but Saturday, except the bride and her mother who would stay there Friday night as well. The only other function to be held at the Inn would be a catered rehearsal supper "for about a dozen people". I won't bore you with the details of how difficult it was to have her reveal the room assignments, or the endless changes in rooms needed for other nights. Nor will I go into any details of what a nasty woman she was, generally. But let me tell you about the actual wedding.

On Friday, the bride and her mother arrived about mid-afternoon as expected, but so did four other couples for whom we had no reservations. We had to find accommodations for one couple elsewhere because, as mother well knew, we had other guests for that night who had nothing to do with the wedding. That evening, 35 people showed up for the rehearsal dinner that had been scheduled "for about a dozen". Mother had remembered to tell the caterer but "forgot" to let us know. Weddings are such a busy time, you know. There was a last minute scramble for tables, chairs and place settings, and just before dinner was served, she had the gall to suggest that things weren't "going as smoothly" as she had hoped.

Well, we got through that all right, with many unexpected hours of extra work cleaning up and returning the rentals, but that was easy by comparison to the next day. Two of the couples, plus mother, came down a half hour after breakfast ended on Saturday morning. The mother of the bride (I'll refer to her as MOB, but it would be more accurate to refer to her as SOB) was incensed that we wouldn't reopen the kitchen and serve them a full breakfast—even though we put out fresh fruit, muffins and coffee for all. Right in the middle of that, a large truck pulled into the parking area. I went out to see what they were doing and the driver very innocently said that they were there to erect the tent. When I went back in the house to find MOB, my blood was boiling. She insisted that this had been fully coordinated with us. However, through questioning, she admitted that she hadn't personally coordinated with us but she was sure that her sister had. Bull!!

She insisted that we would "spoil her only daughter's wedding" if we were to cancel that portion of the festivities. And besides, there were only going to be about 25 or 30 close friends there in the evening after they had the reception and dinner at Wheatleigh, a magnificent (and incredibly expensive) five star inn and restaurant. So the 40' x 40' double peaked tent went up among the stone fences and gardens on our beautiful lawn, and after that came the tables and bars, and all that goes with it. When those setting up came to me for an electrical connection so "the band could power their amps", I knew we were in for trouble and we were on the verge of exploding.

At 11:30 that night, I personally counted over 100 "guests" in and around the tent and they were still coming—complaining, of course, that there was no place to park. People came into the Inn in streams, not just to use the toilets but to ask for all manner of things from ice to Band-Aids to snacks—and late in the evening, aspirin or Tylenol. Finally, when the church bells across the street struck midnight, I sought out the father of the bride. Until this time, he had been all but invisible (probably because he had divorced the bitch years before), and told him that I would give them 15 minutes to close down and disperse, or I would come out and do it for him. He called his wife over who immediately began her spiel about "ruining her only daughter's wedding" again. I just looked at my watch and said, "You now have 14 minutes left," and turned and walked back into the house. It was actually a half hour before things calmed down.

Breakfast the next morning was no better, but we were a bit calmer because they were all leaving in a matter of hours. Of course the parents of the bride stayed in their rooms two hours beyond checkout time—without requesting a late checkout. When they came to the desk, in addition to their room bill, I presented them with a bill for $850 for "unscheduled services rendered". The sweet little MOB looked at it and, with as close to a snarl as she could muster, said, "You did your best to ruin the biggest day in my daughter's life. You'll hear from my lawyer on this!" and without another word, she stormed out the door.

It's four days later and we're still fuming. I have a detailed record of what happened and, of course, a copy of the original contract. I'm looking forward to hearing from her lawyer. Cheers to you both, from the folks who now hate weddings.

Dick

We did hear from her lawyer, who happened to be her brother, a partner in a very prestigious law firm in "the city". In keeping with the family character that had previously been displayed, he suggested that they were probably going to file a suit against us for "mental damages" that his sister suffered in dealing with me. And coincidentally, he thought that the suit should ask for about $850 in damages. Needless to say, that was passed on to our dear old "country lawyer" who, after about a month and four phone calls, produced a check for us for $500. We earned every cent of it, and more.

But in all honesty, I must admit that the majority of weddings that we hosted were "the best of times".

Because of the wonderful setting and the special ambience of the town, there are hundreds of weddings in Lenox each year, and like the rest of the country, June is the peak time for weddings—though they occur year round in Lenox. Those who choose to have a church wedding generally take their choice of a number of very nice locations. The Catholic Church, St. Ann's, is about 200 yards down the hill from us, and it is a beautiful old Gothic edifice made of locally quarried stone. The Episcopal Church, near the center of town, is equally historic and lovely. It, too, is a classical structure built of the local granite.

But it seems that most people are attracted to The Church on the Hill, which is across Main Street from us. It is nearly 200 years old and has that marvelous colonial appearance, both inside and out. It has changed Protestant denominations a number of times over the years and it currently represents the Church of Christ. I'm not sure what the criteria are for holding weddings there, but it seems to me that they are as close to non-denominational as can be. At least from the number and variety of weddings that are held there, mostly by out-of-town couples, I would have to guess that religious affiliation doesn't matter. In any event, because of our proximity to the church, we received many requests for holding wedding functions at the Inn.

Now that can be very good business, but once again we had to learn the hard way in order not to be overworked and underpaid. Our income derives from selling rooms, not from holding luncheons, dinners and receptions. But our propensity, in the early days, to sign on to just about anything that would make a few dollars was where the school of hard knocks training began.

For the first couple of wedding events that took place at the Inn, we did only the supper or reception. So while we didn't fill the Inn for the weekend, we found ourselves working our buns off while the few guests we had were badly inconvenienced by the crowd of short timers that filled the entire public area. And while we understand that wedding guests wish to celebrate and have fun, these people were usually oblivious to our business concerns or our guests.

As experience taught us, we started making some pretty firm conditions for holding wedding related activities. The most important was that we would not even talk to anyone about a wedding unless they booked the entire Inn. That rule began with one night, but after the experience related about dear old MOB, we required a two-night minimum. And we added a surcharge to the cost of the rooms and had those that booked agree, in writing, that all activities not specified precisely in the contract would not be allowed. We probably lost some business that way, but we certainly kept our sanity.

But lest I sound like an unreformed Scrooge, let me tell you about two very delightful weddings at the Birchwood Inn.

The first was one that didn't fall under the normal rules for a wedding because only a handful of people was involved. The Smiths, both of whom were in their late thirties, had stayed with us at least twice. As they were checking out the second time, they asked if they could get married in front of the huge fireplace in our library, three weeks from the following Saturday. They said that just one other couple would be involved—the best man and matron of honor—and there would be no other activity than the wedding and a champagne toast afterward. They even asked Joan if she would help out by finding a Justice of the Peace to perform the ceremony. We were happy to agree and, as if she were the mother of the bride, Joan interviewed four JPs before she found one that she considered minimally acceptable.

As it turned out a month later, the wedding was especially nice. The bride looked lovely and blushed as if she were a 19 year old. The groom, too, was clearly excited by the event, and in a state of exuberance two hours before the wedding, he placed a note under the door of each guest room inviting all the other guests in the Inn to witness their ceremony. We could have wished for a more personable official, but the JP did the job for which he was hired, and the newlyweds couldn't have been happier. And Dan, who is an excellent photographer in his own right, was in his element recording the event on video as well as on stills.

The groom clearly planned his extended invitation in advance, because he and the best man went out to their car right after the ceremony and returned with a cooler containing a half dozen bottles of chilled champagne, two good-sized trays of canapés and a box of two dozen champagne flutes. Stranger as she might have been to all the other Inn guests, the bride received the traditional kiss from all who were there and everyone enjoyed the brief reception that continued for the next hour. (We never told them that we also had hors d'oeuvres and champagne waiting in our kitchen to help them celebrate. But we put the champagne in their room later, while they were out to dinner.)

But that wasn't the end of the story. Each year, for as long as we owned the Inn, they came back to celebrate their anniversary with us. They booked the same room, the bride always wore her wedding dress and they went to the same restaurant each year. And though we rarely used the fireplace in the library, we made sure that it was always burning brightly for their return.

But the second best wedding that was ever held at our Birchwood Inn occurred in our fourth year there. (I'll tell you about the best wedding a little later.) The bride and groom, John and Sarah, were two of the nicest young people that we were to meet in all our years at the Birchwood. They came one afternoon in early summer and asked if we hosted weddings—everything from the rehearsal to the ceremony to the reception. They too thought a ceremony in front of the fireplace would be just right because their planned wedding day was the 31st of October, Halloween. Sarah insisted that instead of the traditional white wedding gown, she was wearing black and John would dress in an orange mourning suit. Her dark humor had a basis.

When we stated our willingness to discuss the matter, they suggested that we start from the beginning. The couple had met as students at the University of Notre Dame and had fallen in love there. Sarah, it turned out, was from an old Boston family with a lineage that went back to the Pilgrims. John, by contrast, was a New Yorker, the son of Italian immigrant parents who had been quite successful since coming to America, but still had many old country ways about them. Sarah's parents were devout Episcopalians and forbade her to marry in the Catholic Church. John's parents threatened to boycott the marriage and disown him if they weren't married by a Catholic priest.

Perhaps an insolvable dilemma, but not for these kids. They found a renegade Catholic priest from New Hampshire who had, long before, married and formed his own Catholic order of priests—and then appointed himself their bishop. He would be happy to officiate at the wedding and both parents seemed minimally appeased that their terms had been met. The Bishop would come to the Inn to witness their marriage, and in fact, as he told us later, there was nothing that he enjoyed more than serving as the vehicle to bring a loving couple together in wedded bliss.

With a slight amount of trepidation, we agreed to give it a try. And we were delighted that we did. It turned out to be most memorable. The arrangements leading up to the big day were all completed by telephone. Once again, Joan busied herself with caterers, furniture rentals, flowers and endless other preparations—getting Sarah's approval each step of the way while enjoying every minute of it. And things couldn't have gone more smoothly. When the big weekend arrived, we collectively held our breath, hoping for the kids' sake more than anything that all would go smoothly when the parents met.

It was a big wedding, the (second) biggest we ever held. Most of the guests were relatives and, depending on which family they were tied to, they knew one another well. The bride and groom were animated for the entire day leading up to the 6:00 PM ceremony, and their enthusiasm—and love— were infectious. We witnessed the first meeting of the Boston Brahmins and the New York immigrants, and it was tentative at best. But Sarah did her magic and before anybody knew it, both families were intermingling and laughter and genuine friendliness became the order of the day.

I honestly didn't think the ceremony could possibly get off on time because Sarah and John continued to circulate among the crowd until nearly 5:30. But just on time, the lovely bride came down the stairs—wearing off-white, not black—and I cued up "The Wedding March" on the ground floor stereo.

The ceremony was one of the nicest we had ever witnessed. Prior to the exchange of vows, three brothers or sisters of both bride and groom gave a brief tribute to their siblings and the joy that their union brought to all. Then Bishop Michael, in his slight French-Canadian accent, proved why weddings were his specialty. His homily was just right. It touched all the right bases, and probably all the hearts of the witnesses. Then Sarah and John, in loud clear voices and broad smiles, recited the beautiful vows that they had written themselves. There was scarcely a dry eye in the room when they finished, including the innkeepers—and two fathers who had been determined that the wedding would never take place.

Shortly after the wedding we received one of the loveliest notes imaginable from Sarah, crediting us and the Birchwood Inn with being the catalyst that made their dream a reality. It seemed more to us that it was two outstanding, ingenious and determined youngsters, whose love and generosity were irresistible, who guaranteed their own success.

And a little less than two years later, Sarah and John returned to show us their gorgeous little six month old girl, complaining jocularly that the child's grandparents—on both sides—were spoiling her terribly. Somehow Joan, Dan and I are absolutely convinced that, with parents like Sarah and John, this lovely little girl will grow to full maturity in the happiest of homes.

*   *   *

July 25, 1994
Dear Chris & Tom,

After the terrible row that occurred during our first summer together, we have tried especially hard to treat Dan as a co-equal adult, rather than as one of our "children". I suspect that he's the only competent judge of whether or not we've been successful, but at least we try and it is something that takes priority in our conscious actions.

Since he was a very young teen, Dan has been rather closed-mouthed about what he does when he's not around us, who his friends are, and, in general, his private life. From all I've read, that's a common characteristic of teenagers and the habit continues after they have broken the apron strings and become independent. And perhaps this is a valid explanation for the fact that, even though he's now well into his 30s, Dan continues to be very private with regard to his personal life. That is what makes the events of last Sunday morning all the more amazing.

As we were cleaning up from breakfast on Sunday, Dan seemed to have something on his mind. He puttered around a bit and then he'd stop what he was doing and just stand by the center island looking from Joan to me and then back again. Then he'd putter around for a while and repeat the process all over again. Finally, after two or three repeats, he broke out in a rather embarrassed grin and blurted out, "You probably never thought you'd hear me say this, but I think I'm in love!"

I was elbow deep in dishwater and Joan was at the computer desk rechecking the telephone log book against our reservations and confirmations. We were both dumbfounded, stopped dead in our tracks, and just stared at him. His grin became broader, he nodded affirmatively and then said with a chuckle, "Yes, you heard me correctly."

The only thing either of us was able to say in reaction was Joan's rather excited plea for him to tell us more. He went on to tell us that he had been dating an English college student who had been in the Berkshires for the past month or so working in a student exchange program at a nearby inn. In the British equivalent of our college programs, she is between her junior and senior year at Plymouth University on the south coast of England (the port city from which the Pilgrims were alleged to have departed) and she will be here until early to mid-September. He also volunteered the fact that she and he couldn't be more in tune to one another and he feels "antsy" when he's not with her. Sounds serious, if I recall those feelings correctly.

Joan told him that we'd be delighted to meet her any time that he would like to introduce her to us, and we'd be especially pleased if he would bring her to dinner some night. Dan said he had hoped Joan would say that because he had already invited her to come over to dinner the next evening (last night). Looks like he knows and anticipates his Mother pretty well, doesn't it?

Well, she is everything he said she is. Anne Marshall came to dinner last night and there was no doubt that she is a very lovely young woman—nor any doubt that they care for one another very much. There were none of the "falling in lust" indications that you often see with young people. There was too much evidence of mature respect and emotional affection. And after an evening of conversation with her, we quickly discovered the many fine qualities that had drawn Dan to her—and a minor mystery was solved at the same time.

Over the previous couple of weeks, both Joan and I had taken a call or two from a woman asking to speak to "Don". We politely told her each time that there was no one by that name living here, all the while thinking that it might have been one of the telemarketers who are becoming increasingly irksome. In fact the calls had come from Anne whose lovely English accent had broadened the "a" in Dan so that it sounded like Don. With that discovery, you can be sure that we won't make that mistake again, and we'll also try our best to call her "Ahn", as she prefers, rather than the Americanized pronunciation of her name.

They may have known one another for just a short time, but it is very clear that their romance has gone well beyond the "pleased to meet you" stage. They are talking vaguely about a possible tour of the eastern U.S. in the fall, before she returns to school in England. She seems remarkably interested in the States, in general, and in seeing as much as she can of the major cities, in particular. In addition, there was an undercurrent in our conversation that would indicate that they have also talked about the future well beyond any mere travel together. If that's the case—and I fully admit that it's a bit premature to judge on our part—then Joan and I will be most supportive. She's just delightful. We'll keep you informed.

All the best,
Dick

As it became very obvious in the next six weeks, they were most assuredly more serious than they initially let on. And as we got to know Anne better, we were convinced that the romantic notion of "being meant for each other" wasn't an exaggeration at all in their case. They complement one another beautifully and they are both blissful in one another's company. We'd never seen Dan so happy and he certainly wasn't far off base when he described himself as being "antsy" when she wasn't around.

Dan did not accompany her on her tour of the major cities east of the Mississippi, but he made sure that a friend was on hand to escort her in every location where he knew (and trusted) someone. With all the friends he had left in the Washington area, she practically had a phalanx guard of honor for her visit to D.C.

After she returned to England, Dan's evenings were filled with writing long letters every night instead of watching TV during his evening duty sessions. He labored assiduously over each letter because, as he claimed at least, he didn't write well. That had hardly been our previous impression of his writing ability—we thought he was rather articulate as a matter of fact—but writing to the one you love is special and it deserved only the best.

The first indication of just how serious they had become was evident a short while later when Dan suggested that, if we had no problem with his doing so, he wanted to go to England for the Christmas holidays. And of course, that indicated that approval from Anne's parents was clearly in the offing, along with meeting all of Anne's relatives and friends. He did not seem daunted by this prospect in the least, but the next few months were anxious times for both of them—they couldn't wait to be back together again.

About this same time, Dan was in the process of having a new artificial leg constructed. His current prosthesis was old, was getting a bit worn and was causing discomfort and irritation. So the coincidence in timing of his trip to England and the completion of the new leg was certainly fortuitous.

The new leg was, in fact, ready for him just a week or so before the scheduled departure. And it was a beauty. It incorporated all the latest materials technology and was especially designed with increased abilities for him to participate in sports. According to the prosthetist, he would be able to run, ski or do virtually any other sporting activity and the leg would not only hold up under the added strain, it was designed so that it would enhance his natural ability.

So we were shocked less than twenty-four hours after his departure when he phoned from London to say that he needed us to send him his old leg, ASAP. When he was boarding the plane in Boston, simply walking along the jetway on to the aircraft, the new leg had broken in half, dropping him to his knees in the crowd of boarders. The flight and ground crews were most solicitous and helpful, and asked him if they could book him on a later flight. "No way," said he, so he arrived at Heathrow to meet his prospective in-laws in a wheelchair, with carry-on bag—and broken leg—in his lap.

It didn't take a lot of judgment on our part to realize that getting the old leg to him took top priority. While I packaged it up for shipment, Joan called all the overnight shippers in the immediate area and explained the situation, asking for the quickest way to get the leg to him at Anne's family home. To our astonishment, none of the carriers would accept the prosthesis for shipment because they were prohibited by policy from shipping "body parts". Despite Joan's protestations that this wasn't a "body part", it was a prosthesis, each remained adamant.

We had barely five minutes to get it to the post office before it closed so Joan called while I headed off with the package. Our postmaster proved why his office had been chosen the best small P.O. in the nation, year after year, when he stayed open and held up the shipment to the regional depot in Springfield so that we could get the package off to Dan. With a promised two day delivery, the package reached him in at Anne's family home in Southampton less than 36 hours later. Everything had gone splendidly as they bided their time at home; and now he was ready to get out and meet the far-flung relatives and friends throughout southern England.

I wouldn't be telling this story, of course, if all hadn't continued to go smashingly well, both during that visit and beyond. Dan returned to England the following spring for Anne's college graduation and she received an exemption to come back to work at the same inn the following summer, even though the exchange program was ostensibly for undergraduates. And they both remained very "antsy" while they were apart. They had made the firm decision to marry—with the enthusiastic approval of families and friends on both sides of the Atlantic—and when she returned to Lenox, they got used to their new state by sharing an apartment together.

Like most little girls, as a child Anne had pictured her wedding as something very special. She thought that there could be nothing more romantic than marrying on a great cruise ship and sailing off to the tropical islands for a honeymoon. And while that was completely feasible for Anne as a grown woman—and Dan agreed as well—they both realized that they had many friends and loved ones who would, of necessity, be omitted from sharing their joy with them. And thus was born the concept of not one, not two, but three weddings, one of which was to be the best wedding that the Birchwood ever saw.

The first wedding, and in reality, the only wedding ceremony, was to be on a cruise ship, just as Anne had imagined as a child. They searched diligently for the cruise line that would meet their expectations, as well as their pocketbooks, and chose a ship out of Port Canaveral, FL. The big day was to be the 14th of March 1996, and Roy and Janet Marshall, along with Joan and me, were privileged to be their only witnesses. As the ladies helped Anne to ready herself for the ceremony which was to be conducted by the cruise line's chaplain, Dan, Roy and I toured the ship briefly and then decided that a small libation would be in order at the outdoor bar on the top deck.

As we sat there enjoying the surroundings and talking about the things that worldly men discuss just prior to one of them getting married, I noticed Joan motioning to me from behind where Roy and Dan were seated. Something had clearly gone wrong and she didn't want to worry the other two. And something was wrong, indeed. The port immigration officer had decided that Anne did not have the proper visa to leave the country and return again. They could still get married on the ship, if they wished to, but if Anne sailed an hour later, she wouldn't be permitted back into the United States. Obviously, she was an undesirable alien that had to be denied re-entry into the country.

The irony of the whole situation was galling. Anne and Dan had anticipated every detail of their marriage and honeymoon well in advance, and had begun the whole Immigration and Naturalization Service process, by the book, 18 months previously. They could have cut corners and just married and then backed into the paperwork for Anne's "green card" (alien registration card) but chose to apply for a fiancée visa—the proper procedure. Anne had returned to England months earlier with the express purpose of expediting her background investigation through the

American Embassy in London. They had made numerous telephone calls to INS offices in Washington, Boston and White River Junction, VT (an influential senator managed that one, no doubt) to make sure that all had been properly done. They made three trips to Boston to the INS office there, waited in lines for hours only to be told there was another "i" to dot or "t" to cross. They even postponed their marriage one month to be sure that all would be in order. Finally, nearly six weeks before their rescheduled wedding date, they were told that all was in order for their marriage. Now, on their wedding day, they were faced with a last minute veto by an officious clerk.

I tried to reason with the lady and told her exactly what they had gone through. I assured her that the Boston office had cleared everything and asked her to call there to verify this fact. I even gave her the agent's name in Boston. Finally after much wrangling, she decided, on her own, that Anne could re-enter the United States as scheduled after the honeymoon, using her still-valid student visa. I asked that she put a memo to that effect in Anne's passport, just in case she weren't on duty when the ship returned.

Then, wiping away Anne's tears of frustration and disappointment, we had a lovely little wedding. The champagne was poured, the wedding cake cut and the ship sailed—without the parents, of course. Our job was done.

But the INS wasn't. When the newlyweds returned to port at 0630 (that's maritime time for 6:30 AM) a week later, Anne was once again called to the ship's administrative office and informed that she was not eligible to go ashore—she didn't have the correct visa. It was clear that the agent on the out-going leg of the cruise left no record of what had transpired earlier. After an hour of harassment, more tears, growing anger and frustration, Anne was allowed to disembark but admonished to go to Boston immediately and get her visa situation straightened out—or face forced deportation. She stepped ashore, feeling more like an unwanted criminal than she felt welcomed to her newly adopted land. On hearing of her added difficulty, I could only feel shamed by this incompetent, bureaucratic nonsense.

But I said there were two more weddings, didn't I. And indeed there were. One was at a 14th century Anglican Church in Kent, England, a month later—and after the visa situation had been corrected once and for all time. The vicar, a young female minister, did a splendid job of consecrating their marriage for Anne's family and friends who came, literally, from all over England and Ireland. Among them was Anne's aged grandmother, Nan, who lived in the nearby village and would have been devastated to miss her favorite granddaughter's wedding. Joan and I were fortunate to be present as well as four of our friends who came across the channel from Belgium for the occasion.

Following the ceremony, a grand reception was held at a private club nearby and the festivities continued far into the night. Then the following noon, Janet and Roy hosted a wonderful family dinner at the hotel where we were all staying. With all the celebrating, we needed the long flight back to the States to rest up for reopening the Inn that had been closed for two weeks,

The other "wedding" was at the Birchwood Inn and it truly was the finest that was held there. Bishop Michael came back to do an equally touching and effective "renewal of vows" ceremony in the library that was packed, elbow to elbow. Most of the family members that had been present for that first Thanksgiving were there, and a few that weren't. Anne and Dan had made many, many local friends and few, if any, declined the invitation. The rafters shook with gaiety and laughter into the wee hours of the morning, and the amount of food and drink that was consumed was prodigious. It was one marvelous party.

The following day, Janet and Roy, who had come from England for this iteration of the weddings, and Joan and I got the two kids together. We assured them that, god help us, should anything happen to cause a split in their marriage, we were going to insist that they go through three divorce proceedings. It would only be fair after three "weddings". But seeing the happy couple today, it's certain that the need for three more "ceremonies" will never ever be an occasion for their concern or ours.

*　　　　　　　*　　　　　　　*

September 28, 1994
Dear Chris & Tom,

When we are old and gray, as the old saying goes, and we look back on the days as innkeepers, I doubt that we'll dwell very much on memories of the two couples that I had to kick out of the Inn or the eight year old kid who wanted to bisect his little sister with a samurai sword. While those events will probably stick with us as long as our memories continue to function—and from what's been happening lately, that may not be much longer—we will surely look back with a nostalgic smile on the very, very nice people who have crossed our paths.

Two of the nicest of those have crossed our paths every summer since our first one. In fact, they were two of the very few people who we "inherited", in that their reservation had been made by the former owners. This special couple is perhaps eight to ten years older than Joan and I, and they come from Queens, out on Long Island. I think Joan will probably remember Molly if for no other reason than their first meeting. When they came into the Inn that first summer, Joan met them to check them in. She introduced herself and told them that we were the new owners. Molly looked at Joan, cocked her head and looked from a different angle, and then after a brief pause, she got a quizzical look on her face and said, "Don't you belong to our temple? Aren't you a member of my Hadassah group?"

Joan was tempted to suggest that, as an Irish Catholic, she probably wouldn't qualify for membership, but instead, just mentioned that we had recently moved to Lenox from northern Virginia.

That first year and each year that they came back, Irving very carefully selected his time and engaged me in a serious discussion on some topical subject. Often, the subjects related to politico-military affairs, but not always, and our discussions usually went on for an hour or more. He is clearly very well read and has both great breadth and depth in his knowledge. He is a retired lawyer, specializing in international law, and I found myself looking forward to our chats each year when they come back. The sessions that we had were never in the least bit contentious and were more in the vein of sharing knowledge and opinions. Both of us have a tendency to illustrate a particular point with personal anecdotes, a fact that probably adds to our enjoyment.

This year, we got into a deep discussion on the situation in Somalia and, in particular, my belief that there is an unhealthy parallel between the current situation there and our initial involvement in Vietnam. Coincidentally, an op-ed piece, which I had just written, was published in the local newspaper last Saturday in which I expressed caution about our impending involvement in Bosnia. He had read it and that, of course, took our conversation all over the map. I expressed my great concern that we are getting entangled more and more overseas while, at the same time, the military forces of our nation are being drastically cut each year. He was in strong agreement with that point and, from then on, our thoughts focused on how we can possibly get out gracefully now that we're involved in so many places. Unfortunately, there was no resolution worthy of forwarding to Washington.

Normally, when Molly and Irving leave at the end of the weekend, they both come to the Dutch door to say goodbye—always adding some kind words of appreciation. This time, Irving came alone, and began with his usual compliments and some last minute after—thoughts on the talk we had this year. Then, changing the subject abruptly, his eyes became a little moist and he told me that, for as long as he can remember, he has said a traditional Jewish prayer each night when going to bed. While I can't quote it exactly, it went something along the lines of:

> *Dear God, I thank you for this day and I ask that I may live to see my grandchildren. Next year in Jerusalem.*

Then, with a slight smile through watering eyes, he told me that, finally, their son got married in his late thirties and just last spring he and his wife had presented them with their first grandchild, a boy. He said that he feels that he can no longer say that prayer each night or the Lord will think that he's too greedy. Now, he went on, when he goes to bed each night his modified prayer has become:

> *Dear God, I thank you for this day and for permitting me to see my grandson. Next year at the Birchwood Inn.*

And with that, he quickly turned his back and headed out the entrance door.

I don't think I've ever been touched quite like that before. This nice little man probably gave us the finest compliment that we've ever received and I didn't even get the chance to say thank you. Perhaps the watery eyes were going to flow more heavily and he was embarrassed. But whatever the reason that he rushed away, he imprinted a memory on my mind that will never be erased.

Love to you both,
Dick

And, indeed, Molly and Irving came back each succeeding year until we left. He was aging noticeably and rapidly but his mind remained sharp and the chats continued each year. Sometimes we'd even squeeze in two sessions during a weekend. In the later years, Molly would occasionally apologize for his "taking up my time", alleging that he had started to repeat himself too often. And while she was, perhaps, right to a certain extent, I never became too busy to sit down with him to talk for an hour or so. And I always enjoyed it. I still think of that great little guy from time to time and realize that Molly and Irving, and many others like them, were the folks that made all our efforts worthwhile.

And thoughts of Irving bring another little Jewish man to mind. Herbert was also short in stature, but like Irving, was indeed a giant of man. He and his wife, Rose, also came back year after year. Herbert had been an architect-engineer for most of his professional career, and was the project engineer for some of the more recent major construction achievements in New York City. Late in his career, he had begun writing mystery novels and when he won The Edgar, the prize named after Edgar Allen Poe that is awarded annually for the best mystery of the year, he gave up engineering and devoted full time to writing.

Well almost full time. He also spent much of his time creating technical innovations and, like Irving and politico-military affairs, he loved to get me aside to discuss his latest high tech marvel. And just like Irving's wife, his wife, Rose, was forever scolding him for taking up too much of my time. But I thoroughly enjoyed these talks as well.

On their last visit to the Inn, he asked if I had any contacts in Washington with whom he could discuss his latest invention. He was concerned that this one was a real winner and he might become the victim of industrial espionage. His invention was something that he had been working on for nearly five years, and we secreted ourselves away in a corner of the front porch so that we could review the plans that he had brought with him.

The design was remarkably impressive and, during the following week, I unhesitatingly put him in contact with three people in Washington that I was certain would find his plans interesting—and could be trusted. The feedback that I received from these friends shared my enthusiasm and they foresaw endless possibilities for applications of his design. Unfortunately, Herbert died of a massive heart attack just a few months later and was never able to pursue his breakthrough. Someone did, however, since Honda and Toyota have recently produced the automobile of the future which is powered by a hybrid gas-electric engine that produces over 70 miles to the gallon of gas and is the cleanest automobile engine ever produced.

This same hybrid engine combination was Herbert's pride and joy back in the mid-90s. Whether it was pure coincidence and Herbert was just slightly late to the table, or if, indeed, he became a victim of the industrial espionage he feared, we may never know. But I, for one, saw the engine on paper long before there was ever any mention of it in the trade journals.

No recollection of memorable couples who came back to stay with us each summer would be complete without mentioning Margaret and Charles. They lived in the hills of northwestern New Jersey, an area that they described as being very much like Lenox and the Berkshires. As we get along in years, I suspect that almost all of us become creatures of habit. But Charles carried this to an extreme.

Each February, Charles would call within a few days of our sending out the annual schedule of concerts for the Tanglewood Festival the following summer. He would request reservations for the same weekend each year, and he would specify the same room that he had booked the previous year. They arrived with unerring punctuality at the same time every year, requested reservations at the same restaurants, and had us purchase the same picnics from the same caterer. And while that didn't make them especially unusual, one other thing that Charles did clearly set him apart.

Each year when he would check out, he would express his appreciation for our hospitality, leave a generous tip for the housekeepers and then ask, plaintively, "Isn't there some way that you can get those darn church bells turned off at midnight or earlier? They keep me awake every single night and just about the time that I get back to sleep, they ring again."

He was referring to the bells in the steeple at the Church on the Hill, which ring each hour around the clock. As the crow flies, the steeple is about 200 yards from the room that he requested year after year. And in addition to his rhetorical question to me, he would also write a letter to the pastor of the church each year, making a more formal request to silence "those darn church bells". With equal regularity, she would write back to him to tell him that she would be delighted to accommodate, but she didn't own the church. It belongs to the Town of Lenox and is rented to the Church of Christ for a nominal annual fee and their promise to maintain its structural integrity and appearance. And no, the Town had considered many requests for turning off the bells, but continued to decline each one. They wouldn't think of defying centuries of tradition.

It was well toward the end of our innkeeping tenure that we discovered what to us, at least, is a strange irony: Charles is a minister himself and his church also has a bell that chimes the hour. Perhaps he doesn't live quite as closely. Finally, in our last summer at the Inn, we convinced Charles and his wife to change rooms to the far side of the building. He conceded that the bells were less bothersome than they had been previously, and he had slept a lot better—but he still preferred his old room.

The final tale about memorable characters and events is about a couple that we hardly knew. They were not regular returnees. As a matter of fact, they were walk-ins one weekday winter night early in our career. But every once in a while, one of us will start laughing over the memory of the family tradition that they left us

While it certainly wasn't the cold, snowy night that might provide the story with a more melodramatic aura, it was a very cold night and it was after dark. We had no guests at the Inn that evening, and as was our custom, we were using the public area of the Inn and treating ourselves like real people. And it wasn't just Joan, Dan and me. Seamus and the two cats were in the public area as well and we were all acting just like we were a family in the comfort of our own home. There was even a roaring fire in the fireplace to set everything to rights.

Suddenly, there was the familiar sound of the bell that signaled that someone was coming in the entrance door. Well, so much for our family evening together. When the intruders came into the desk area, it turned out to be a couple in their mid-40s perhaps, both very nice looking people and exceptionally well-dressed. The woman was especially attractive and as soon as she said hello, it was clear that she had a heavy accent, which turned out to be Spanish—a true lady of Spain, not a Hispanic from the Western Hemisphere. We were later to learn that she had only been in the States for less than a month.

As she stood midway between the desk area and the den, chatting amiably with Joan, Big Kitty's curiosity got the best of him and he slinked around the corner to see who had arrived on the scene. Now saying that Big Kitty slinked is the highest form of compliment because, at the time, he tipped the scales at 22 pounds—even though he has since slimmed down to a svelte 15 pounds. When our newly arrived guest caught sight of him, she stifled a gasp with her hand and exclaimed, "Oh my, what a big cat!" with the pronunciation of "cat" sounding more like the Spanish pronunciation "gaht-to".

I was standing nearby and laughed at her apparent amazement and replied, "He certainly is a moose, isn't he?"

She looked at me very strangely, pondered what I said for a moment and the blurted out as if to explain her comment, "Well he looks like a cat to me!"

Her husband, who was an American, broke the ice and began to laugh first, and we all chimed in with him. Then he sweetly and patiently explained, in perfect Spanish, that "moose" is American slang for something or someone who is very large. And then, finally, it became clear to her and she was able to join in the laughter as well.

Still today, when Big Kitty slinks around a corner and regally saunters into a room, some one of us more than likely will say, "Oh my, what a big gaht!"

*   *   *

November 30, 1994
Dear Chris & Tom,

You probably remember the informal name that we came up with for room 5—the Loving Room. That's the room in which the memory book reads like a steamy, dime-store romance novel, the spot where people have recorded their most personal reflections (or fantasies) about the great love affairs that have transpired there. I suspect you also recall the instigator of all of the torrid entries into the book, the young man from "the city" with whom we plotted the unusual engagement rite up in Kennedy Park. Well, that happy (erotic) couple has been heard from once again.

This past weekend, we had another young couple from New York who came and stayed in the Loving Room. Saturday morning when they came down to breakfast, the young man had the memory book from the room in his hand. He set it on the table beside him where it remained throughout the meal. Joan thought that perhaps they were reading it over breakfast or were going to make an entry in it after they ate, but she really didn't pay very close attention.

Finally, after they had been served and the dining room had started to empty, he picked the book up in his hand and said to Joan, "Would you mind if I borrowed this for a week or so and sent it back to you later?"

Joan was a bit surprised by the request because no one had ever asked anything like that before. But she was instantly reminded of our bad experience with our library books. We started out with a willingness, bordering on eagerness, to share our very nice book collection with any guest who might be interested. During our little orientation tour, we would tell guests that if they found a book that interested them, they were welcome to take it home and return it at a later date. All we asked is that they tell us that they were borrowing it and return it within a few weeks. After a year of serving as an informal lending library, we found that fifty or more books were missing, which included some of our more valued ones that had been inscribed and autographed by the author. And we didn't have the slightest idea who had taken them. Even a few of those who had told us that they were borrowing a book later ignored repeated written requests for them to send the book back. Needless to say, we discontinued that practice, and it also prompted Joan to deny this young man's request.

Undaunted, he asked if he could just borrow it for the day so that he could get some pages copied. This peaked Joan's curiosity—was he going to try to turn our memory book into a steamy, dime-store romance novel?—so she asked him why. The answer turned into one of the more humorous ironies of our many bizarre experiences.

It turns out that the "hero" of the original erotica, the co-author of all the grunting and groaning of that memorable engagement weekend, was a co-worker of the current occupant of the room in a Wall Street brokerage house.

Those young professionals are apparently just as avid about their play as they are about making money. The firm's semi-annual party was scheduled for the following weekend, so the chap holding the book thought it would be especially humorous to stand up at their affair and read the many pages that had been penned in the book over two years previously.

But that wasn't really the essence of the irony. For our young hero of yore, as it turned out, had broken up with Laurie less than a month after they were engaged. And from the talk around the water cooler at the office, most of his co-workers thought that the whole thing had been a ruse to "score" with the reluctant maiden that Laurie was reputed to be. Since Romeo had achieved his goal—and bragged about it openly with the guys—our current guest thought it would be particularly fitting to air the great romance openly at the office party. He punctuated that belief by telling Joan that the hero was now engaged to another female employee of the firm and, rightly or wrongly, most of the others in the office were pretty well convinced that this was another attempt by the young Lothario for a repeat conquest.

Ah, the difficult moral dilemmas that we sometimes face. Joan was so irate at the crude brashness of the rogue that I think she might have been willing to go to New York and read the excerpt herself. But she was also torn by his right to privacy, so she elected to be Solomonic in her decision. She told our guests that, no, she didn't think that it would be very ethical to let him take the book to get copies made. But on the other hand, she certainly could not prevent them from taking all the notes that they wanted. In fact, she would be happy to lend them a legal pad and pen if they needed one.

I would have given anything to have been at the office party the following weekend to see the reactions. Particularly, as we were to learn, because both Laurie and the new fiancée were employees of the firm and both were expected to be at the celebration.

Hope you had a nice Thanksgiving and we'll be talking to you before the Christmas holidays. And by the way, be careful of what you put in writing. It might have a way of coming back to haunt you.

Cheers,
Dick

But this wasn't the only time we had experiences with alienated affections. Often, a young, very attractive woman would stay with us on weekdays while she was in the area. She was the sales representative—I think we used to call them traveling salesmen, but I like the new term better—for a major national firm and her territory covered a good part of New England. She was one of the easiest guests we ever had. She was ready to go out the door by 7:30 each morning and a blueberry muffin and coffee would suit her just fine. She also had dinner out each evening and rarely returned before we secured for the night, so it was almost as if she weren't even there.

One morning when she was checking out from a three day stay, she mentioned that she really loved Room 1, so much that she thought it would be a wonderful place to come back to for a relaxing weekend. Only if she did, it would be with her fiancé. She checked availability for the following month and promised she'd call back in a day or so to book. She just needed to coordinate their schedules.

And sure enough she did, but it was not for just one weekend. Though I can't say for certain, it seemed that every time her future business brought her back to the Berkshires, she would plan her stay so that it merged with the weekend and then her fiancé would join her on Friday night.

But after two or three such weekends, we didn't hear from her for nearly a year. We weren't sure whether her territory had changed or, perish the thought, we had done something to cause the Inn to lose its appeal to her.

But finally, she called. Yes, she had not been around for a while but she was coming back. And she would like to extend her business stay through the weekend, as had been her recent habit. But then she paused. Finally, she stammered slightly and asked what other luxury room might be available that weekend. It seems that Jeff was not going to be with her that coming weekend—or ever again—and Room 1 contained far too many memories for her to feel comfortable there with her new friend.

On another occasion, while alienation of affection was not involved, at least that we are aware of, we had one more look at the unusual way in which some people view the world around them. These guests seemed to be a bundle of contradictions. He and his partner checked in late one Friday. If you say wife or husband these days in our business, you're probably going to be wrong close to half the time. And during the orientation, their questions implied to us that they expected to find all the opportunities and amenities of New York City right here in our little village. They wanted to know if there was theater (meaning Broadway style legitimate stage productions) available. Were there any unusual ethnic restaurants in the area? They never passed up the opportunity for off-beat dining, but our local Italian and Chinese restaurants didn't seem to fit that expectation.

So it was all the more amazing to us when both of them came downstairs on Saturday morning dressed in the latest Abercrombie & Fitch safari gear, complete with shorts and bush jackets—with, I suspect, the sales tags just removed. Only the pith helmet was missing, but they were headed out to the nearby wilderness in early fall, so the likelihood of sunstroke was probably at seasonal minimums.

When they returned for wine and cheese that evening, they were both flushed with the excitement of one who had seen nature up close and personal. And they liked what they saw. They had seen a flock of wild turkeys that just ran, rather than flew, as they approached. They had seen a deer from a distance and they even thought that they had seen a wolf—more than likely a coyote since there are no wolves in the area. And they found the fall foliage to be a miracle of nature. These city folks had clearly enjoyed themselves and we were delighted to have had the experience.

But when they checked out, we were to discover that they had another experience, far less pleasurable than the others. Dan did the honors, and in a style that we had seen more than once, the man approached the desk while checking rather furtively in every direction to see if anyone were in hearing distance. Then he leaned over the desk with one hand cupped beside his mouth and said, "I'm very disappointed with the cleanliness of your rooms. There was a bug in my bed last night."

Dan was stunned to say the least and asked him what kind of bug he had found and where it was. The man checked in all directions for eavesdroppers once again and said that it actually wasn't *in* the bed. It was a tick, he thought, and "….it was attached to my scrotum." In fact he had pulled it off and there it was in a small pill vial that he withdrew from his pocket.

Dan confirmed that it was, indeed, a tick while doing all he could to avoid breaking out into paroxysms of laughter. And as diplomatically as he could, he explained that the man and his wife had spent a good part of the previous day out in the forest—wearing short pants. He went on to say that deer ticks are very common in the woods, especially at this time of year, and that those of us who live here, because of the ticks, would never wear shorts in high grass or a forested areas. Rather, we would wear long pants and tuck the bottom of the pants into heavy socks to prevent the ticks from doing exactly what had probably happened to him. And we always check for ticks when we come in from the woods, Dan told him, just to make sure that one of the little devils hadn't breached our defenses.

Our intrepid woodsman didn't seem completely convinced that the Birchwood Inn wasn't at least partially responsible for his inadvertent hosting of the tiny parasite. But when Dan went on to explain the deer ticks carry Lyme disease and it would be a good idea to get to a physician for tests when he got back to the city, the man paled and looked faint. This last cautionary note made him forget all about the source of the tick and he and his wife beat a hasty retreat out of the Inn and back to the big city.

Dan never volunteered to look at the site where the tick had attached itself for the tell-tale circular red rash that comes with Lyme disease, nor did we ever did hear how he fared after that. But we strongly suspect that the Abercrombie & Fitch outfits have probably been donated to Goodwill, or at best, reserved for an occasional expedition through Central Park, perhaps in search of elusive new ethnic restaurants.

*   *   *

February 26, 1995
Dear Chris & Tom,

As I've mentioned to you before, one of the side benefits of having chosen Lenox for our home base as innkeepers is our proximity to both Joan's and my families. So far, the ability to be within shouting distance, so to speak, has all been pleasurable. Now we find ourselves in a situation that can hardly be associated with pleasure but our closeness has certainly been important.

Joan's Dad and her Aunt Dorothy and Uncle George, who became her foster parents after her mother died when she was ten years old, all live in the Boston suburbs. All three have entered their eighties since we bought the Inn. With advanced age, of course, comes an increased likelihood that serious illness or even death is more imminent. But, believe it or not, George's mother, who Joan calls Aunt Beth, is also still among the living and she recently celebrated her

100th birthday. With genes like that, one never knows, but we have felt a lot better being in the nearby area just in case.

Not too long ago, Uncle George had a fairly serious stroke and it was good that we were close enough to respond. He spent a number of weeks in a rehabilitation hospital, and though his ability to walk, as well as his speech and comprehension, received irreparable damage, he had recovered fairly well—well enough to join us for Thanksgiving, which has long been a tradition in Joan's immediate family. But recovery after a stroke as serious as the one he suffered is, unfortunately, usually just an interim reprieve and ten days ago he had another, more serious stroke.

Thanks to Dan's running the whole show by himself, Joan and I have spent the better·part of the intervening time in Boston, taking our turns at the death watch. The doctors told us that he would be a complete invalid, and possibly in a coma, if he were to survive, so it is merciful that he passed away a few days ago.

The transition for Aunt Dorothy was hardly easy, but she has always been the matriarch of the family, so she continues to be the level-headed, strong soul that she has always been. I know she has been most grateful to have Joan to lean on from time to time, especially in that difficult no man's land between death and recovery. But she has already restored herself as the solid foundation on which the family depends and she seems to be coping with the situation very well. Joan was also fairly well resigned to the probability of death and though there were tears and sorrow, she and her cousin, Bill, have attended to most of the details related to the funeral.

So we didn't need the additional crisis that hit us the day before the funeral. About 4:30 AM the phone rang and it was Dan calling from the Inn. The phone was right beside my ear and nearly scared the wits out of me when it rang, but it served to awaken me sufficiently so that I was fully alert. It reminded me of my days as a base commander when calls in the wee hours were common. As Dan related the story, the fire and security alarm had gone off about an hour before, and he was out of bed like a shot looking for the source of the problem. He checked the master panel first and found that the alarm had been triggered on the ground floor, so he made a thorough search of the whole area. When he approached the entrance door, he discovered what had probably set off the alarm, but that discovery just opened the door to an even greater mystery.

He found that water was streaming down the walls and through the ceiling and had, in the process, shorted out the alarm sensor that was in the ceiling at that same point. Now, where was the water coming from?

As you can imagine in a house that was built before running water and electricity were commonplace in any structure, the control valves for the water shutoffs are scattered all over the place, from the basement to the second floor. We had made previous efforts to locate all the valves and label them according to the area that they controlled. But tracking the right one down was going to be a nightmare for Dan, so he very wisely went down to the basement and turned off the water main to the whole house. He apologized for waking me— certainly no apology was necessary—but had only called to find out if the heating system might be endangered if its water supply was cut off. It wasn't.

I could have hugged him through the phone for keeping his wits about him and taking exactly the right action. And I told him that I would be on my way as soon as I could get dressed to help him to get the situation under control.

By the time I made the two hour trip back to Lenox, Dan had discovered the cause of the flood. Directly over the entrance to the Inn, on the third floor, there is a common bathroom that is shared by the guests in the two tiny rooms, 8 and 9. The ancient antique cold water faucet in the sink had finally given up the ghost, and because of the water pressure that is augmented by circulation pumps, it simply broke off at the base. Water had been flowing from the broken *fixture apparently for hours and hours and had flooded the bathroom. A good chunk of the third floor was also in standing water and a good deal of it had then flowed down through the second floor walls and ceilings to the ground floor—and even into the basement as we were to discover later.*

Well, the first priority was clean up, and that was going to be followed by repair (and in some cases, restoration). Fortunately, the ceiling at the entrance door was a drop ceiling with acoustical tile overhead, and while it looked like an ungodly mess with the broken, wet tiles all over the place, it was better than having a plaster ceiling come down. At any rate, we spent most of the day cleaning up the portion of the mess that was most evident, replacing the ceiling tiles and installing portable heaters all over the place to try to dry out the carpets and the walls.

By 8:00 that evening, I was back at the funeral home helping to greet the hundreds of mourners who had come to George's wake. As a former fireman, he was known by everyone in the suburban town where they had lived all their lives. He was a grand guy, and we are very sorry to lose him, but considering the alternatives that the doctors had predicted, his passing was a blessing.

As for the damage to the house, things have begun to dry out pretty well, but we haven't yet had the chance to crawl into some of the nooks and crannies to make an accurate assessment. At first blush, I don't think things are going to be quite as bad as they looked initially, but it's not going to be a piece of cake getting things back to normal. The wonders of owning an old property can't possibly be overstated. I'll keep you posted on the final verdict. Meantime, enjoy your balmy Monterey Peninsula weather while we freeze in sub-zero temps.

All the best,
Dick

Fortunately, no serious structural damage was done by the flood and, over time, Dan and I were able to handle most of the repair work ourselves. The highest priority first step was to replace all of the antique plumbing hardware to prevent any recurrences. And while we tried hard to select new hardware with an antique appearance, things never did look quite the same again. But, of course, we didn't have any surprise floods again either.

The longevity of the older generation did not turn out to be as promising, however. Not too long after she buried her only son at age 82, Aunt Beth died peacefully in her sleep and moved on to her reward. There was never a finer woman to grace the face of the earth and she left a legacy of love and respect that even the most successful and fortunate among us might envy. Adult great-grandchildren still speak of her as a guiding light in their lives and as one who set the standard for living a good life. Once again, we were gratified that we were close enough to be able to spend many hours with her in the final years. It was especially nice to be able to help her celebrate the centennial of her birth, and we felt fortunate to pay our last respects to her when she passed away.

Joan's father, Eddie Nobis, spent his final years in much the same way that George had done. But he suffered from congestive heart failure rather than as the victim of strokes. Eddie had married again late in life, well after Joan and I were married, and he and his Nonie were like youngsters in their shared joy in having found one another. They lived a full and good life together, and they were completely devoted. When Nonie passed away unexpectedly in the late '80s, Eddie began a slow but steady decline that was painful to watch, and most likely even more difficult for him to bear.

He insisted on living alone and, aggravated by depression and a fading sense of love for life, his personality underwent a change. He had gone from the jolly, positive person who never had a bad thing to say about anyone to an increasingly glum and critical man. Our proximity gave Joan the opportunity to allow him to take a look at himself and the changes he was undergoing and it helped. Often, when we weren't particularly busy, he would came to the Inn for a few days by himself and he seemed to like very much just to be around his daughter and her family. His attitude and outlook became more positive over time, but he never fully regained his zest for life nor the buoyant attitude that had characterized him over the 40 years I had known him.

A series of four congestive heart failure incidents over the next year put him on an irreversible course to the end. He very nearly perished on his own living room floor after one incident but was rushed to the hospital in time to save him. After each incident, Dan was always the stalwart holder of the fort while Joan and I hurried to Boston in hopes that we would be in time. And while we were, each time, we knew it was only a matter of weeks or months before he would be gone. After the fourth incident, while he lay in the cardiac care unit barely able to speak, he looked at Joan with a look on his face of abject surrender and whispered that he was no longer good for anything and it was time for him to die. She leaned over, kissed him and, though her throat that was badly constricted by sorrow and pain, she whispered in response, "It's OK, Dad. You can let go if you want to." And within a matter of minutes he was gone.

Eddie was laid to rest a few days later beside his beloved Nonie and we are certain that everlasting happiness has been granted to them both. And so the third member of the senior generation in Joan's family had passed away within just over a year. Only Dorothy, the matriarch of the family, was left.

She too had a stroke shortly before we sold the Inn, leaving her severely incapacitated and nearly blind. But in her stubborn, determined independence, she has refused to leave the small apartment that she and George shared over the last decade of their lives together and, with the occasional assistance of her many friends and family in the nearby area, she continues to persevere.

When we sold the Inn, we debated whether to follow our plans and move to the southwest or to remain, temporarily, in the Boston area. She kindly settled the dilemma by telling us that we have a long life still ahead of us and we had earned the happiness of putting down roots for the first time in our 43 years of marriage. And so, with her blessing, we made our final move. Joan returns to Boston every six months or so to be with her and she calls her every other day on the telephone. And knowing how determined and independent Dorothy has always been, I wouldn't be the least bit surprised if she outlives us both.

My family has been a lot more fortunate even though my older brothers and sisters have all entered their seventies. Brothers-in-law have undergone extensive coronary artery bypass operations and others have had surgery to correct normal, and some not so normal, consequences of aging. But my sisters, Nancy and Paula, still persevere as if they were in their forties.

As we were getting ready to turn the Inn over after the sale, Nancy and Paula were once again there to lend a hand with the final clean-up. Everyone busied him—or herself in various parts of the house, doing the various chores that each would expect to have done if we had been buying the Inn rather than selling it. But when I found Nancy and Paula on their hands and knees scrubbing bathroom floors, I drew the line. They protested loudly that this was the only way to get the floors completely clean, but there was no way I was going to let my older sisters do what I refused to do myself. As the two of them had proved over and over throughout our ownership of the Inn, "they threw away the mold" when they were created. I'm not sure if they are still scrubbing floors on their hands and knees in their own homes, but they are both indefatigable and indestructible, so nothing would surprise me. May they stay that way forever.

*　　　　　*　　　　　*

April 4, 1995
Dear Chris & Tom,

I don't think I mentioned it to you previously, but last summer we had a couple of robberies. We keep our operating cash in a strong box in one of the drawers in the computer desk, and there is usually a few hundred dollars in small bills in it. One day last summer, I had just been to the bank where I had cashed a check for $400. The next morning, I went to the drawer to get change for a guest and found only a few singles remaining in the slot where the paper money was kept and all the rest was missing.

We quickly concluded that it was an inside job, probably one of the new kids that we had hired for the summer who had seen us go to the drawer and couldn't resist the temptation. Foolishly, I figured that a padlock on the strong box would preclude that from happening again, and went back to the bank for more petty cash. However, the second time it happened, the padlock was no challenge. Whoever it was had taken the whole cash box, containing not just the petty cash but all the cash receipts from the guests and a few personal valuables.

Though it took more than a thousand dollar loss for me to learn my lesson, we finally did it right. I put a hasp and a large padlock on the on the drawer where the cash box is kept. And in an effort to nab the thief or just create a greater deterrent, I bought a small area motion sensor with an alarm that would wake the dead, and installed it in the corner of the kitchen, behind a blind adjacent to the desk. Last one out of the kitchen sets the alarm each night and the first one to arrive in the morning has to disable it. You have about ten seconds after it "sees" you to turn it off, so Joan insists that I have to be the first to arrive in the kitchen each morning.

Fortunately, we have had no repeats of the robberies, and whether that's because of the preventive measures or because the summer help is gone, we'll probably never know. And while I reported it to the police each time, I'm sure they're not going to find out who did it. I can't visualize them grilling some teenager under hot lights the way Joe Friday used to do it on "Dragnet". But the relatively new alarm has been the cause of some rather humorous incidents. I do not include the times that either one of the cats has decided to go prowling in the middle of the night and managed to set off the alarm. I haven't yet found the trip over to the kitchen from my warm bed to turn off the klaxon in the wee hours the least bit humorous.

But last weekend, the alarm incident that took place really took the cake. About 3:00 AM the motion sensor was triggered in the kitchen and, fully convinced that the cats had done it again, I got up rather slowly to silence the alarm. But as I turned on the light, here were both kitties, sound asleep in their beds, or at least they had been until the ruckus and the lights had disturbed their rest. And then they just glanced up briefly to find out what was going on. Perhaps this one was going to be the real thing. When I reached the kitchen, there was no one there and everything looked to be in order. So it was back to bed again, but I still had a bit of nagging curiosity over what had triggered it.

It seems as though I had just barely put my head back on the pillow when the alarm went off again. No necessity to awaken this time or force the sleep out of my eyes. This time I was going to catch the perpetrator and I ran over to the kitchen. The room was empty as before, but this time as I silenced the klaxon, I heard the faint sound of the pantry door closing and what sounded like footsteps leaving the dining room. I followed the noise, turning on all the lights as I went. As I reached the library, I was amazed to find a young woman crouched behind one of the overstuffed chairs—barefoot and clad only in a filmy shortie nightgown.

As it turned out, she was the female half of the young couple staying in the ground floor suite of the carriage house. And the story that she unfolded for me, explaining how she happened to trigger the alarm, not once but twice, was a masterpiece of confusion.

I'm afraid that both she and her partner suffer from a preoccupation with personal security. I certainly do not say that as a criticism because, if I lived in Manhattan, I suspect that I'd be far more security conscious. But their concern for security was clearly what had led to her meanderings in the wee hours.

The carriage house suite that they occupied has a lock on every door, both the interior and exterior doors, and those on the interior are all one-way locks. In other words, you can lock the door using the button on the handle to prevent someone from intruding. You find these locks on most all bathroom doors. In this suite, the bathroom has two doors—one leading to the sitting room and the other leading to the bedroom—and both doors lock from inside the bath. The entrance door to the suite from the outside is a standard lock set that can be locked from either side. But just inside the entryway to the suite is another interior door to the sitting room with a one-way lock that locks only from inside the room. And none of these locks automatically open when you turn the knob. If you lock the door with the push button, you must unlock it manually.

I'm not sure exactly how it happened, but in their apparent concern for security, they locked every single door in the suite before they retired for the night. Unfortunately, as they were to find out some time in the middle of the night, they had locked themselves into the bedroom and couldn't gain access to the bathroom—or anywhere else for that matter. They had apparently changed into their night clothes in the sitting room, because everything they had was on the other side of two locked doors, including the key to the entrance door to the suite.

Perhaps they drew straws to see who was "it", or perhaps the young woman had volunteered for some reason. But she had climbed out the window of the ground floor suite, clad as I said in only a shortie nightgown, and had made her way over to the mansion in search of another key. One big problem. We had an early spring snow storm the day before and there was about eight inches of snow on the ground through which she had to travel in her bare feet in order to reach the mansion. She wasn't about to travel all the way around the driveway to the entrance door so she entered through the kitchen and, bingo, she set off the alarm.

As she was later to explain, she was too embarrassed to reveal herself the way she was dressed and was certain that she could find another key at the front desk. So she never rang the night bell to ask for help. And she was right. She had found another key, and between the time that I had silenced the alarm the first time and its second mournful pealing into the night, she had gone back to the suite entrance only to find that she could get in only as far as the entrance foyer. Not surprisingly, they had locked the interior door from the foyer into the sitting room as well. She wasn't quite sure what she was looking for in her second foray into the mansion—and she clearly hoped that I hadn't reset the alarm after it went off the first time. But here she was, very pointedly showing signs of the cold through her scanty clothing and ready to break down in despair.

I found her one of Joan's coats for her to slip on and some boots to put on her feet. And to be polite, I went back to the hovel to put on a shirt. It wouldn't do for the two of us to be found in relative states of undress the way we were. Then I also put on a pot of water for tea so that she could warm up while she told me her tale of woe. Finally we headed back to the carriage house, with the proper tools this time to open all the doors that they had locked—and eventually get us both back to our respective beds so that we could gain back a little of the sleep we had all lost.

I never did see the husband or boyfriend, whatever he was. You don't suppose that he had slept through the whole thing, do you? People are certainly funny sometimes.

Take care of yourselves,
Dick

That incident was not the first contact that I had with this couple under circumstances that were less than normal. When they arrived and checked in the evening before, the man told me that he had a "little trouble" getting up the driveway and wondered whether it would be OK for him to leave their car where it was. When I went outside to check, I found their little old Dodge Colt nosed deeply into the decorative hedge that surrounds the side parking lot, with the rear end athwart the driveway so that no one could get in or out. A quick look at the tires on his car made it evident why they had trouble getting up the driveway. All four of them were bald—not just low on tread but completely smooth with not a trace of tread to be seen. It's an absolute wonder that they were able to complete the three hour drive without a blowout or skidding off the roadside in the snow. And needless to say, Dan and I had to remove the car from the predicament that he had put it in.

But they were hardly the only guests we had that we remember for goofy events associated with locked doors. Some of them were even celebrities.

Two of the nicest people that we ever had at the Inn also happened to be long-time stars of rock and roll music. They had come to the Berkshires to do a benefit concert for the National Music Center. In fact, they were two of the co-founders of the parent Foundation and they were in Lenox with Dick Clark and many others music celebrities to do a free performance for the community. Joey Dee and his wife, Lois Lee, had been stars on the popular music circuit for three decades and they were especially well known for their great classics of early rock and roll, "Peppermint Twist" and "Shout". Since they had paid their own way to the Berkshires and were doing a benefit performance, we thought it was only fair to put them up for the night as our true guests—as our contribution to the Foundation.

Like most performers, they were "night people" but Joey had committed to doing a 9:00 AM interview with a local oldies radio station. We had blocked off the library for the interview, and since he was going to be so close at hand, Joey had quietly dressed and left the room while Lois continued to get her beauty sleep. The scheduled half hour live interview apparently went very well, for both Joey and the announcer, because it continued on for a second half hour and then yet another.

Finally, one of the guests came to the Dutch door and said, "There appears to be something wrong with the woman in Room 1 and I think you had better check. She keeps yelling, 'I'm locked in here. Would someone please unlock the door and let me out'"

It was Lois Lee of course. When Joey had tiptoed out to the room, he had locked the door out of force of habit and taken the key with him. Because of the extended length of the interview, he was way behind schedule getting back to the room to free his imprisoned wife. Lois said later that it was a lovely room and she enjoyed sitting in the silk chaise lounge reading the magazines that were in the room. But after a while the room seemed to be getting smaller and smaller and she found herself becoming claustrophobic. Their life on the road in show business had more than likely seen more than a few incidents of this nature in the past. And like the trooper she was, she took it very good-naturedly. But she wasn't going to let Joey forget about it right away.

One of the great surprises that we had throughout our innkeeping careers was the distinct lack of emergency calls in the middle of the night. I suspect that a lot of credit for this—at least as far as the young couples on a getaway were concerned—goes to their careful selection and preparation of the babysitters who were caring for the children while they were gone. There were endless calls during the daytime, usually from children with complaints that the sitter wouldn't let them do such and such, or was trying to make them do so and so. But we almost never had any emergency calls in those wee hours between midnight and dawn.

One call that did come in the wee hours was memorable, however, if not because of the rarity of such calls, at least because of the reason for the call. It was, without question, a marvelous illustration of the differing perceptions of what constitutes an emergency.

This particular call came shortly before 4:00 AM and it was from a young woman who asked for one of our guests by his full name. She said she was calling from Paris, France, and could I please hurry up. I reminded her of our local time and asked her if it was truly an emergency. As if that question opened the floodgates, she began to sob and told me she didn't care what our local time was, THIS IS AN EMERGENCY.

I went up to the room of a very nice couple in their forties who had been with us for the previous two days and told them, through the door, what the situation was. When the man came out of the room, he had an expression on his face that told me that he knew this wasn't a real emergency. But he had been in the habit of humoring his daughter so long that he wasn't going to choose this particular moment to try to break that habit. I brought him down to the kitchen where I had left the phone line open, rather than putting the young lady on hold, so that the overseas connection wouldn't be interrupted.

Before she could explain anything, Dad asked her the number that she was calling from so that he could call her back from the cellular phone in his car. And while he went out to the parking lot to continue the call, I made a pot of coffee and waited to see if there were anything that I might do to lend a hand.

When he returned to the kitchen, he had a wistful smile on his face and he accepted the coffee gratefully. It seems that his 17 year old daughter was calling from Charles de Gaulle Airport near Paris to inform him that "somehow" she and her friend had just missed their flight home to the States. They had "misread" the departure time on their tickets and besides, they didn't know that they were supposed to arrive "that early" for check in. And the aircraft had just taken off without them.

He told me that he very patiently reminded her that he had provided her with a credit card, with no spending limit, so that she could handle any situation like this. He advised her to go back into Paris, find a nice hotel— the George V or Le Bristol, perhaps—and enjoy an extra day or two in Paris until they could book another flight back home. "You'd think that most kids would be delighted to get a couple of days extension on their vacation in Europe," he told me, "instead she just cried all the harder."

After questioning her further to find out what her real problem was, he discovered that she had a date the following night with the "real hunk" that she had wanted to go out with for months. She was afraid that he'd never ask her out again if she stood him up. Her Dad went on to say, "I think she truly expected me to tell her to come home on the Concorde, or better yet, that I'd send a charter flight after her. But I think we're well past the time that she needs to learn to live with the consequences of her own actions."

Then raising his coffee cup as if in a toast, he said, "Well I realize that your problems are no where near as serious as hers, but you've still got to get up in an hour or so to face a full day's work. I'm sorry you were disturbed but I appreciate your help very much."

I haven't yet figured out a way to get someone to tell me to spend a couple of days in Paris at the George V, but that doesn't mean that I'm not still looking!

*   *   *

June 22, 1995
Dear Chris & Tom,

With all the experience that we've all had in dealing with people and their problems, I still get knocked off my pins when some bizarre expression of human nature comes along. I know most of the generalities, like most women will fiercely defend their children and most men will react very defensively if you question their manhood. And I'm even familiar with the tendency of some people to stretch the truth or even lie when they are caught in a compromising position. But this business is revealing facets of human nature that are new and a bit strange to us—even though most are funny in retrospect.

We had an incident that extended over the past six months that illustrates all of the above. Back last fall, we had a young couple from North Jersey staying with us for the weekend. I'd guess they were probably in their late twenties or early thirties, and they were nothing out of the ordinary. Just quiet and congenial people who showed every indication of having enjoyed themselves when they checked out.

Two weekends later, we had another couple with us who made a point of telling us right off the bat that they were best friends of the couple who had been with us just two weeks previously. And they came from a New Jersey town that was fairly close by the home of their friends. They too were excellent guests, seemed very satisfied with their weekend and even made a point to tell us that they "owed one" to their friends who had recommended us to them. Therefore, it was quite surprising when we received a series of telephone calls from both of them that began a short while later.

The male member of the first couple called to tell us that he thought something was amiss at our Inn. They had just received their Visa credit card bill and discovered a charge at a restaurant in Pittsfield for nearly $150 and he insisted that they had never been near that restaurant nor had they even heard of it. In fact, the man said, the only time they had used that particular card that particular weekend was when they checked out from the Birchwood. As we discussed the matter, the man was very careful not to blame or even suggest that Joan, Dan or I might be responsible for fraudulent use of his credit card number. But he was equally pointed is stating that he thought "one of our employees" had probably copied down their credit card number and gone out to have a big dinner for herself. No mention of the other couple, their friends, was made in the conversation.

Then, two days later, the other man—I'll call them couple # 2 for clarity—called with precisely the same story. Their card had also been used fraudulently at the same restaurant, only this charge was for $165. They too had only used the card to check out of the Inn and the second man also implied that we were responsible for the charge, somehow or other. Since the name of couple # 1 was still fresh in my mind, I asked him if he knew that their friends had called with the same complaint. He hesitated perceptibly but then admitted that they had all talked about it.

As nicely as I could, I asked him what he thought should be done about the situation. He started his response by saying that he just wanted us to know that we may have some dishonesty in our staff. But then he quickly got around to saying that if I sent him a check for the total amount that he had been charged, we could "call it square".

Not being terribly enamored of that idea, and having gone through the reverse situation with Visa a few years ago, I told him that the proper way to resolve this was to call the Visa customer assistance line. He should tell them that an unauthorized charge had been made to his bill, and to instruct them not to honor the restaurant charge. I went on to tell him that the restaurant owner would then receive a "charge back" from Visa and would be required either to provide evidence of the card imprint and a signature, or they would be responsible for the fraud and receive no payment. In either case, he would not have to pay the bill. I was quite taken back when he listened to all I had to say, but then became insistent that he "didn't have time for all that paperwork" and it would be much easier all around if I would just send him a check.

I was so puzzled by his strange reaction, that I called couple # 1 back again and went through the same explanation to him of the way to initiate a charge back. I also told him that I would appreciate both couples sending me a copy of the paperwork that they received from Visa, particularly the signature copies of the receipt, so that I could initiate an investigation by the local police. I assured him that if I had a dishonest employee, I was going to get to the bottom of this situation and see that she made restitution. As if he were reading from the same script as his friend from the next town, this guy also insisted that he thought it would be handled much easier if I'd just send him a check for the amount charged.

The coincidences of the situation were just too eerie for the allegations to have much validity in my mind. Knowing the restaurant that they alleged as the site of the fraud, those charges must have been a down payment on buying the place. The bills were much too much like one would expect in New York City to have very much meaning in Pittsfield, Massachusetts. And of course, the only complaint of this nature that we had ever had in our innkeeping experience just happened to come from two "best friends" who were with us during the same month. And those odd coincidences, though significant in themselves, overlook the very suspicious aspect of both men declining the remedy that was offered to them and asking me to send them a check.

I left a little note to myself to follow up on this situation, so last week I called couple # 1 to find out the status of their actions. After the woman expressed total ignorance of the entire situation, she handed me off to her husband. I told him that I was very anxious to launch a police investigation before there was no chance to follow up on the evidence. The man sounded very evasive and confused by my call and I practically had to go back step by step to refresh his memory. Finally, he said, "Oh yeah, I remember that. It's no big deal. Why don't we just forget about it." And then as quickly as he could, he closed off the conversation and hung up.

I'm still puzzled by the situation. Either they are so well off that a hundred and fifty bucks have no significance to them. Or they were two rank amateurs who were trying to pull a little scam to manage a free weekend for themselves. I know it's not very nice to view one's fellow man through a jaundiced eye, but I get the feeling after all of this that if there was any dishonesty involved, those two guys deserved the credit. And to top it off, it irritated me all the more because they apparently figured I was dumb enough to jump at the chance to "save our reputation". Naïve I may be but I don't think I'm that stupid.

All the best,
Dick

The aspect of the allegations by these two guys that bothered us more than anything was the aspersions that it cast on our two housekeepers. After our original housekeeper, Paula, had left us to go back to school, we hired Susan to replace her. She was in her forties, lived with her mother within walking distance of the Inn and had formerly been the head bartender at Joe's Bar in the village. As one might expect with that background, Susan tends to be blunt spoken and a bit rough around the edges. But she also has a great sense of humor and she usually has a ready retort for anything that one might say to her. We were soon to learn that she also had a heart of gold, was absolutely loyal and dependable and was a pretty fine housekeeper as well. Better yet, she wasn't the least bit afraid of dogs and was a doting "godmother" to Seamus.

After we experienced the robberies in the previous summer, we also decided that summer hires were just the luck of the draw, so we hired a second housekeeper, Dianne. She was still in her twenties and also living with her mother. Fortunately, she was willing to take "part time" literally, and while we needed her at least five days a week in the summer and fall months, she found that just a couple of days on weekends was acceptable in winter and spring. Like Susan, Dianne also rewarded us with unquestioned loyalty and trust for all our remaining years at the Inn. We frequently left the Inn in the care of either one of them while we all had to be away from the Inn for business. They were also our "inn-sitters" when we all went out to an occasional meal in the evening. With little training, both became skilled in taking reservations or answering inquiries. We had no doubts whatsoever about their personal integrity, for both Susan and Dianne had repeatedly demonstrated their complete and total honesty.

It was therefore incomprehensible to us that either of them would suddenly compromise themselves with credit card fraud and the more I thought about the accusations, the angrier I became. We felt obliged to let them know that their integrity had been questioned—even though we were having none of it—and when I broached the subject with the two of them, Dianne had the best answer. She pointed out that her reputation was worth a lot more to her than $315 and, "…besides, I wouldn't eat in that dump if they were giving the food away."

Every time we thought we had seen the end-all of expressions of human nature, something else would come along to get our heads shaking in disbelief. Like the lady who called the day before her reservation to cancel her booking. Dan informed her that she would have to forfeit her deposit if we didn't resell her room and she seemed shocked. Dan happened to have taken her reservation himself and distinctly remembered advising her of our cancellation policy, as we' did everyone who made reservations. "Yes, I know you did," she told him, "but at that time I had no intention to cancel so I didn't pay any attention to what you were saying!"

Another situation was to be repeated many times, but we never ceased to be amazed each time that it occurred. It seems that there are three Birchwood Inns in this great country of ours, at least as far as we know. Of the other two, one is in New Hampshire and the third is in Michigan. But we were the only Birchwood who had a toll free 800 telephone number for reservations. One evening, Joan took a call for reservations, and went through all of the details with the lady, recording them all in our log book. Finally, just as she was about to terminate the phone call, the lady suddenly said, "Oh, I almost forgot. We'd like one of the rooms that overlooks the lake."

Joan chuckled to herself and told the caller that perhaps she had called the wrong inn. Not only didn't we have any rooms that overlook the lake; the nearest lake to us was about three miles away. "But of course you have a lake," she responded, "We stayed with you last summer and our room overlooked the lake. It was just beautiful."

Joan went on to explain that there is more than one Birchwood Inn and she was probably trying to reach the one in Michigan or New Hampshire. But that seemed to go right over her head and she still insisted that she was correct. After all, she had called AT&T directory information and this was the number that they had given her. Certainly AT&T wouldn't give her the wrong number.

After gently arguing with her for a good two or three minutes, and just before Joan was beginning to conclude that she was never going to win, the lady closed off the conversation by telling her that, "I don't know why you're being so difficult with me. All I want is a three night reservation in July, but if you don't want to help me, I'll just have to look elsewhere."

But the other side of that same story is the surprising number of calls from people who were calling to cancel reservations that they never had made. They would tell us the day and date and the number of days they had reserved, but we couldn't find the least shred of evidence that they had called us previously. And it wasn't that this occurred only once. It was a regular occurrence every summer. We came to suspect that people called a number of places for information and when they finally made a reservation someplace, or at least thought they did, they wrote down the wrong inn.

We were certainly not infallible and we discovered our own mistakes from time to time. Usually these discoveries occurred when we were making a periodic audit of reservations by cross checking the log book with our master schedule. That was a wise practice, by the way, because we actually would find an occasional error in an audit. But 99% of the time, the error was easily corrected and the guests never knew that something had temporarily dropped through the crack. The phantom reservations, on the other hand, were another thing entirely and the total absence of any information in either our telephone log or the reservation book made it clear that, in these cases at least, it had not been our error. Finally, after a number of calls of this nature, we got to the point where we simply thanked them for calling and hung up.

We also had calls from people that typically went, "I have reservations at a Lenox inn this weekend but I forget where. Am I supposed be at your place?" If they weren't booked with us, the follow-on question was usually something akin to, "Could you name some other inns in the town? One of them might sound familiar."

The excuses for canceling a reservation were also quite interesting, occasionally unique. But most of them had a single purpose in common: they were clearly designed to avoid forfeiting the prepaid deposit. The death rates went up each summer to the degree that we were beginning to think that a reservation at the Birchwood might be a family jinx. But we came to know pretty well which death reports were faked and which were genuine. When someone voluntarily offered to send a copy of the death certificate, you were pretty sure that the cancellation was legitimate and we always told those folks that it would be unnecessary. In addition, we took the matter seriously, always expressed our commiseration and before the person had a chance to bring the subject up, we told them that we never wish to profit from someone else's misfortune and we will refund your entire deposit. We went on to offer our hope that they might come to stay with us again sometime, under better circumstances. It was always gratifying to discover the number of who people did come back under better circumstances and each was careful to remind us that they rebooked partly because we had been kind to them in a moment of grief.

The subject of human nature and telephone interaction with people would not be complete without a mention of solicitations for charitable causes. Somewhere along the line, the idea blossomed that a weekend at a lovely country inn would be an ideal prize to offer at a blind auction or a raffle. That idea grew so fast and so pervasively that rarely a week went by when we didn't have two or three requests for us to donate that wonderful raffle gift that the winner would so thoroughly enjoy—the requestor's pitch, not mine.

We certainly didn't mind when the local Pittsfield Rotary Club made such a request for its annual fund raiser or the high school cross country ski team or the local churches approached us for a donation. Those requests were usually made by people we knew and we certainly were familiar with both the institutions and their causes. And we always responded positively. But when requests of this kind came over the 800 number from eastern Massachusetts, Florida, Kentucky and dozens of other states, from people who had never seen the Inn but merely got our name from an inn directory, it was a bit much. It wasn't that the callers didn't represent a worthy cause. But it was hard to justify our donating to a small charity that we knew nothing about, in some other part of the country. Not to mention the fact that scams had seemingly become and increasingly popular way to "plan" one's holidays.

We have always been the type of people who find it hard to say no to a worthy cause, so we eventually had to come up with an answer for some of the nuisance requests we received. As it turned out, our response was effective and it eased our consciences at the same time. When we received these requests, we started offering a $50 gift certificate toward a stay at the Birchwood Inn. We also mailed out a nice little certificate to confirm that offer. We felt we were being minimally charitable while not worrying too much about someone coming from Florida or Kentucky—or even eastern Massachusetts—to claim a $50 discount on a $200 per night room. But I guess our clever solution is just one more off-beat example of human nature, isn't it.

*   *   *

September 28, 1995
Dear Chris & Tom,

We may not be right out there on the leading edge of a new business movement, and perhaps even a little late getting started, but it appears that it's time for us to venture into cyberspace. I suppose a statement like that might indicate that this is a momentous decision based on months of study and absorption of great amounts of technical knowledge. But I'm afraid that nothing of the sort has happened.

In fact, the only reason that we have reached that conclusion is that more and more callers are asking if we're "on the net". At first, our answer was, "On the what?", but we have done enough research to learn what the term means, at least. We now know, for example, that "the net" is really shorthand for the Internet, and it must be something worth looking into with the increasing numbers that are inquiring about our presence there. My next challenge is to learn a heck of a lot more about the Internet and what it can do for our business prospects.

You probably recall from your visit with us that we already have a computer. It's a six year old Tandy something or other, and it has less capability than today's hand-held calculators. About the only thing I ever learned to do with it is to write letters, do some minor calculations and to keep a running account of our financial data, primarily for periodic government reports and tax purposes. Terms like processor speed, hard drive, RAM, ROM, and gigabytes of storage capacity might just as well be in a foreign language for all I have understood about their meaning. But now that's all changing.

If we're going to join the evolution toward Internet marketing and reservations, it is first of all going to mean a new computer. Our old Tandy doesn't even have the power to hook up to the Internet, so we need to get something that does. Not only that, the new computer is going to need to have some shelf life to it. I read recently that the president of Intel Corporation predicts that computer capabilities are going to double every 18 months for the next ten years, so there's no sense starting behind the power curve, so to speak. But buying at the high end also means that prices go up significantly for each incremental step of capability that you buy. Ah, the dilemma of the costs of upgrades.

I picked up a few books recently that give some pretty good information on buying a new computer, what the internet is all about and how to use it for business purposes. They are hardly as engaging as Tom Clancy's latest novel, especially after a full day around the Inn. But one of the new books is entitled "The Internet for Dummies" so that's probably going to be pitched at just about the right level for me.

Microsoft is about to introduce Windows 95 which they guarantee to make computers more user-friendly, so I think we'll hold off until that software becomes available. Joan and I both took a course in MS/DOS that is the operating system for the Tandy. That literally is like learning a new language and it's a huge challenge for your memory—either that or you have to look up everything you want to do in a reference book. The new Microsoft system is supposed to use plain English and "talk" back to you so that's more my speed. We'll see.

As far as I know, none of the other inns in the village is on the Internet yet, and I'm not sure whether or not anyone is planning to venture in that direction. While we are all pretty good about sharing ideas and giving referrals to other inns when we're full, I plan to be a bit closed mouth about telling people that I am going to do this particular thing. On the one hand, a little competitive advantage will certainly give us a leg up for a short while—something we can certainly use. But on the other hand, if it's a big investment with little or no return, then I'm not very enthusiastic about being responsible for steering people in the wrong direction. But, in the final analysis, it just sounds too promising to me not to give it a try.

Let me illustrate what I'm talking about. Some time ago I told you that the conventional wisdom was that it was a waste of time to advertise in the Boston area. We decided to defy that wisdom and give it a try and Joan was very creative in finding a publisher that does a separate weekly newspaper for all of the suburban towns surrounding Boston. The cost of a year of ads, which are published in over 30 individual papers each Thursday evening, is roughly equal to the cost of one ad in the Sunday edition of the New York Times. No exaggeration!

When we started this new advertising campaign, the response to our ads was tremendous. We got calls by the dozens from most of the towns and the bookings have been wonderful. On the whole, it has been a great find. Or perhaps I should say was. Joan has been very generous to other innkeepers by passing on tales of our success in marketing to eastern Massachusetts. So about every week we have found that more and more Lenox inns have ads in those same papers and it appears that the mother lode is now being mined by more than a few of us.

Consequently if, in fact, we are the only ones moving to get on the Internet at the present time, I have decided not to make a big deal of broadcasting the results to other inns. All of the other innkeepers are bright and up on the news, so they'll get around to this new means of marketing quickly enough. But we'll let them reach that decision on their own. We will, of course, keep you up to date on our progress. And if you get on the Internet along with us, we can change our future letter writing to the latest craze, e-mail.

All the best,
Dick

It took a little longer than originally forecast for Microsoft to release their new Windows 95 operating system, but after we found out that the first reviews were favorable, we bought our state of the art computer and joined the Internet. Despite the considerable amount of reading that I had done in the interim, every step of the way seemed like a new adventure—a bit scary in its own way, but rather exhilarating at the same time. It was a mind-boggling experience to log on to the Internet in those early days and discover the incredible amount of information that was right at one's fingertips.

By a pleasant coincidence, at the same time that we went on-line, we started getting a lot of mail which solicited our ads on various sites that were being created on the internet. Some of those solicitations were from the authors of travel guides and inn directories who were anticipating the new wave of the future, the same as we had. Other ads were from folks who were establishing web sites on the Internet for the exclusive purpose of promoting inns and each was intent on getting our business.

The most remarkable thing about all of these offers was the low cost of Internet advertising. Many of the directory publishers offered to put us on their site simply if we renewed our agreement to appear in the forthcoming edition of their book. We knew which ones of those had been the most beneficial to us so it was a no-brainer. The other offerings were mostly from start-up businesses and their usual "introductory offer" was for a four page ad on their site for as little as $50 per year—to include the creation of the four pages. These sites also show a running total of the number of people who have looked at our ad—referred to as "hits" in the newly emerging *lingua cybernetica*. You can't get better feedback than that. Having weathered annual advertising budgets of nearly $15,000 in our early years, we jumped on every one of these solicitations. Even if they failed, the cost was a drop in the bucket by comparison to most print ads.

The public response to these new Internet sites was remarkable, both in the excitement of watching the use of the medium grow as more and more homes joined the Internet, but also in the volume of inquiries and bookings that it meant for us. The importance of the Internet as a marketing tool grew way out of proportion to our expectations, to the point that within a year of our beginnings on the net, it became by far our primary advertising medium. And that became an even more important factor as the other Lenox innkeepers joined the rush to cyberspace.

As we previously suspected, it did not take long at all for the more progressive of the innkeepers to realize that Internet marketing was the wave of the future. The decision to move in that direction became solidly reinforced in our minds when we began to discover that many people "shopped" for a weekend getaway exclusively on the net. There were still a lot of die-hards who read the ads in weekend newspapers or religiously purchased a new guide book each year. But the younger folks who worked with the Internet in their day to day professions didn't have the time or wouldn't think to make an inn reservation any other way.

The combination of all these factors brought about the birth of The Six Inns. As the name implies, these were six Lenox inns that teamed together to offer packages and share the wealth in order to enhance the off-season bookings. For years in our local innkeepers' association meetings, we had talked about how successful cooperative advertising was in other locations. "Sell your town or location first and then sell the individual inns" seemed to be the theme of the effort, and places like the resort town of Cape May, New Jersey, had proved that it can be a most effective strategy. But until now, we could never reach agreement for all the inns to join such an effort so we never pursued the idea further. The Six Inns would change all that.

The whole cooperative effort was founded on trust because, in essence, we were still in competition with one another at the same time that we were working jointly. We purchased our own domain, www.lenoxinns.com, and paid top dollar to have the web site designed and advertised to the growing number of search engines, like Yahoo and Altavista. We all had a picture of our inns and a short blurb about us on the main site, but also had email addresses and links to our own home pages so that the curious could get more information. Our collective Internet advertising essentially promoted the town of Lenox as a destination and, with the all-important picture and link, we "paid our nickel and took our chances" on which inn a potential customer might select.

When word of this new venture got around town, a great deal of hard feelings surfaced. Some of the very innkeepers who had earlier subverted any efforts to do something of a cooperative nature were angered that they had not been given a chance to join in this undertaking. However, when the costs became known, the furor quieted down in a hurry. For not only did it cost each inn thousands of dollars to get our collective site up and running on the Internet, it also cost significantly in time and effort. Innkeepers took turns answering telephone inquiries from hundreds of callers, each of us promising to be as objective as possible when recommending a specific inn. It also meant a great deal of leg work in soliciting cooperation—as represented by discounts—from restaurants, ski areas, spas, athletic clubs and other attractions in the local area so that we could develop package programs.

The initial results were impressive. Not only did we manage to put together a very enticing image of the town and the area, we also put together a nice variety of packages that would appeal to all—from the lovers to the jocks and the gourmands. When we launched, we were pretty confident that we had made the correct moves, but we all knew that time would tell whether the investments of money and effort would prove their worth.

As things turned out, we never did develop a method to measure in precise quantitative terms the success of The Six Inns effort, or even to determine whether the up-front costs were ever completely amortized. It was also impossible to tell how much the non-member inns benefited from this co-op program. But it was clear that, on the whole, off-season business improved considerably in Lenox and it continued to improve as each year went by. For our parts, we marveled that the combination of the Internet and a handful of risk takers proved that a cooperative effort can work, and that it could be fun in the process.

As far as we know, some version of this cooperative Six Inns effort is still in being and we have been told that the new era of e-business for Lenox inns gets better each year. One of the highlights in our own book of memories is that we were one of the successful pioneers in bringing about this dramatic change in the way modern business is done—well, in Lenox at least.

*   *   *

December 15, 1995
Dear Chris & Tom,

Well, we had hoped fervently that it wouldn't happen, but it now appears that we will be forced into making some major structural changes to the Inn. If you recall, a couple of years ago I mentioned to you that one of the new Lenox innkeepers had incurred the wrath of the local innkeeping establishment. They had gone to the Town Inspector of Buildings to determine what needed to be done to the property they bought to meet the specs for an Inn. It turns out that it was the opening of Pandora's box and we are all going to have to meet the same specifications. At least, that's what it seems.

Back in February of last year, all of the innkeepers were invited to a meeting in the Town Hall regarding the building code. The meeting was called by the Chairwoman of the Town Planning Board and when we got there, we found that she was joined by the state fire marshal, the state building inspector and our local inspector. The whole session was pretty innocuous and, in fact, showed some real promise that everyone was working together to minimize the impact of any decisions that might eventually be made.

Right at the beginning, the fire marshal made two key points: there is no code in existence for the types of country inns that we all own; and the specifications that exist for hotels are far too rigid for them to impose on inns, especially since most were converted houses or mansions. All of the panel members insisted that their over-arching criterion was to minimize the impact on small business owners. They also pointed out that Lenox had been chosen as the test site, so to speak, for the state because we have the highest density and broadest cross section of inns of any community in the entire state. They promised that the revised building code, adapted for inns, would be published within the next few months. For the most part, we were guardedly optimistic (to use a term from the diplomatic field) when we left the meeting.

The short version of the story is that, here it is nearly two years later, the revised code has never been published, and as far as anyone knows, there is not even a draft in the works. The ball has been totally dropped. So in view of this, our local building inspector has ordained that he's going to take things into his own hands. He sent out a letter recently in which he used the same type of wording—they want to minimize the impact on the local small business owners—but he made it clear that there will be a new building code for inns, and none of the existing inns will be grandfathered. That includes those inns—such as ours—that have a certificate of occupancy from an earlier inspector that states that the structure meets all code requirements.

Of course, it remains to be seen what the requirements are that will be imposed, but the rumors are already flying. The one that bothers me the most is the likelihood that every inn is going to have to have a sprinkler system installed. Now I'm doing my best to avoid listening to rumors and I'm certainly not going to take any precipitous action on that basis. But it makes good sense that this will be a requirement and, much as I dislike the idea of unfunded government mandates for which Massachusetts is notorious, I can almost see it coming.

For the time being, we have all been directed to provide the inspector with scale drawings of our inns to include a floor plan for each floor, plus the basement and attic. We also need to send him a plot plan for our property showing the exterior footprint of the building. My engineering drawing courses over 40 years ago are going to come in handy because I'm not planning on hiring an architect or draftsman to do this for me.

The irony of this whole situation is that whenever this locally produced code is imposed, the first to be required to comply are those inns that are being sold or otherwise changing hands. Apparently, it will be a condition of sale that the property either has to meet code prior to the sale or a clause in the sale contract must acknowledge that code requirements will be met by the new owner and conditions for meeting the code must be specifically stated. When we decided that we were going to become innkeepers, we promised one another that we would sell and leave the business after five to eight years—the time period in which working innkeepers are alleged to burn out. Well, we're coming up on that five year point, so as our luck would have it, just about the time we're ready to score, the goal line has been moved. Seems like that's the story of our lives.

We hope you're both well and are excited about the coming holidays.

Dick

Actually a new building code for the inns was never published in writing, and the enforcement of the case-by-case code that came into being was slow to evolve, even when there was no input or participation by the state authorities. As a matter of fact, if you were to go to Lenox today to ask to see the code that is being applied to the inns in the town, you wouldn't be able to find one. Instead, the building inspector has chosen to judge every case individually, extrapolating from the existing hotel code that was judged too rigid to be imposed on small businesses. And though there is a constant risk that case-by-case judgments can be arbitrary and perhaps even capricious, I'll have to admit that it is probably a rational approach to the situation.

One additional requirement has been imposed, a requirement that was merely hinted at during the February 1994 meeting. At that time, the

Planning Board Chairwoman introduced a Stockbridge architect, whom she described as a building code expert, and suggested that each innkeeper would be well advised to hire this or another well-qualified architect to assist in the code compliance process—whenever. That is no longer a suggestion. The building inspector decided that he couldn't waste his time discussing code issues with innkeepers who know nothing about the code, so he made it mandatory that a registered architect represent each innkeeper when the decision time arrived. Another unfunded government mandate that escalates the cost. But, of course, the local architects have raised no objection.

As things turned out, after I submitted the drawings for our property, we heard nothing specific in response. About once a year, the building inspector sent out another letter in which he stated his intentions with respect to the inns, but little occurred other than that. Meanwhile, a bit of a stir was raised by some of the inn owners over the "home stays". These are the private homes that are allowed to "play" bed & breakfast during the Tanglewood Festival to compensate for the shortage of lodging. The point was made that home stays are not licensed, as the inns are, they collect no taxes for the state and the town as the inns do, and now they were going to be exempted from code compliance as well. And while this was certainly true, it was not going to take the pressure off the inns.

At roughly this same time, the Federal government issued an unfunded mandate of its own, the Americans with Disabilities Act, or ADA. This law requires that people with disabilities of any kind be afforded equal access to facilities and services. And while this civil rights law is well intentioned—it was enacted on behalf of people with physical disabilities that weren't previously able to go to restaurants, theaters, hotels and the like—it is so poorly worded that it is becoming a legal nightmare. People who claimed to be alcoholics are even filing suit against bar owners for serving alcohol in their presence.

It occurred to me that ADA was directly contradictory to the legislation governing the establishment of the National Register of Historic Places. For example, someone might charge us with not providing equal access to the Inn for not having exterior ramps constructed and the entrance porch and door modified to accommodate a wheelchair. Yet, as owners of a structure on the National Register, we were specifically prohibited from making any exterior modifications to the building. So out of curiosity more than anything, I sent a letter to the Justice and Interior Departments in Washington who were responsible for compliance with the ADA and NRHP laws, respectively. I asked them for a coordinated decision to tell me which law takes precedence.

After about six months of waiting, when I had just about given up hope that I would receive an answer, an official letter arrived from Washington. It was, indeed, a coordinated position between the two cabinet agencies and it soon became clear why it took so long to receive it. The letter was perhaps the most masterful example of legalistic government bureaucratese that I had ever seen—and I had seen a bunch in 30 years in the military. After many readings, the meaning became fairly clear—I think.

The letter was written by the Justice Department lawyers and it said that, as civil rights legislation, ADA could not be invoked directly by an ordinary citizen. If someone believed he or she was not afforded equal access to a facility, they must report that to the Justice Department who, in turn, would investigate the charge and bring suit against the business owner, if appropriate. The letter went on to say that if such a charge were leveled against the owner of a facility on the NRHP, the contradictory laws would *probably* be taken into consideration and *probably* no suit would be filed by Justice. The letter went on to advise, however, that we should do all in our power to improve access to our property without, of course, doing anything to violate the laws governing the National Register. Our mandate seemed pretty clear. Don't do anything.

Now that the local building inspector was tightening down the requirements, it would be interesting to see how the decision by the Justice Department would play with respect to the revised building code for the inns.

The factor that bothered us, and all the other innkeepers for that matter, was how this new code is going to affect us financially. In a series of meetings among innkeepers, we gradually began to figure out where the inspector was going to focus. And as suspected, the installation of a sprinkler system was right at the top of the list. The next highest priority appeared to be the stairways or, more specifically, the chimney affect that would occur in open staircases going up to the second and third floors. These would have to be corrected by enclosing the staircase—a terrible blow to those owners with broad, majestic stairways leading up from the entrance to the inn—and fireproof doors would need to be installed at ever level.

And the third "sure bet" on the inspector's priority list appeared to be a fire and smoke detection system. This would have to be a hard wired system with sensors in every hallway and room in the house, including the basement. It would also have to have an enunciator that set off alarms outside the building and automatically called the fire department or a security service on the telephone. Battery operated fire and smoke detectors in each guest room, which most inns had already, would no longer be adequate.

The fourth consensus requirement was the need for an external fire escape. Interestingly, it appeared that this fire escape could be constructed of wood—indeed, a strange material for fire safety—but it must be a stairway, not a ladder. We already had a steel ladder, accessible from both the third and second floor, but this would no longer be acceptable—at least in the consensus of the group that gathered to discuss the situation.

Well, one-half out of four isn't very good. We already had a hard-wired fire and security system with an enunciator but it was installed only in the hallways on each floor and in the basement. Battery-operated detectors were elsewhere in the house, including each guest room, but we had no sprinklers and our stairway was not enclosed. Just to avoid facing the shock when we couldn't stand it, we had estimates made of the cost of meeting just these elements of the code. There would unquestionably be more. To our chagrin, the total came to just under $100,000. This just happened to be about half of our gross annual income. We made a profit that year of just under $5,000 so at that rate, it was going to take us 20 years to pay for these upgrades.

We did have another choice of course. We could elect to be forced out of business for non-compliance and then have the Inn taken over for default on our payments. And this, apparently, was what the Town regarded as the "minimal impact" of the new code. Well, that was something that we would have to face later. We'd just have to hope that something might happen to ease the situation.

*   *   *

PART V

Getting Tired

The traditional belief that we had picked up in our original innkeeping course—that burnout for full-time innkeepers begins at about the fifth year and becomes too much to contend with by the eighth year—was showing signs of cutting in. This belief in the five to eight year burnout was reinforced each time one of us went to an innkeepers' convention, the most important and well-recognized of which were sponsored by our original mentors and PAII, the Professional Association of Innkeepers, International. As a mater of fact, these conventions even featured seminars on recognizing burnout "in time", and ways of coping with effects.

During our eight years in the business, we went to only three of these conventions. Early on, we both went to one in Gloucester, Massachusetts. Joan went to one in Lenox and another in Manchester, Vermont, the latter of which was close enough so that I could join her for the last day and evening. It was at this affair that we learned of a rather shocking irony. Back in the fall of 1990, when we attended the seminar that was to determine our fates, we stayed at the host inn in the Pocono Mountains of Pennsylvania, an inn which was run by a couple about our age. I mentioned previously that the man seemed to have gone beyond the time that he should be in the business because he was rude, impersonal and an out-and-out grouch. His attitude apparently was too much for his charming wife to bear because, not long after we stayed with them, she became a suicide victim and their inn was sold at auction. This sad tale was our sole topic of conversation on the way home from Manchester, and neither of us had any intention of allowing ourselves to fall into such a predicament.

It wasn't that we weren't enjoying the vast majority of our experiences. And we were becoming more skilled in our abilities to improve our offerings with less effort and time. But the Inn was beginning to seem like a bit of an albatross around our necks. There was no getting away from the pressure of our responsibilities nor was there much time when, in good conscience, we could get away from the seven-day per week grind. We had our annual ten-day ski trip at Mammoth Mountain with Chris and Tom each March. We also managed a two or three-day weekend to Cape Cod or the Maine coast in the late fall. And there were many overnight weekday trips to Boston, even though most seemed to involve a family medical emergency of one sort or another. But we were always accessible by telephone and never really got away.

Though not for the same exact reasons, Dan was also ready to change careers. He and Anne had found one another, and their three weddings were about to take place, so his outlook on life was taking a turn toward other directions. After all, he had additional responsibilities himself and it was not really fair to his new bride to bring her into the business that clearly had a finite limit to it.

So after many hours of discussion, we decided that it was time to begin the process to sell the Inn. Most innkeeping veterans agreed that it normally took about two years for an inn to sell, once it went on the market. Our past observations convinced us that this was not an unreasonable estimate and we agreed that chances were that it could take us at least that long—well into our seventh year by that time—particularly with the threat and expense of the revised building code hanging over our heads. We would cross that bridge when we needed to, but for the time being we agreed that it was time to invest in a few ads in innkeeper journals just to see what would happen.

February 8, 1996
Dear Chris & Tom,

Today is Joan's birthday and in addition to the normal card, flowers and a nice dinner in one of our finer local restaurants, we chose a once in a lifetime way to celebrate. We officially put the Inn on the market. We all decided that the time is ripe for us to start making preparations to leave the business, so we have placed our first advertisement in one of the major innkeeping journals. As we told you previously, there seems to be about a two-year period for the sale to take place, so we aren't starting to pack our bags yet.

If all of our past guests who have expressed a yen to become innkeepers were the least bit serious, we might be inundated with buyers. However, we're convinced that for most people who say they're interested in owning an inn, it is just a romantic notion, idly stated, that has little or no sense of reality or intent associated with it. I compare it to the dog that loves to chase cars. It's the chase that he enjoys and he wouldn't know what in the world to do with a car if he ever caught one.

So we're ready to hunker down and wait until the right person comes along. The economy is starting to pick up and the interest rates are going down gradually, so that is one thing—the only thing?—in our favor. We already recognize that selling the Inn is not just a business transaction, it is an emotional one as well. A unique quality of innkeeping is that each property has its own, individual personality that has to mesh perfectly with the personality of the buyers.

We experienced that sensation when we looked and looked before finding the Birchwood and we're sure that there are people out there who will become equally as attached to the place as we were. We hope that whoever they may be, they will also let the emotion of finding the "right place" take priority over the more pragmatic business considerations, as we did. But on the other hand, we've improved the property and the customer base so dramatically that this is now not just a viable business but a prudent investment.

Our biggest concern is the unknown impact of the revised building code. The nice round figure of $100,000 seems to be the rough amount of what we will need to spend to satisfy the new code. From what I've been told, there will be two choices over the next few years. We will either have to find the money to accomplish the upgrades before the place is sold or, using contractor estimates for the work remaining to be done, we can reduce the final sale price. The new owner, as part of the sales contract, will have to make a commitment to complete the upgrades within three years of purchase. Either way, we're going to come out the big losers. We had hoped that we might earn a return of between $100,000 and $150,000 when we sell, considering the physical improvements we have made and the sweat equity that has gone into making this a healthy, going business. But the way things now appear we'll be lucky to break even, especially when the state and federal taxes are included.

But enough of the glum outlook that money brings. The actual process of putting the Inn on the market has had a most positive effect on our outlook. Not a single thing has changed except for our sending an ad—and the accompanying check—to the publication, but it gave all of us a sense of elation. Like that old saying, we must have received a bit of a lift from seeing the "light at the end of the tunnel". Let's hope that the counter culture version *of that old saying—the light is actually a train bearing down on us at full speed—doesn't come into play.*

We could probably blanket the market with ads in every trade journal associated with the business but we're not doing that right now. We have intentionally chosen to take a gradual escalation approach (where have we heard that expression before?) and gauge the reaction from this first ad. In fact, we're actually keeping the whole idea of selling to ourselves for the time being. It's probably some subconscious concern over the thought of being regarded as "lame duck" owners that is the strongest influence, so we're just not broadcasting the fact locally or to guests. That, of course, will change over time, unless some angel comes out of the weeds soon—and very unexpectedly.

At the same time that we feel that buoyant sense of relief at having "done it", there is also a nagging sense of having made an irrevocable decision to put our baby up for adoption. There has been so much love and anguish and creativity put into this old place that we have a deep-rooted sense of guilt that we would ever consider giving up what we have created. Conflicting emotions of the first order. Wouldn't a Freudian shrink have a ball with this letter! Despite saying early on that we're not packing our bags yet, I'm beginning to sound like the movers are going to show up in the morning. So it's time to let your eyes get a rest and for me to get to bed. Hope all goes well.

Love to you both,
Dick

It was clearly very premature to start becoming either excited or remorseful because it was going to be some time before we even saw our ad in print, let alone received any calls expressing interest in our property. The most important next step, we soon realized, was that we needed to prepare a brochure to send out to those who called to ask for information. The advertising professionals advise that a brochure that is designed to attract guests to the inn should use as little print material as possible. Wow them with pictures is the secret to success, they say. But for a sales brochure, we concluded that we needed lots of written information—a pre-emptive answer, if you will, to most of the questions that a prospective buyer might have.

We began with a lot of brainstorming and a considerable amount of effort in organizing and building a brochure that would "sell" the area as well the property. We benefited greatly from the not too distant memories of what we might have liked to know about the Inn when we were shopping, but had to learn for ourselves. We also still had access to the very extensive business plan that we had put together to convince the bank to loan us the mortgage money. Eventually, with the help of the new computer, we put together a pretty fair 40-page brochure that provided reams of information and a little of the glitter that only color photos can offer.

The subject material covered the waterfront, ranging from market assessments to the history of the town and plenty of detail on our property. We included information on both the property itself as well as the business. We were pretty well convinced that the final package satisfied the most important questions, at least all of those that we were able to surface during our brainstorming sessions. We pitched the information in the same manner that we would have liked to have available to us during our decision process. Our emphasis was on the niceties of the rooms and the decor for the distaff side of the buying couple and a lot of technical information about systems, structure and maintenance that most men would find of interest.

Joan also added an excellent attachment to the brochure that highlighted her efforts as our advertising manager for the previous five years—a whole section on advertising and promotion. Included were sections on where we advertised; what our success (or lack of success) was; what professional memberships we held; what directories we appeared in, with differentiation between those we paid to be in and those we were chosen to be in. She also listed our accomplishments, such as our selection by *Country Inns* magazine as one of the "Seventy-five Top Inns Across America". Later on, this attachment was expanded to include the many internet sites where we had an advertisement or a home page.

So now we were ready for the thundering herd to beat a path to our door, all anxiously competing with one another to have the privilege of buying the Birchwood Inn. But of course, that never happened. Sure, we received some phone calls right away. Most were from curiosity seekers and we quickly learned to differentiate between those and people who might have a genuine interest in entering the profession. For the merely curious, we soon developed a two-page flier that we sent to them, along with the regular inn brochure that was sent to prospective guests. To no one's surprise, we never heard from any of them again.

But the serious seekers were another story. You knew when they called after receiving the brochure to ask for detailed financial data that their interest had been aroused. We were most willing to send them general data such as one-page profit and loss statements. But we usually told them that more detailed financial data such as income and expense statements or corporate tax returns was privileged, and it would only be made available to them after we started into preliminary negotiations for the property sale. We also wanted them to know that we would be looking for some indication that they were in a financial position to qualify for buying the Inn. First, however, we advised that it might be a good idea to look at the Inn personally and decide whether, in fact, they were interested in our property. Because, we explained, if you're not excited by the property, no amount of financial excellence was going to change your minds.

Most callers understood that this made good sense, but occasionally, there was the person who insisted that he (usually) wasn't going to waste his time visiting the property unless he was certain that the business was financially sound. Usually, this sort of reaction came from businessmen who were planning for a corporate retirement and their wives were interested in innkeeping. They were determined to look at the bottom line in the same way that they had done in their current business. I didn't waste the time trying to convince them that a country inn was different or that, while we were on a sound footing, there were not going to be great profits to be had from running an inn. They probably couldn't relate to the idea that the bottom line, though important, is not the primary measure of success in innkeeping. Still, I've often wondered since then if any of these financial managers ever did get into the innkeeping business. If they did, chances are they're miserable.

It wasn't too long before our advertising began to show some tangible results. For many months after that first ad, we had people call in advance and make an appointment to come and look at the property. Some came by for an hour or two while others made reservations and stayed around to see the Inn in operation. Each wanted (and deserved) a complete tour of the property which was difficult on weekends when most of the guest rooms were occupied. But we usually found that Sunday afternoon was the best time. We weren't busy with guests as most had already checked out, and we were able to devote full time to the interests of the potential buyers.

In many cases, we found ourselves in the training business to a certain extent. With some of the prospective buyers, a major portion of their questions related to the "how to" of operating an inn as opposed to the things they might need to know in order to formulate a decision on a purchase. We gave them the time for these answers willingly and happily. Again, we were motivated primarily by a willingness to provide information that we would have liked to have had as beginners. Even if we didn't sell them on the idea of buying our Inn, we gained a lot of satisfaction from helping them to become more knowledgeable about the business, in general, and the lifestyle of an innkeeper.

For some strange reason, Dan usually ended up getting some of the more difficult lookers. Joan and I were making a lot of day trips back and forth to Boston for family emergencies and the aftermath, and he was left with the responsibility to look after the Inn. At one point we almost concluded that somehow, perhaps ESP, people were just waiting until we headed off to Boston before coming to inquire about buying our business. In due deference to Dan, I'm certain that his concerns were influenced most by his reluctance to do or say anything that was incorrect with regard to the sale. He was a partner in every way, but he was conscious of the fact that the investment in the business—and the final decisions on the sale—were Joan's and mine.

It was not difficult to separate the curious from those who were truly looking for a place to buy. This latter group not only came well prepared with questions about the property, they were also very inquisitive about our day to day operations and the lifestyle that we led. We were tempted as time went by to assure these folks that it was an idyllic existence and every day was a barrel of fun, but we had a lifetime of honesty behind us that wouldn't allow us to be other than realistic in answering their questions. We're not sure how many we chased away by this frankness, but we wouldn't want to sell the property under false pretenses.

We also came to realize over time that we were very selective about whom we wanted to buy the Inn—a luxury that we could ill-afford, of course. When someone would leave after an afternoon or a weekend, our first appraisal was never oriented to whether or not we thought the visitors were likely prospects or not. We always began by deciding whether or not these were people to whom we would like to sell the property—to adopt

302 • The Loving Room

our baby if you will. We also wondered, as time went by, whether our attitude came across to those who didn't fit the image of our preferred successors. We jokingly decided that we would always be sentimental slobs, no matter how hard we tried to become shrewd businessmen.

As a general rule, those who had done a significant amount of homework prior to shopping for an inn were very nice people and would be perfectly suited to this change in career paths. These were the people who were clearly going to buy an inn somewhere, if not ours. Many of those who visited us had great potential for becoming our friends and we would welcome them as colleagues in the business. In the past, I had a habit of paraphrasing Will Rogers to say that I never met a skier that I didn't like. (I don't say that any more, by the way.) It was interesting to discover that we found people who were serious about becoming innkeepers usually fell into a similar category. Which makes sense, of course. If you're even interested in the business, chances are very good that you're friendly, gregarious, and you enjoy being around other people.

But for all the nice, friendly folks we had met, more than a year went by and no one really showed any sign of wanting to go forward with the purchase. There were a few who came back a second time to look. There were others who called back with questions and still others to whom we were willing to give some basic financial performance data. But no one was in a buying mood. We added a few advertisements to the original one that we purchased and while that stimulated more interest, it didn't change the outcome. We were probably going to have to modify our strategy if we expected to sell. But that would have to wait because we were back in the thick of summer and autumn and there was little time for anything except the care and feeding of the multitudes.

*   *   *

April 22, 1996
Dear Chris & Tom,

After making the decision to put the Inn up for sale, some of the things that we've been struggling for years to accomplish are suddenly starting to fall into our lap. According to the innkeeping experts, a great money-maker, and also a great way for people to learn about your inn, is to host corporate off-site meetings. And thanks to two very helpful neighbors, one of these off-sites has recently been scheduled for the Birchwood.

Debbie and Dick are models of good citizenship, in our judgment, and they give a great deal of their time and effort to the community. (Perhaps I should use the more modern term, paradigms of good citizenship, to show that I can still speak bureaucratese.) Both of them are professionals: he is a professor at Rensselaer Polytechnic Institute which is about 40 miles west of here in Troy, NY. And she is a management consultant who works a great deal of the time with General Electric Co. at their regional headquarters in Schenectady, NY, about 15 miles west of Troy. So with their daily commute, it is all the more commendable that they are always involved in civic affairs in the Town.

Dick and I first met when he became a candidate for political office. The Chamber of Commerce sponsors a debate each election year among all the candidates for town selectman and I usually end up as the moderator. Dick was one of the candidates in the last election. "Debate" is probably not the right term to use because these sessions usually entail a series of questions—which I solicit around town in advance—posed to each candidate. The candidate gives his or her answer, and then the other candidates get an opportunity for comments or a rebuttal. The audience also gets involved with questions from the floor and the attendees usually come away from these Town Hall debates with a pretty good feel for the candidates' positions on the issues of interest.

To my way of thinking, Dick was clearly the best candidate that was running in the last election. He was very well prepared and had a solid grasp of the details of the issues. He was poised and sure of himself and gave very lucid explanations of what he hoped to do and how he hoped to do it. In my own mind, it was clearly he that I would vote for and I thought he would run away with the election. But that was hardly the case. Up until then, I didn't realize that how long a candidate had lived in the town, whether or not he or she had attended Lenox schools, etc., was at least as important as the candidate's position on the issues and qualifications to serve. Since Debbie and Dick were relative newcomers to town, it was pretty much a foregone conclusion that he would lose the election; and he did, by a fairly substantial margin.

In an effort to maintain a public posture of neutrality as the moderator of the debates, I never told Dick of my support for him until after the election was over. And then it was more in the fashion of commiseration than support. During our later conversations, I mentioned that I had received a graduate degree from RPI and we joked a little about the graduate school in which he was now teaching. I mentioned that my classmates and I were only the second class to graduate from the RPI School of Management and, in my judgment, there was a lot of fine tuning that needed to be done to the curriculum at that time. As a matter of fact, I told him, my thesis was a critique of the School, primarily because they were teaching quantitative management techniques with almost a total disregard for the most important consideration in the management equation—people.

He laughingly told me that my critique must have done some good because that situation was hardly the case anymore. He was teaching courses in group dynamics, as a matter of fact. Over time, this rather slender thread of our RPI connection seemed to serve as a basis for kinship and friendship between the two of us.

A couple of months ago, Dick called me on the phone and told me that the RPI School of Management was going to host a four-day workshop for management school faculty representatives from universities all across the country. He said that the project director was looking for a place to hold the workshop, possibly Lenox, and Dick asked if we thought we could host such an event. Our answer, of course, was an immediate agreement and in a matter of days, we had the project director and some of his staff knocking on the door to see what we might offer.

Naturally, I wouldn't be telling all these details to you if we weren't selected as the host Inn. The three of us had put together a very extensive and comprehensive package to outline our offerings, but Joan deserves the lion's share of the credit for making our offering especially attractive. She also made a lot of the other innkeepers happy, because the RPI people expected between 40 and 50 attendees for the workshop. Obviously, we can't put up that many people in our place, so the overflow is to go to at least three other inns and possibly a fourth.

So, in a couple of weeks now, we are going to be full to the rooftop with college professors from all over the country. The project director told us that it is planned as a very relaxed and informal affair, but the RPI folks are also very intent on making it a big success. They have visions of turning this seminar into an annual affair, but much is going to hinge on how well this first one turns out. That sounds great to us—especially if we continue to be the host inn—so we are equally intent on seeing that it is a big success as well. There are seemingly thousands of details to attend to, beginning with limousine pickups at the Albany and Hartford airports and delivery of each guest to the right inn, but we'll be able to handle it with little difficulty. It's a bit like being the logistics planner for a military exercise, except that we will be responsible for execution of the plan as well. I'll let you know how everything turns out.

Best regards,
Dick

Everything turned out just fine, as a matter of record, so much so that RPI had a hit on its hands and the same conference was held every year thereafter. Last we heard, the Birchwood is still the site of choice and the Inn once again hosted the workshop this past spring. (We had left all of our planning data and schedules for the new owner and that continuity probably had a part to play in the selection.) And while I was supposed to be the professional planner during my military career, Joan was unquestionably the hero of these functions. We all worked together on the details, of course, and what I might have come up with on my own would certainly have been adequate and acceptable. But she and Dan added touches all around that made our collective efforts very special. And the attendees were most effusive in letting us know that they noticed and appreciated all that we did.

The other inns that were involved simply provided for lodging and breakfast of the overflow guests. And of course, we provided rooms and breakfast for a full house of participants at our Inn as well. All of the working sessions, coffee breaks, luncheons, cocktail parties and evening review sessions each day took place at the Birchwood. Only the dinners each evening were held elsewhere, at a different local restaurant each night—another unexpected weekday bonus for other businesses in town. RPI has managed to make a lot of business owners in Lenox quite happy, as a matter of fact.

Joan's special contributions came in the form of her superb coordination of individual events along with her creativity in developing the luncheon and break menus. With a fairly bountiful luncheon each day and coffee breaks each morning, afternoon and evening, she never repeated the same offering twice and all of the presentations were outstanding. Despite the fact that we had received approval for all of these events from the RPI hosts in advance, they were still a bit surprised and pleased to see how well they actually were prepared and presented. The three of us did all the cooking and serving for every event held at the Birchwood and we were convinced that this touch was what impressed the attendees the most.

Those who participated represented an honor role of the top universities in the United States. As might be expected since they were so relatively close by, professors from Harvard and MIT were among those participating. But they came from the far reaches of the country as well: Duke, Stanford, Southern California, Cal-Berkeley, Michigan, Florida State, Georgia Tech and Texas were just some of the other schools that were represented. There was even a young professor from one of Canada's most outstanding colleges, McGill University in Montreal. When we received the roster of attendees and their time and airport of arrival, it was our turn to be impressed at what a fine job the RPI organizers had done in promoting their workshop.

All the sessions were held in the great library, with some people using the sofas and chairs while others—usually the younger ones—sprawled out on the floor with huge throw pillows for comfort. All of the guests insisted that they were completely comfortable and, in reality, I think the informality of the room and general ambience of the Inn contributed greatly the success of the workshop.

But the sessions were anything but informal. They had a very extensive agenda to tackle each day and the moderator of the workshop kept them precisely on schedule. We were a bit concerned before the first session that our timing for meals and other services might be thrown off by sessions that ran over. But that was never in doubt after the first morning. It might have been a military operation, it was so precise and went so smoothly, and I for one was quite impressed with the ability of the moderator and his small group of assistants to stick to the schedule. Each day, they proved that they just didn't teach good management practices, they were able to demonstrate them as well.

As far as I know, they deviated from the agenda only once in the three and a half days of meetings. Just before the afternoon coffee break on the first day, the moderator asked me to come in and tell the tale of my Master's thesis at RPI. They all seemed particularly amused when I told them that the Dean decided that he would be my thesis advisor and he gave me the only "B" of my final semester.

Of all the various events that we hosted at the Birchwood over the years, I think we all enjoyed doing this first RPI workshop more than anything else. The guests couldn't have been nicer. The whole affair couldn't have gone more smoothly, despite two attendees being called home early for family emergencies during the first conference. And each successive workshop turned out to be the most profitable of any venture that we undertook—even though, once again, Joan refused to cost out our labor as part of the itemized bill that we sent to the college.

The aftermath of hosting this first affair also turned out to be profitable in the longer run. Of course, most important was the fact that the workshop came back to Lenox and the Birchwood each year thereafter. There were different project directors each time and the character of the events changed accordingly, but each one continued to be especially well run and a relative joy for us, personally and financially.

After the initial event, an article was published in the journal of the School of Management, a publication that was circulated to the School's alumni and other interested parties. The purpose of the article was clearly to enumerate the results of the seminar and publicize its success as an inducement to attract attendees for future iterations. But embedded in the article was a most complimentary few paragraphs on the Birchwood and the way in which we contributed to the achievement of their goals. And though the distribution of the magazine was somewhat limited, we benefited continually, both from other organizations who wished to host similar events, as well as individuals who came to stay with us on their own.

But even before the article was published, we saw positive results from our efforts. Dick was so impressed by the positive feedback from his colleagues at RPI that he passed the reviews on to his wife, Debbie. Just by coincidence, General Electric was planning an off-site for its senior executive managers and as a consultant, Debbie recommended the Birchwood as the site for GE to hold its discussions. The guidance that she gave us as the point of contact with GE/Schenectady was simple. "Just do it the same way that you did it for RPI," she told us.

In the years after that first seminar, we were to receive contracts for other off-sites and each one was a significant amount of work but well worth the effort in the short—and long-run. We never argued with the conventional wisdom that said we would burn out as innkeepers between our fifth and eighth years, and saw the wisdom of this idea as each week and month passed. But we still are not over the irony of the fact that these off-sites were tremendous contributors to the profitability of our business—yet we were unable to attract this critical contribution to our business until after we had placed the Inn on the market for sale. Better late than never, of course, as the old saying goes.

*   *   *

June 8, 1996
Dear Chris & Tom,

Once I told you that to be elected to an important political office in Lenox— and I used the office of a selectman as an example—you practically had to be a native of the town. I later had that perception confirmed by one of my friends who is currently serving on the Board of Selectmen, a very nice guy about our age whom you'd like as much as I do. He told me that when he first ran for office, he made the comment in a campaign speech that, although he had been gone for a number of years for professional reasons, he was, after all, a Lenox native. No sooner had he said that than someone in the audience jumped up and said, "Joe, that's a damn lie. I know for a fact that you were born in Pittsfield!" As you well know, Pittsfield is three miles north of Lenox. Not a native of Lenox, indeed.

Perhaps my assessment of unofficial residency requirements for Lenox office holders is still accurate, but it apparently doesn't apply to state offices. I received a somewhat mysterious call a couple of weeks ago from one of the better-known businessmen in the region who asked if he and one or two others might come by the Inn to discuss an "idea" with me. This fellow is a prominent banker, I had met him a number of times, previously, and had always found that I liked him. So I asked if there was a specific subject that he wished to discuss. He added to the mystery by telling me that he'd rather not talk about it over the phone.

The delegation showed up as scheduled and I vaguely knew the other two who came with him. All three are very much involved in community affairs and from all that I have figured out over the past few years, they are among a small handful of people who are the primary movers and shakers in Berkshire County. I was beginning to get an inkling into why they were visiting but I still didn't know for sure.

Lately, I have been doing bi-weekly op-ed pieces for the local newspaper and the paper has published most of them. Virtually all of the articles have been in the category of politico-military affairs commentaries and they have been generally critical of the Clinton Administration polices of committing military forces to police actions, for which the troops are not trained. I have been particularly outspoken about the open-ended commitments of troops overseas, in areas where our strategic national interests are not involved, with seemingly little consideration for spreading ourselves too thinly. From my perspective, the biggest drawback has been the adverse affects of constant overseas deployments on the morale of military personnel and their families. Well, apparently those articles had made an impression on my visitors.

It turned out that the delegation was from the Berkshire County Republican Committee, and they had been sent by the chairman and the board of directors to convince me that I should be the Republican candidate for state senator in the up-coming election. The current senator who represents Berkshire county in the statehouse in Boston is a young woman in her late twenties named Jane Swift. She is an outstanding legislator, despite her youth, and has done a wonderful job representing this area in the Senate. From all I've heard, she is also one of the most popular people in the State House and is universally admired on both sides of the aisle, as well as in the governor's office. Jane has decided to campaign for the U.S. House of Representatives and will not be running for re-election to the Senate.

Without question, trying to fill her shoes would be a challenge and it was one of the nicest compliments that I've had, not only in the Berkshires, but also at any other time. But without giving the idea any further thought or even discussing it with Joan, I told them, no. I was flattered by their offer, but I had no desire whatsoever to get involved in politics. In the ensuing discussion, it became clear that they were instructed not to take no for an answer and they continued to press the idea with more convincing arguments.

If they weren't going to accept my aversion to becoming involved in politics, then I'd have to use the most important secondary excuse that I could think of—I couldn't take time away from the Inn. But that didn't seem to satisfy them. After all, I would receive a decent salary as a senator and I could hire a manager to replace me in the Inn. Finally, I had to allow the cat out of the bag. I had to tell them that the Inn was for sale, which they immediately took as a good sign. There went my excuse for attending to my business affairs. But when I went on to tell them that we did not intend to remain in Berkshire County or even in

Massachusetts after the business was sold, the argument was clearly at an end. They couldn't, for the life of them, imagine why anyone would want to leave the most beautiful area in the world. But they also accepted the fact that their offer had been turned down, finally and firmly, and there was no reason to stay around any longer.

This whole thing reminded me of the old days when we were still on active duty. One of the guys in my office in the Pentagon was heading across the Potomac on a one-year Fellowship with the State Department. We had the usual sayonara party for him and our boss got up and said a lot of nice words about the things this guy had done and how well he had done them. In conclusion, he made a comment that broke up the house.

"Remember, Darrell, when you get over to the State Department, you'll find that those guys are a little different than we are. The first thing you need to do is to learn is to say 'That's amazing!' instead of 'Oh, bullshit!'" That same advice probably applies to the political arena as well and I'm not sure whether or not I could pass that test.

I'll have to admit that their offer was quite a compliment and I suppose, in truth, I was even a little bit tempted. But better judgment quickly prevailed. Perhaps I'll wonder from time to time in the future what might have been. Knowing my luck, however, I probably would have been defeated in a landslide by the professional politician whom the Democrats had already nominated. And I certainly would not like to live with that hanging over my head for the rest of my life. As the old saying goes, I had my chance and I blew it. But right now, I'm glad I did.

Your ex-politician friend,
Dick

As it turned out in November, the Democrat did, in fact, win in a minor landslide, defeating another professional Republican politician who was the ultimate nominee. It was, from my viewpoint at least, an uninspired campaign that seemed to end up being the essence of so many political races lately—a choice of the lesser of two evils. Not to say that I would have done any better because I may well have been regarded as the worst of three evils. You never know until you try, but that's one thing that I have no intention of trying—ever.

Jane Swift, unfortunately (again in my judgment), was also defeated in her race for Congress. Very shortly after the election, the Governor appointed her to a significant position in the Republican administration in Boston and her appointment was readily approved by her former Senate colleagues. The usual hew and cry of political patronage went up from the opposition but that died down in due time. Her defeat was hardly the end of Jane's political career, however, because she was elected as the lieutenant governor of the Commonwealth of Massachusetts in 1998, and she still serves in that position. I daresay that Jane will one day become a nationally known political figure, if she chooses to remain in politics—and I'll be right there cheering her on from the sidelines and telling my geriatric friends that I knew her when.

Over the years since I had become the president of the Lenox Chamber of Commerce, I found myself becoming more and more involved in local business and government affairs. And it seemed that the more I did, the more I was asked to do. In all my preoccupation with donating time and effort on community projects, it finally dawned on me that a lot of important things were not being done at the Inn.

Joan and Dan had picked up the slack of my frequent absences, and they encouraged me to become involved. But there were just some things that only I could do. Among the most important of these things was focusing our collective efforts on selling the Inn. So with the exception of some board of directors positions that rarely took up more than a couple of hours per month, I resigned from all the committees and other groups that I was serving on and declined to be talked into taking on any more civic responsibilities. I firmly believe that everyone has a duty to give back to his or her community, but the time had come for us to break the ties and move on.

There was one final footnote to my political career. My good friend, Leo Mahoney, the Lenox Town Moderator, approached me in the spring of 1998. He had things all worked out so that, in the fall election, I would replace him as the Town Moderator. Once more I had to reveal our plans for selling the Inn and leaving the area. Though disappointed, Leo was much easier to dissuade than the others guys had been. And with this refusal, I drove the final nail into the coffin of my volunteer community service and any political ambitions I might have had. I haven't regretted it for a single moment.

*   *   *

November 12, 1996
Dear Chris & Tom,

We're coming up on a full year that we have been doing print advertising for the sale of the Inn and we still have no one whom we regard as good prospect for buying the place. We've had plenty of the curious come around to get their tours and a brief course of instruction on how to run an inn. We have also had a number of realtors from Lenox and the surrounding towns who would be just delighted to get our Inn as a listing. At a ten percent commission (which is alleged to be the going rate for commercial sales) on a million dollar property who wouldn't be delighted? But we can't point to a single looker that could be called a "hot prospect", or even a tepid one, for that matter. So it's time to shift gears and go into phase two of our campaign.

Our gut instinct has brought us around full circle and we are now leaning toward a company in Brattleboro, VT, to be our agents in the sale of the Inn. This is the same organization that conducts the seminars on purchasing and operating a B&B—the seminar we took in the Poconos six years ago—so quite naturally they have a ready made client base for buying B&Bs. And while they are neither realtors nor real estate brokers, they have a consulting service, as part of their operation, to assist both buyers and sellers in coming together on the purchase and sale of an inn property.

If you recall, these were the folks who led us to Lenox originally, even though we bought the Birchwood through a local realtor. Despite a number of factors that mitigate against doing so, we're inclined to commit ourselves to hiring them as consultants on the sale. Hopefully, they can get something moving beyond the curious stage.

Back over a year ago, this company contacted us with a reminder that they did evaluations of inn properties. Over the years, they have devised a method to combine both the property value with the worth of the business, based on income and occupancy rates, in order to give the owners a good feel for the market value of their inns when the time comes to sell. Their results, we understand, are well-regarded in the somewhat narrow inn real estate industry. They charge $2,500 for their evaluation but that amount is subtractive from the fee that they will later charge for consulting during the sale—if you hire them as consultants, of course.

After receiving their reminder, we figured that we were entering the go-no go zone and we had them do their evaluation as of the five year anniversary of our purchase of the Inn. We chose to do so then for a couple of reasons. First, we wanted to see just how much the market experts thought of the improvements we had made to both the property and the business during our first five years in the business. And of course, the five year mark was the threshold of when we had promised ourselves to start thinking about selling, so we wanted a point of reference in establishing our asking price whenever we got around to calling it quits. The results were not as promising as we had hoped, and to be perfectly frank, no where near what we expected.

They claim that their evaluation is very "scientific" in nature. At least there is a fairly complicated formula that the company uses to crunch all the data that we provided to them—five years worth of financial performance records, kept on a monthly basis. But there is a bit of a twist to this scientific method. Had they done their calculations precisely in accordance with their own formula, the value of our Inn would have appreciated by around 20%.

But the fly in the ointment is that the head of this company then puts his "expert judgment" on top of the formula results, based on "what the market will bear" in the region where the inn is located. And when he applied this expertise to our property, we ended up with less than half of the appreciation that the formula had given us. In other words, after five years of hard work and plowing every cent we've made back into the business, building a moribund operation into a going concern, we have improved the combined worth of the property and the business by only 2% per year—according to them.

So if you put their estimate of the scant increase in the value of the Inn along side the possible $100,000 it is going to cost to bring the property up to the revised building code for Lenox inns, it looks like we're going to take it in the shorts. That's certainly a prospect that doesn't excite us very much. Such a dilemma! The options right now seem to be a choice of the least of three evils. We could turn the property over to a local realtor and face an additional 6 to 10% fee for their commission—and probably take a lot longer period to sell. We could continue trying to sell it ourselves, but the past year has hardly shown any signs that this is a promising course of action. Or we can involve the *organization that has a pretty good track record, even though we stand to face proceeds from the sale that are, at best, break even.*

But there's one thing we know for sure. We simply won't have the staying power to remain in the innkeeping business much beyond that eight year mark. Unless we win the lottery and become gentlemen innkeepers, of course. But that's the least likely prospect of the whole lot because we don't even play the lottery.

Unhappily yours,
Dick

As it turned out, it was late January of 1997 before we finally made up our minds and drove to Brattleboro to sit down face to face to negotiate a contract for their "consulting services". The contract called for $10,000 up front as a down payment and another $20,000 when the sale was completed. We had already paid $2,500 for the evaluation so we were into them for only $7,500 right away. This is a chunk of money right off the top—certainly a lot more than we would have to pay if we sold the place ourselves—but a flat fee of $30,000 is a lot better than a realtor's 6 to 10% commission which would more than double that amount.

Their sales pitch promised to take a considerable burden of time and effort off our shoulders. After receiving our down payment, they said they would prepare a marketing brochure and do all the advertising for the sale, though we would be expected to pay for the mailings that they sent out. And the key provision—they would serve as our agents for every aspect of the negotiations with prospective clients.

This latter provision was apparently the most important to them because they stressed over and over that owners become too emotionally involved in the sale of their properties and, more often than not, this emotion will serve to negate any deal, rather than reinforce it. In fact, they said, they want us to have as little contact with a potential buyer as possible. And the idea made a lot of sense—at the outset at least. But it was soon to be very obvious that all of the showing of the property was to be our responsibility. And how in the world can you show your property to prospective buyers, answer their questions and yet not have any direct contact with them?

The only major sticking point in the entire contract negotiation was the sale price. We had experienced over a year of greatly improved performance—better occupancy rates, an 8% improvement in gross revenue over the previous year, and a significant reduction in expenses, in general, and advertising costs, in particular (as a result of shifting almost exclusively to the internet). Yet our new agents wanted to increase their previous estimate of the asking price by only $4,000, less than one-half of one percent. This made the job easier for them, of course, since that was their "guaranteed" sale price.

They also strongly recommended that we make a number of capital improvements in the property, such as building a new set of owner's quarters, centrally air conditioning the mansion and completing all of the code upgrades that were going to be required by the Town. We pointed out to the agents that those were all projects that would enhance the sale of the property, but a back-of-the-envelope estimate indicated that we were talking about a quarter of a million dollars in order to complete these projects. Would they also guarantee that we would not only recoup this amount in the sale, but also recoup the interest on the loan that would be needed to make it happen? Or was this just another suggestion that would cost us money but make the Inn more marketable? Oh well, I guess you can't blame a guy for wanting to make his job easier.

As it turned out, the support that we received from our agents was minimal. For example, after we were billed an additional $800 for the mailing that they sent out to their "A-list" of prospective inn buyers, we realized that we never received a copy of the brochure they sent out, nor were we even given the opportunity to approve it in advance. When we finally did get a copy, the reasons why were immediately evident. They had essentially used all our material, the same 40-page brochure that we had developed the year before. And in addition to that, the brochure had understated the asking price for the Inn—the one we had agreed to in writing—by $10,000.

As we were to look back on our arrangement later, we would have been far better off canceling the contract right then and there. However, we knew the reputation of this company—a very good one—and once the ball started rolling toward the sale of the property, we kept assuring ourselves that they were the right people to handle things. In reality, we were probably too anxious to sell not to continue in the direction we had chosen. We hoped against hope that this was just a bad beginning and things would pick up from here on. Our stock in trade had become wishful thinking, and we made a conscious decision to stick it out to the bitter end. We were going to sink or swim with these people, so we might as well keep our game faces on and make the best of it. At least for the year's duration that the contract had to run.

We had a number of "lookers" who came to the Inn over the following year, most of whom were sent by our agents, but no one ever came remotely close to making an offer. Nor did we have a greater number of lookers than we had previously when we did our own advertising. We would normally hear from Brattleboro a day or so in advance that a certain couple was coming, sometimes wanting to stay with us and others just to look around. It seemed that about a third of those times, Joan and I were off to Boston, looking after some aspect of her family's health problems. Dan was still uncomfortable having to give the tours himself, and even though it was the luck of the draw he seemed to get the less pleasant people most of the time. And a few of those were beauties.

One couple, for example, had feelers out in every direction imaginable. They had originally contacted us directly from their home in Great Falls, VA, a very affluent suburb of Washington, DC. As was our newly acquired habit, I referred him to our agents but the man spoke to me a number of times after that. He told me that he was about to sell a mega-million dollar business and his multi-million dollar house, and as soon as that was taken care of, he was going to "buy" our Inn because it was "exactly" what he and his wife were looking for. Wow! Our brochure was that good?

But they turned out to be "users" instead of lookers. Our agents endorsed their credentials enthusiastically. But we were to find out later that they were, along with us, also clients of the same company, only as buyers rather than as sellers. We were encouraged to give them comp rooms—let them stay with us for two nights at no charge—because they were such "promising prospects". They stayed with us, at a reduced rate, and dominated our time for the entire period, always pandering to our high hopes by prefacing many of their questions with comments like, "When we become the owners,...". And most of their questions had little to do with buying our Inn, but instead were primarily oriented to detailed instruction in how we operated our business.

As it turned out, these people had made a habit of doing this at many inns all across New England, and most of the time they succeeded in getting comp rooms at the place where they stayed. And they gave the same spiel at each inn that they had given us. The place was exactly what they were looking for and they planned to buy the inn just as soon as they got their business affairs straightened out. I tend to doubt that our agents were aware of what they were doing as they went from inn to inn, but we found their conduct to be at least unsavory, if not fraudulent. We learned later that their great wealth was even more greatly exaggerated than their other claims and that they ended up buying three-bedroom guest house off the beaten path in a small town in California.

On two or three other occasions, our agents alerted us to the effect that this prospect or that one was really hot. A single woman who had just quit as the chief financial officer of a major computer firm near Boston was one of those. She came to look at our Inn, and we received no feedback either from her or our agents. After a lot of prodding, we were finally told that this supposedly very wealthy woman (a description that we had no reason to disbelieve) had narrowed her search to our Inn and one in California. And she was on her way to the west coast to try to make up her mind. The next report was that she had definitely decided against California, leaving the Birchwood as the only place that fully met her standards. We were told that we could probably expect to receive a written offer within a week or so—and our adrenaline really began to pump. But that was the last to be heard from her and even our agents had no further explanation.

And so it continued into the fall of 1998. We probably showed the Inn fifteen to twenty times during that period, and despite the insistence that we leave the discussions of the sale to our agent, a representative of the company never once came to the Inn for that entire period. And of course, we did all the talking. We were getting tired—both as innkeepers and with our sales agents—and perhaps it was time to start looking in other directions if we ever going to become former innkeepers.

*   *   *

September 23, 1997
Dear Chris & Tom,

After all the roller coaster rides of false hopes that we have had over the past many months, this is probably just one more of those. But at least this "prospective buyer" is quite a bit different than the usual lookers that we get. For the most part, each of the couples or individuals who have come to look at the Inn over the last year or so have appeared to be quite affluent—a very good starting point, of course. They also seemed to have a pretty good idea of what is involved in running an inn—they don't suffer from the Bob Newhart Show message that all is a barrel of laughs—and they seem to have a good idea of what they want. But the guy who came today doesn't fit that image at all, at least as far as appearing affluent is concerned. The other qualifications are yet to be determined.

Late this afternoon, a man pulled into the parking area and got out of the official looking car that he was driving. At first, as he came toward the door, I thought it might be a police officer, but as he came closer, his hat gave him away. He was a fireman—from Pittsfield, I was to learn later. But my first thoughts were not very charitable. Great, I thought, first the building inspector is coming after us and now the fire marshal is going to make life miserable for us too. But that wasn't the case at all.

The fellow's name is Tom Foley and he is indeed a fireman. But he wasn't here to do an inspection or anything to do with his profession. He was here on personal business. After he introduced himself, he said, very simply, "I have heard around town that your Inn is for sale. Is that true?"

When I answered that it was, he broke into a grin and told me, "You know, I've lived in the Berkshires all my life and this old mansion is the most beautiful in the area. I told myself as a little kid that someday I was going to own it and I think I just might be in a position to do that now. And besides, my wife has wanted to be an innkeeper for years and this way we could make both of our dreams come true."

We hit it off right away and not just because he was interested in buying the Inn. It turned out that he was an Air Force Vietnam veteran, had learned his fire-fighting skills as an airman and saw considerable use for his abilities *during the Tet offensive. He still obviously carried himself as a military man and after we started swapping a few war stories, we both nearly forgot why he had come in the first place.*

One of the things I liked about him right up front was his candor and honesty. He asked me what our ball park asking price was and when I told him that it was in the million dollar neighborhood, he appeared neither surprised nor taken back. He just nodded as if that were the answer he expected. Then he really impressed me by suggesting that I should probably be very skeptical of a fireman walking in off the street looking to buy a million dollar business, because he would be too, if our roles were reversed.

He went on to tell me that his grandfather had sat him down while he was still a teenager and convinced him that he needed to begin a comprehensive savings and investment program. So he began, before he went into the Air Force, investing in real estate. His grandfather had told him that this would be his wisest investment and, so far, he hadn't been proved wrong. Tom is what he, himself, described as "quite well off" as a result of thirty years of borrowing from the local banks to buy land, apartment buildings and commercial properties, and using rents and systematic savings to pay back the loans.

I was impressed by this openness and while it appeared quite evident that he was financially able to buy the Inn, he gave no impression that he was boasting. This guy had obviously followed a plan for his whole adult life and worked hard in the process. While he was probably not as sophisticated and refined as the wealthy lawyers and stockbrokers who had been looking at the Inn, he was certainly in their same class otherwise. As my old Navy friends would say, I "liked the cut of his jib" from the moment I laid eyes on him. And when he mentioned that he also owned a small construction company, which he himself operated on his off-duty and evening hours, my respect for him jumped up another notch.

He stayed for perhaps a half-hour and we didn't get into much more detail than his telling me that he was interested and qualified as a buyer. In turn, I told him that I was interested in selling to him, but there was an agency involved and he'd need to contact them. At that, he looked a bit disappointed, saying he hoped that perhaps we might work together and leave out any middle-man. But when I assured him that the fee for the agent was totally my responsibility—he would pay no commission of any kind—that seemed to ease his concern somewhat.

Since there were no guests in the Inn at that time, I asked him if he'd like to look around the place. He smiled and said he didn't need to right now, but would bring his wife back in a short while—after they had a chance to talk things over. And with a bit of distaste showing around his eyes, he added, "And after I have a chance to talk to your agent." With that, he was gone, with a vague promise that he'd "be in touch".

As I mentioned at the outset, we hate to allow ourselves to get enthused or even let our hopes get stirred. But we all had similar feelings this evening. Wouldn't it be nice to have him as the new owner: a local boy who had made it by his own hard work and sweat, one who had wanted to own the place since he was a child. It almost sounds like a fairy tale, or at least a Frank Merriwell type of story. But you know how often those sorts of stories come true! Keep your fingers crossed. After just a half hour with the man, we have a gut feeling that this may be "it".

Hope all is well,
Dick

As it turned out, he didn't come back in a "short while" nor was he in touch. A good six weeks went by without a word from him and Joan and Dan started dropping very unmistakable hints that I should give him a call to see if there were anything to his initial visit. But while my hopes had waned considerably, my feeling was that he seemed so earnest about wanting to buy the place that I didn't want to appear like I was pushing. And besides, we finally rationalized, even though he didn't blink when I told him the asking price for the Inn, he may in fact have been put off by the price. Or, looking at the glass as half full, maybe he was still trying to see his way through to raise the capital.

Finally, he returned in early November, just about the same way he had arrived the first time—in uniform, on his way home just as he was getting off duty. He had a bit of a sheepish grin on his face when we met and, in his usual candor, asked rhetorically if we had given up on him. Very quickly thereafter, he asked if we had written a contract on the sale in his absence. The grin broadened when I told him that we hadn't.

Then he became serious when he got down to the business of why he was there. "I'll be completely honest with you," he began, "The primary reason that I haven't been back is that agent of yours. They've done everything they could do to talk me out of buying the place. They don't believe that I can afford it. They claim that it's more than we can handle, since we've never been in the business before. And they were damned rude when they spoke to my wife—or spoke down to my wife is more accurate. That's a helluva lousy agent that you have, as far as I'm concerned. I'll tell you straight on, I just flat refuse to deal with them anymore, even though we're still interested in buying the place."

He had clearly placed the ball right in my court and it was time for me to make a decision. I would be nuts to adhere blindly to a contract that was about to expire in a few weeks, especially since the agents had done nothing for us in the previous eleven months. And now the only luke warm prospect that we had was being alienated by a combination of their disinterest and discourtesy.

Sure, I told him, I'll deal directly with you for the time being, but I had to be as candid as he was. "If it comes down to a situation where it looks like we have a deal, I will probably have to bring the agents back into it, at least for the contractual formalities. But I will deal with them directly, and you won't have to." What I didn't say was that neither of us would have to deal with the agent after our contract expired. The expiration was likely to happen quite some time before we would sign a contract.

He reached out his hand when I said that, and offered, "If you say so, that's good enough for me," and we began what was to be a series of handshake agreements over the next six months.

My decision became a bit easier to live with a short while later when he asked me what bank held my mortgage. When I told him, he brightened and said that the current bank president had given him his first loan when he was 18 (with grandfather as co-signer) and he had been dealing with the same bank ever since. He offered that he didn't think he'd have a bit of trouble securing a loan to purchase the Inn—it was just a matter of deciding which properties that he wanted to sell and which he wanted to use as collateral for a second trust.

Things began to look more serious and I was convinced in my own mind that we were on to something good. And we couldn't be happier that a nice guy like Tom was beginning to look like the future owner of the Birchwood.

The next few months passed rather routinely. Tom came by the Inn almost on a weekly basis. He brought his wife by to go through the rooms with a fine tooth comb and she and Joan hit it off as well as Tom and I had. We spent a fairly significant amount of time on the detailed estimates of the upgrades that had to be performed as well as a couple of deferred maintenance projects that had to be factored into the final price of the property.

As we approached February, I pointed out to Tom during one of his visits that we had been proceeding as if we had reached a deal on the sale and yet, not only did we not have a contract, he hadn't even made a firm offer thus far. We should probably begin by reaching an agreement on the sale price, at least, particularly since he had mentioned a number of times that they wanted to take over by mid to late May. They wanted time to get their feet on the ground before Tanglewood was upon them, so it would be a good transition time. As residents of the Berkshires, they were well aware of how our sleepy little community changes after the Boston Symphony arrives.

Meanwhile, we heard not a word from our agents. Not only had they failed even to inform us that Tom had made an official inquiry about purchasing the Inn, they didn't have any leads for us whatsoever. No one else had come near the Inn to look. We therefore concluded that it was no random coincidence when one of the partners from the agency called—a week to the day before the contract was due to expire—to ask why they hadn't received our revenue and occupancy report for December. And, oh by the way, did I realize that our contract was due to expire in another week, and if it was OK with me, he'd just invoke the automatic renewal of the contract for another year.

The timing of this call, the lack of any contact from them for nearly two months, the manner in which they had treated Tom and his wife and probably just the tone of voice infuriated me. No, I told him, I didn't think that would be necessary since the couple that they had driven away—and not even spoken to us about—were about to sign a contract with us for the sale and I didn't think their services would be required any longer. As a matter of fact, I went on, if it will ease the burden of all the hard work that they had done for us, they could consider the contract dissolved as of today.

His shock was almost palpable over the phone and there was a long pause before he said, "Well, we talked to those people last fall and there's no way that a fireman can come up with the money to buy the Birchwood."

Really?, I said. Well, perhaps you'll be surprised to learn that his loan is already approved and we're going to close on the sale around the 15th of May. As a matter of fact, I taunted him, the only thing left to be done is to have a joint walk-through of the property with the building inspector and agree on the selling price. Since we had handled everything else by ourselves—without any rancor or emotion—this last hurdle looked like it would fall into place fairly easily.

Again, the pregnant pause made it clear that he was flabbergasted, but finally he blurted out, "Well I hope you realize that whether or not you cancel the contract now, you still owe us another $20,000. There is a clause in the contract that says you pay us even if you find a buyer yourself, and I'm going to hold you to that even if we have to take you to court."

I was absolutely furious. "You son of a bitch," I hollered at him, "I'll look forward to that. You're not getting another cent from us and, as a matter of fact, our counter suit will give us a chance to get back the $7,500 that we paid you which we might just as well have pissed down the drain for all you've done for us." And with that, I did something I can never recall doing before or since. I hung up on him.

The next time Tom and I got together, he delighted in my telling him the story of the parting of the ways with our agent. He seemed more pleased than I had ever seen him before, but we still had a good bit of work to do before we had a contract. And time was a-wasting if we were going to make that mid-May hand over.

*　　　　　*　　　　　*

February 12, 1998
Dear Chris & Tom,

After five consecutive years of enjoying your superb hospitality, and getting a much needed recharge of our batteries at the same time, we may well need to back out of the reunion at Mammoth next month. It's about the last thing in the world that we want to do. I think I've been looking forward to it since the day after we left Mammoth last March, but the activities related to the sale of the Inn are really beginning to heat up.

Tom Foley (the guy who plans to buy it) is away from the area fairly frequently, much more than I would have thought he would be. But in addition to being a lieutenant in the fire department, he is apparently a nationally recognized innovator in the fire-fighting business and spends a lot of time at conferences and seminars around the country. While he is away, all progress ceases, but when he is around, we have to work overtime to make up for his absences. The Foleys still want to have the closing around mid-May, and we're still a long way away from having the deal sewed up.

While I would very much like to be farther along than we are, I have every confidence at this point that it's going to go through. Though I must admit that we still haven't agreed on the sale price so we're no where near having a contract or, using the proper term, a Purchase and Sale Agreement, which local lawyers and realtors call a P&SA. Sounds like the military with all the abbreviations and acronyms, doesn't it?

The reason for the lack of a final sale price or a P&SA is a bit complicated. The whole deal hinges on the final definition of what needs to be done to satisfy the building inspector. When he makes his decision—which must be negotiated by a registered architect, a process from which both Tom and I are excluded—we will then have to go to a number of contractors to get written estimates of the cost. With those estimates, we'll decide how the costs are to be apportioned and our share of those costs will, of course, be deducted from the final sale price. All of this will be delineated in detail in the P&SA so that there'll be no doubt in anyone's mind as to the buyer and seller responsibilities.

We have done everything that we can, so far. We have hired the architect, the same person who was introduced at the fateful building code meeting four years ago and Tom and I have agreed to split the cost of her fees. Now it is up to her to get the joint inspection scheduled and the negotiation conferences done and over with. We will, of course, get the estimates after that, and I don't see any real difficulty completing the process once those initial bases have been touched.

The building inspector is the primary bottleneck, without a doubt. In actuality, he is only the part-time Lenox inspector because he holds the same position in Pittsfield through a joint agreement between the two municipal governments. Since Pittsfield is considerably larger than Lenox, most of his time is spent there, and it takes a good amount of time to get on his schedule for inspections. Tom knows him personally, both as a fellow city employee and as a contractor, so I hope this will get us some priority consideration. It will be necessary if he and his wife are going to be in business before the end of May. I suspect that there probably aren't more than 20 hours involved in getting all of this done, but when each of those hours is a week apart because of various peoples' schedules, it's going to be a tough journey ahead.

And that, unfortunately, is the reason that we won't make it to Mammoth this year, dammit! I feel especially bad since you have always arranged the reunion according to our best availability, as you have again this year. However, let's look at the bright side. If everything goes as it should, we won't have to be accommodated in the future. We'll be free to come anytime that is convenient to you. We hope this late withdrawal won't inconvenience you or the others too much, but I'm sure you understand.

Love to you both,
Dick

As it turned out, we made the reunion after all, because everything was at a stalemate. We couldn't schedule the inspection with the building inspectors until early April. I guess that shows that fellow municipal employees don't get any priority consideration. But Tom also had a couple of conferences he had to attend which made it convenient for both of us to be away in early March.

Just before we both left town, however, he apparently thought that we should get the ball rolling a little bit because he made a formal letter of offer to buy the Birchwood. When I saw it, my heart sank because it was for $10,000 less than we had paid for the Inn seven years previously. I couldn't believe that we had gone on for months in our discussions and he had the audacity to think we would sell at a loss.

I called him on the telephone immediately and asked him to stop by the Inn before he (and we) headed out of town. This offer was not even worth considering and if it were the best he could do, we might just as well drop the discussions right then and there. But I wasn't going to force such a critical juncture on the telephone—this was something that needed to be broached face to face.

Tom arrived with that sheepish expression on his face that I had become accustomed to seeing over the past few months. And as was his normal mode of operation, he got right to the point. "I guess you didn't think much of my offer," he said, as if he knew for sure that would be the case before he even presented it to me.

"No," I told him, "as a matter of fact it was bordering on an insult, if I can be perfectly blunt. You know very well what we paid for the place because it's spelled out in detail in the county records. And since you have lived in the area a lot longer than we have, you also know what condition the place was in when we bought it and what it's condition is now—even though you may not know that we built the business up from next to nothing." But he knew those details as well, because, by now, we had shared all the financial data with him back to day one of our ownership.

He chuckled a bit and told me he was sorry that he had pissed me off. He hadn't meant to do that. But he did want to show that he and his wife, Connie, were dead serious about buying the Inn and he thought that an official offer, regardless of its acceptability, would indicate their intentions and give us a place to start from. He paused a moment, chuckled again and added, "And, I'll have to admit, maybe I wanted to see just how eager you really were to pack up and call it quits."

When we both returned from our absences, I had an answer for him. I gave him a counter offer with an increase of $125,000, plus an offer to put $70,000 more in escrow to cover my half of a 50-50 share of the upgrades. We were certain that the upgrades and repairs wouldn't come to more than $140,000. If our share was too much, the escrow holder could return the unused balance to us after the projects were completed. I also gave Tom a blank P&SA contract that I had laboriously copied from the 15 page contract that we had signed in 1991, amended to incorporate the conditions and agreements that we had already reached. To my pleasant surprise, he studied the counter offer briefly, stuck out his hand and said, "That's just about what I expected to agree to and it sounds good to me. Why don't we just call it a deal with the condition that it will be amended according to the results of the inspection."

When I asked him if he wanted me to put it in a format that we both could sign, he said that as far as he was concerned, he fully trusted me and hoped that I felt the same about him. He would like to have a copy of the counter offer as it was but that's all that would be necessary as far as he was concerned. And since it was now late March, we also probably needed to shift our projected closing date to the end of May. Two months should be enough time to get our ducks in a row. I think I "liked the cut of his jib" even more at that moment and I assured him that the handshake was fine by me as well—all the while, amazed at how easily our negotiations had gone.

In the interim period while we waited for the inspection to take place, he and Connie came by a couple of times and they even brought one of their two adult daughters on one occasion. The three gals would be the ones running the Inn, we learned. Tom was pretty certain that he was going to spend most of his time in the background, taking care of the maintenance requirements and doing any upgrades that he could. He still had another year to go until retirement from the fire department, and perhaps things might change when that happened. But more than likely, his energies would then be directed to his construction business rather than schmoozing with guests at the Inn—a revelation that didn't surprise me a lot because that didn't really seem to be his cup of tea.

Meanwhile, we became preoccupied with our lawyer. By now our wily old country lawyer had retired and turned over all the responsibilities of the firm to his son. We had met Jay before, were impressed by his abilities, and besides, Dad was still right there in the vicinity if any "consultation" was necessary. When I told Jay about my confrontation with our former agent, he became angrier than I had been. He reviewed the contract that we had signed with them for their representation and suggested that we beat him to punch: sue him preemptively for promising to perform both legal and real estate brokerage functions when he was licensed to do neither. I liked his *chutzpah*, but declined and said we'd rather hold that in abeyance for a counter suit if he ever had the audacity to press any attempt to get more money from us.

We spent most of our time on the principal actions related to the sale—getting certification from the state that we had paid our taxes and were not in default on loans or had any other legal action pending. Jay also needed to draft a "modern" P&SA agreement, since things had changed in the past seven years and he wanted a decent document to present to Tom's lawyer. He also advised most persuasively that we hold firm on whatever the sale price that we might agree to and drop any idea of putting money in escrow for the upgrades. "You need to decide right from the start what the costs of those upgrades are going to be," he told us. "When you sell the Inn, you will want to be free and clear of anything to do with upgrading the property, unless you want that hanging over your heads for years to come." We didn't need much convincing.

Finally, the big day for the inspection came. The inspector arrived with the fire marshal to make a joint run through the buildings from top to bottom, but before we started to the basement, he made a little speech. He wanted us to know that they were not there to put innkeepers out of business or to destroy the beauty and architecture of fine old homes. They only wanted to take the minimum precautions to certify that the safety of the guests in our inns was assured. He went on to say that he and the fire marshal would mention everything that they saw that related to safety or the code—the architect should take notes—but that didn't mean that all items mentioned would be required changes. They would only be the basis for a "compromise solution" that would be "acceptable to all".

For the rest of the tour, either the building inspector or the fire marshal seemed to be talking non-stop while the architect furiously took notes. Tom and I looked at one another from time to time as if we both thought that many of the remarks were very petty. The need for a second egress from the owner's quarters (The Hovel) whose windowsills were less than four feet above the outside ground level seemed to be one of the many trivial items. Despite the fact that many areas of the mansion were already up to code, I stopped counting when I came to about 20 deficiencies that were cited.

Over the next four weeks, the architect met with the building inspector on three different occasions, trying to get a definitive answer on what we were expected to do. Each time she met with him, she reported, he would mention some "work around" that would be a cheaper alternative than doing something else. And each time he would give her the task of going back to work out the details of it's effectiveness and come back to him the following week. One of his alternatives, after being shocked (in her words) at the high cost of installing a sprinkler system, was to close the third floor of the Inn to guests. Great idea, like all the rest of his work-arounds, except that closing four guest rooms would cost us roughly 20% of our annual revenue.

Finally, as we approached the second week in May, I told the architect that we needed a drop-dead final answer or the deal was going to fall through. It would be too late to get the Foleys into the Inn for the prime revenue season and that was key to their going through with the deal. She called the next day to tell me "the good news and the bad news". The good news was that we didn't have to install a sprinkler system in the entire house—only on the third floor and in the basement. The bad news was that we would have to do "everything else". Somehow, that didn't seem to be much of a compromise solution to prevent financial ruin, at least from Tom's and my perspective.

Two days later, the architect's rather hefty bill arrived for her services. I called her immediately and told her that I appreciated the fact that she had worked hard on our behalf but I needed her report, the detailed list of "everything else", before I would send her a check for her services. Her answer amazed me. She told me that she had been hired to negotiate with the building inspector, not to write reports, and if we wanted to get a written report, we would have to pay her another $250. But she couldn't do the report for at least two weeks anyway because she was leaving in the morning on a ten day vacation. Thanks a lot! She would hang by her thumbs waiting for a check until we found out the results of her negotiations.

Tom and I sat down the next day to try to recall the details of the inspection that had been held nearly a month before. A walk around the Inn helped a great deal and finally we were satisfied that we had covered everything, at least all the major items. Fortunately, the estimates for the big ticket items had already been done, and as a contractor, he was able to complete the estimates for all the minor construction projects. We had the numbers we were looking for and it was time to get down to brass tacks: the final sale price of the Inn.

I told him that I would work out the details, in writing, that night and if he were agreeable, we would hand that piece of paper to both of our lawyers so that they could get busy on the final, official P&SA.

The next morning, I presented him a Best and Final Offer with the following terms:
  * Closing as of June 1, 1998
  * Buyer assumes all responsibility for upgrades to code
  * Buyer assumes all responsibility for residual maintenance tasks
  * Buyer and seller divide architect's fees equally
  * Seller retains all deposits currently on file as of closing date
  * Net price at closing (a total less than what we wanted but minimally acceptable)

He asked for 24 hours to consider the conditions, and the next day, May 18, Tom accepted the terms as stated. And once again, we shook hands on the deal—this time with a lot more gusto and sincerity—and agreed to start our respective lawyers on the completion of the P&SA, ASAP. Both lawyers shook their heads as if we were asking the impossible of them, but vowed to do their utmost to make the date. Within another week, the date had drifted back to the 6th of June, but all parties agreed that wasn't a problem.

Meanwhile, Joan and I made the final plans that we had looked forward to for some time. We arranged with the movers to come the following week to pick up all of the heavier personal items and to put them into storage with our other things. We would probably not want our 11,000 pounds of household goods, most of which had been in storage for seven years, until next fall when we had found the house of our dreams in Colorado.

We also planned the final family reunion which, considering the time of year, would probably be our generation only, rather than the younger folks. And everyone would likely be involved in packing and cleaning up more than anything else, anyway. And finally, since we would still have a lot of personal items that we'd need in Colorado during our house hunting period, we decided that I would drive a rental truckload of all those things out to Colorado Springs and put these items in temporary storage. Dan and Anne had already offered to drive one of our cars to Colorado, leave it there and fly home, so that we could take our time and have a little vacation on the way out. The feeling of elation was running as high as a kite.

Oh yes, and one other thing. We suggested that we host a hail and farewell party to introduce the community to the new owners and to give our thanks to all the friends and acquaintances that we had made in our seven years in Lenox. The Foleys thought that would be very nice of us and agreed enthusiastically. And meanwhile, while I made the round trip to Colorado, Connie and her daughters would spend the better part of the next two weeks training with us to take over the Inn. And they were to show up at 6:30 AM the Monday morning after the party to start their training.

Our family was, as usual, an inestimable help in getting boxes packed and labeled and segregating those things that were going into storage from those which I was going to drive out west. But we still managed to have the wonderful evenings filled with love and laughter that had been the highlights of our previous seven years. However, my normally stolid brother, Jim, couldn't help becoming a bit maudlin. From time to time he would get misty-eyed and wonder, rhetorically, how we would possibly find a way to continue these reunions, which to all of us, had become a vital part of our sense of family.

The turnout for the community party, which was held on the front porch and the front lawn on a glorious spring day, was large and wonderfully friendly. We concluded that Tom and Connie knew as many of the local people as we did, and probably for a lot longer, but it was a perfect way for us complete the "change of command". As the last guests began to leave, Tom asked if he could speak to me in private. We went into the dining room where we had met so many times trying to work out the details of the sale.

He became very serious and appeared troubled when he said, "You know that clause in our final agreement, the one that says, 'Seller retains all deposits currently on file as of closing date'. I have to be perfectly honest with you. I guess I really didn't know what that meant, even though you were very careful to explain it to me, including telling me that $37,000 was the current amount that was on deposit. I didn't pay close enough attention to what I was agreeing to and I accept full responsibility for that. And I promise you that I'm not backing out of the deal. I just thought you should know."

I honestly didn't know what to say. I had gone to great pains to explain the situation to him, to include telling him that this was a way that I could get an acceptable price for the property while he wouldn't need to take a loan that appeared too big for him. I then told him that I appreciated his honesty and integrity, but an agreement wouldn't have been possible without that clause. I assured him that I certainly wasn't trying to take advantage of him. He said that he knew that and we should consider the issue closed.

I reminded him that I was leaving for Colorado with a truckload of personal items in two days. If he had the slightest thought of backing out at this point, I'd like him to tell me now, because while we would be deeply disappointed if they were to do so, it would save us a lot of time and money if we did so now. In one of our now familiar, earnest hand shakes, he assured me that there was no backing out at this point. He and Connie were committed and were looking forward to becoming innkeepers. He wished me luck on my 2,000 mile trip and on the following Monday, bubbling with happiness, I was off in my 15' Hertz-Penske rental truck toward the great Rocky Mountains of Colorado.

*   *   *

June 16, 1998
Dear Chris & Tom,

Disaster! We still can't believe what has happened, but the Foleys have backed out of buying the Inn. After some additional delays for a variety of reasons, the final date for the closing was set at 10:00 this morning. Tom came to the kitchen door about 6:00 last evening, a bit of a surprise because he usually came in the guest entrance and we'd meet at the Dutch door. Good, I thought, he's starting to treat the place like it's his own, which it will be by noon tomorrow.

But as soon as we saw his facial expression, we knew that something was drastically wrong. He stepped inside the door and just stood there with a doleful, hang-dog look on his face and, for a moment or two, he said nothing. Then, he raised both hands from his sides a couple of times, in a gesture of apparent abject futility.

Finally, he said, hoarsely, "I'm sorry, but we can't go through with it. It just doesn't feel right and I'd rather be damned now by backing out than to have to live with a mistake for years to come. I'm really sorry, and I guess there's nothing that I can add to that."

Joan and I were totally stunned. After all we'd been through trying to put this deal together—and the endless promises that his "handshake was more valuable than his signature"—just like that it was over.

Under normal circumstances, I probably would have been furious, but I guess we were so dazed that all I could do was mumble, "Tom, I can't believe what you're saying. I can't believe you've waited until the eleventh hour to drop this bomb on us."

"I know," he replied, "you have every right to be mad as hell, but as I said, we'd rather be called all the names in the book than to go through with something that's not the right thing for us to do. I'll try to make it up to you—some way, I don't know how—but that's all I can say. I'm sorry." And he walked back out the door.

As he walked down the driveway to his truck, I glanced at Joan and tears were streaming down her face. She looked like a little girl whose favorite doll had just been destroyed, crushed beyond repair under the wheels of the family car. I went over to her—with tears rapidly welling up in my own eyes—and put my arms around her. And both of us just stood there and sobbed. For how long, I don't have any idea.

As the initial shock began to wear off, we just looked at one another. The farewell parties, all our things in storage or out in Colorado, all the farewells—all for nothing. We remained in a daze for most of the evening and each time we'd look at one another, the tears began to flow again. I'm not even sure today what we had for dinner last night or even if we had any dinner. But most of the rest of the evening, until bed time, we spent with our arms around one another trying to figure out answers to the question that will probably never be answered. Why?

Anne and Dan stopped by later in the evening for a "last night" celebratory drink and were, of course, as stunned as we were. Dan's anger came to the surface immediately and he was all ready to "go make that son-of-a-bitch pay for this", but the anger subsided quickly and they soon joined us in the depths of depression.

Today would be another day and today would be the time to tug on the bootstraps and decide what needed to be done. But last night we all gave ourselves over to bottomless despondency and inexorable self-pity. And today, we did start to put things back together and priority one is for me to hop on an airplane bright and early in the morning, head back out to Colorado Springs and bring back that truckload of things that we will need immediately to operate the Inn.

We're going to be fine, I promise. But it's going to take an awful lot of tugging on the bootstraps for the next week or so to get ourselves back into the swing of another Tanglewood season. We'll probably give you a call in a couple of days to tell you that everything is back to normal again—even though things are a long way from normal right now.

Bless you both,
Dick

We were extremely lucky, at that time of the year, to get flight reservations and to be able to rent another truck on one day's notice. We arose before dawn, which was nothing unusual, but this time it was for Joan to drive me to the Bradley IAP near Hartford so that I could begin the reverse of the trip that I had just completed ten days before.

By morning, we found that bitterness had started to replace our depression and while neither is a very commendable mood or emotion, we took it as a sign that we had already begun our recovery. I was concerned about leaving Joan at the Inn by herself, even though Anne and Dan and other friends were near at hand. She was equally concerned about my making the four day return drive by myself, another sign that the initial tug on the bootstraps was beginning to take effect.

Though it may be a strange comparison, I doubt that we had both been so deeply despondent, emotionally, since we had lost our first child at birth in 1958. We had had our share of disappointments and tragedies in our 41 years of marriage, but those were usually traumatic experiences suffered by one of us, the other serving as the bulwark in the recovery process. This had been a tremendous hurt but we tearfully promised each other as I left her at the airport that this, too, would pass and we'd be just fine.

My flight went by quickly because I spent most of the time in deep reflection. My attention focused initially on what I was doing and all the other things that had been done that we would like undone. Clearly, I could recover the personal articles of clothing, furniture and cooking utensils that we had so recently taken out to the Springs. The knowledge that it was going to take me a repeat expenditure of $3,500 and another six days to complete the round trip didn't do much to assuage that growing sense of bitterness. But there had been other actions taken that couldn't be undone.

All of the items that we had brought to the Inn to put our personal signature on the place were irretrievably buried among all our other household goods in North Adams, a town about 30 miles north of Lenox. The movers had taken considerable time (at our expense) breaking the entire shipment down, consolidating and re-packing it in shipping crates for the upcoming move to Colorado. All the art work, furniture, decorative pieces and many of our kitchen tools, appliances and serving pieces wouldn't be seen again at the Birchwood. We were just going to have to learn to get along without them. But the plain austerity of the public rooms probably did more to depress Joan than anything else.

Far more serious was the loss of over a third of our team. In anticipation of our departure into retirement, Dan had begun a very promising new job at another local full-service property where the management responsibilities that he had, and the experience that he would gain, were both going to be excellent additions to his resume. He and Anne had also moved from the Hovel into a lovely little cabin out in Becket, the town where Anne worked, and they were newly settled into the first real home that they could call their own. The first thing that Dan said when he calmed down from the disastrous news was that he would leave his new job and they would return to the Inn. While it was a wonderfully selfless offer, Joan and I couldn't possibly agree to their making a move that would affect their lives so drastically.

In a vein that was more black humor than anything else, I began to wonder what were we going to say to all our friends? All of the innkeeping couples with whom we had been close had recently held a delightful going-away party for us. There was an excellent meal, the presentation of a variety of mementos to include a gorgeous quilt that they had commissioned expressly for us, as well as some very touching expressions of affection on our leaving Lenox. We decided that we weren't going to give anything back. But their delightful farewell party would be "put in the bank" for the time when we actually were leaving—a time that hopefully was not in the distant future.

My reflections then shifted to thoughts of what might have happened to cause this last-minute abortion of a deal that sounded so good for both couples. There were so many little bumps in the road during the course of our negotiations, but none of them seemed to have gone unresolved, and each had been put behind us as a matter of course. Except, perhaps, for one last-minute glitch.

In our conversation following the party that we had for the Foley family a few weeks back, Tom mentioned that he had decided to have an appraiser come by and look at the Inn while I was on my way to and from Colorado. He had made many surveys of the property himself, but because this was such a large and important investment, he had decided at the last minute to seek an outside opinion. Since I had been encouraging him for months to do just that, I didn't think anything further of his sudden change of mind.

I made a habit of calling Joan each night while on the trip west, and the first night I called from western Pennsylvania. She told me that Tom and his inspector had spent most of the afternoon there that day and seemed to be having some very serious discussions.

My call the next night from Missouri was greeted by greater concern on Joan's part because she had received a call from our lawyer telling her that Tom's lawyer was concerned about "serious problems" that were found in the inspection, particularly with the roof. Tom's lawyer thought that the final selling price needed to be reduced by $40,000 to cover the cost of these additional repairs. I found it highly suspicious that this happened to be slightly more than the amount of money that Tom had agreed to allow me to keep in the form of deposits on hand—the same amount that he confessed that he didn't realize he was going to leave to us.

On the day that I returned I got together with Tom and gently chided him about the manner in which he had undertaken to recoup the deposit money. He looked at me with a blank expression and said that if his lawyer had done that, he did it without his (Tom's) knowledge or approval, and he wouldn't have agreed to doing this if he had been asked. Leave it to the lawyers to do their best—in pursuing the "best interests of their client"—to screw up an amicable agreement.

"But now that you brought it up," Tom went on, "you had told me that the roof was fine and it's really not. It's in pretty bad shape and needs to be replaced." His tone and the look on his face gave me a strong impression that he believed that I had intentionally tried to mislead him.

"First of all, Tom," I told him, "I have encouraged you to go into every nook and cranny in the house to look at its condition for yourself." He nodded that yes, indeed, I had done that. "Second, I have asked you at least twice, and probably more times than that, if you had been up on the roof to evaluate its condition." Again, he nodded in agreement. "But most importantly," I went on, "I did not tell you that 'the roof is fine'. What I told you was that the roof was fine for the time being, but it was reaching the end of its days and would probably have to be redone in a few years."

He said that he didn't hear it that way, and of course, such simple misunderstandings have caused wars in the past. So I offered to have a roofer come in, do an estimate on the cost of re-roofing the house and told him I would reduce the final selling price accordingly. This had seemed an acceptable solution to him. The roofer came by a day later and his firm fixed price estimate was for less than half of the $40,000 that his lawyer had given as the estimate. Ah yes, these lawyers!

The only other possible cause that I could think of was Tom's seeming lack of comprehension of cash flow. Most of his construction business was conducted on a cash and carry basis, so he never found himself in a situation where he had to save, when times were good, for the times when income sadly trailed behind expenses. When we were reviewing the Inn's annual financial statements, he would look at the month to month income and expense figures and just shake his head. He appeared not to understand why anyone would be so foolish as to buy a business where some monthly expenses were double the income for that same month. Despite many attempts on my part to help him accept that this was a fact of life for innkeepers, he never seemed very comfortable with the concept.

But as my thoughts drifted from possible cause to other possible causes— probably abetted by the feelings of bitterness that we had awakened with that next morning—I kept drifting back incredulously to the fact that Tom had reneged on so many solemn promises.

Joan and I had come a long way since our early marriage days when we were naive and trusting of everyone we met. It seemed incomprehensible to us, forty years previously, that we shouldn't accept the word of those with whom we served and did business. Too many disappointments in the intervening years had proved that to be a questionable personal philosophy. But we still preferred to err on the side of trust in our fellow human beings than to be perpetually suspicious or paranoid regarding the motives and trustworthiness of others.

Tom was above suspicion from very early in our relationship, as far as I was concerned, and I believe to this day that he meant every word when he said that his handshake was more valuable than his signature. I believe, beyond a reasonable doubt, that he had every intention of meeting each commitment that he had made. And there is no question in my mind that he and Connie truly concluded that becoming innkeepers wasn't "right" for them and they backed out rather than to have to live with a bad decision.

So the roof and the cash flow and those many other things that I had pondered for the first hours of the trip probably weren't the reason for their last second change of mind. Perhaps it was the training program— could that be possible? Perhaps Connie had been one of the many romantics who thought that there was nothing more charming than having a big "doll house" to decorate and meeting all these nice people who came from near and far to spend time at their beautiful inn. Maybe in the two short weeks of her training, she discovered that the romance was only a small part of it. Innkeeping was also long hours and hard work that went on for years at a time. Further reinforcing this train of thought, I recalled that Tom wasn't going to be involved very much in the actual running of the inn so it well may have been Connie who decided at the very last minute that it just wasn't "right" for them. Cold feet might be a more apt description.

Joan still disputes that theory today and insists that Connie was just as eager and enthusiastic on the final day of her training as she had been on the first day. In fact, Joan believed, Connie's increased knowledge and confidence had given substance to her enthusiasm and she and the girls couldn't wait to get started on their new venture. The truth is, we'll probably never know for sure what the underlying cause was for the aborted sale. But the fact that other prosperous, yet more affordable, inns have sold in Lenox in the last two years—and the Foleys were not the buyers—still makes me suspicious that our training successes turned on us and caused the disaster.

Certainly we were foolish and overly trusting for not getting a substantial deposit up front—at least enough to cover the expenses that their backing out had caused—and for not having a signed document in hand that was actionable in court if worse came to worse. That was entirely my fault and I take full responsibility for that decision. But as I said, we have always been trusting and probably always will be.

In the cold light of nearly two years of reflection after the event, we both forgive Tom and Connie for causing us such grief, and for causing a huge, unnecessary expenditure of our money and emotion. Except for one thing, that is.

Previously, I had mentioned that the architect was going to charge extra to reveal the results of her negotiations with the building inspector. A few months later, she apparently saw the ridiculousness of her position—or her lawyer husband convinced her that her position was untenable—and she sent me her detailed notes from the final meeting.

Her final invoice came to $3,000, half of which Tom had committed to pay, without any conditions regarding the consummation of the sale. Since her bill was addressed to me, I paid the entire amount and then sent Tom a copy of her invoice plus an invoice of my own for half the amount. Over the next two months, I sent additional copies of the invoice and left messages on their telephone answering machine (they habitually screened their calls rather than answering directly). Neither Tom nor Connie ever responded, and to us, that abrogation of responsibility is, and always will be, unpardonable.

*   *   *

September 15, 1998
Dear Chris & Tom,

Well, we made it, thanks to a lot of support from family, good friends (like your calls), our close innkeeper friends, two very dedicated and thoughtful housekeepers—and a secret weapon. On the way back from Colorado in the truck, I was getting a bit down and remembered a recent spate of TV ads for St. John's Wort. According to the accompanying spiel, it is a "mood elevator", a natural substance derived from a weed that is essentially harmless but is effective in lifting the spirits—for some people at least.

I still have my doubts about the claims, but I stopped in a drugstore in Kearney, Nebraska, where I spent the first night, and I bought some. Darned if I didn't feel better for the rest of the trip. And instead of feeling sorry for us for the plight we were in, I spent most of my time making mental notes of things we could do to make the load a little lighter when the high season began. When I got home, I suggested to Joan that she try some. She scoffed at the idea and even chided me a little for being so trendy. But later she decided that I was surprisingly upbeat about our challenges so she tried it too. We still don't know whether it works, is purely a psychological crutch or what, but we maintained a "stiff upper lip" for the whole summer and actually found that it was one of our easiest summers on record.

A lot of the ease might be attributed to the fact that we hired people to do a lot of the things that had taken so much of Dan's and my time. Even though Dan received an insulting pittance in his position as a partner, we weren't paying him any longer so we used that money to hire people to do odd jobs. We had a gardener, someone to do the lawn each week, and we had a fine young teenage boy "on retainer" to help with a lot of inside and outside chores. Susan also inn-sat about once a week so that we could get out to dinner or a performance at Tanglewood. In fact we attended most of the Sunday afternoon concerts, a huge change from previous years. All in all, the summer was much less stressful than those in the past—a change for which we're inclined to credit the decrease in pressure and work tempo, rather than St. John's Wort.

Joan has done beautifully for the entire time although she remains considerably distressed over the plainness of the Inn with all our decorative pieces gone. She has picked up a few things to spruce up the looks a bit, some of which stand out particularly sharply. She managed to buy two huge, very attractive oriental urns that stand about four feet high that are now by the bay windows in the dining room where the oriental chests used to be. She claims that they both cost less than $50 and they do a good job of dressing the place up a bit. We also had to buy a lot of new kitchen utensils, but the "replacements" haven't been all that extensive or expensive.

Some of the regular guests have not even noticed the changes but others have asked right away what happened. We decided to be open with them and tell them a one-sentence account of the aborted sale. Some have told us that "they're glad" that the sale fell through, although they're quick to add that they're sorry for us. One or two women, who are realtors in the New York metro area, have offered to "solve our problems over night" as soon as they returned home. They figured it would be a piece of cake to sell such a beautiful place, and of course, they practically salivated openly with the thoughts of the commission. Like the local folks, we politely declined their assistance.

I guess it will come as no surprise that we have heard nothing from the Foleys. No, that's not completely correct. While I was on my second circuit to Colorado Springs and back, Tom called Joan one day, apologized once again for backing out, and asked if he could come over sometime "to mow the lawn or something like that". Joan thanked him for the offer—a bit coldly, she confessed to me after my return—and said that I would call him later if he could be of any assistance. I did not call, but I suspect he now feels that he has discharged his commitment "to help out", the promise that he made the night that he told us the bad news. I'm perfectly happy to have no further contact with him.

The reaction by the townsfolk is a bit strange. Our closest friends have been most solicitous, some even suggesting that they begin a whisper campaign against "that fireman"—which we vigorously declined, of course. But the casual acquaintances have had an unusual reaction. It's almost analogous to a situation where relationships have been warm until your teenage daughter becomes pregnant out of wedlock or your son is arrested for vandalism. They generally feel sorry for you, but there's a lingering bit of doubt that it somehow might be your fault, so the preferred course of action by most is to avoid us like the plague. We also must recognize that many of the natives have been long-time friends of the Foleys—far longer than they have been with us—so they're a bit torn. Since everyone knew of the sale, it would be interesting to know what the Foleys are telling people.

We haven't had any time to put the Inn back on the market throughout the summer, or even to figure out a strategy for marketing the sale, as a matter of fact. Some of the print ads haven't expired, so we still get an occasional call and we've even had one or two couples come by to look at the property. But they were just curious. Our depressed dread, after spending the better part of two years trying to complete a sale, is that we'll have to start the traditional "two years to sell" period all over again. Realistically, I'm sure that everyone who sells an inn runs across disappointments and "almosts" all the time, so I suspect we shouldn't worry about things like that.

Susan is inn-sitting this coming weekend—we refused any reservations for those two days—and Joan and I are off for a three-day break, probably to Cape Cod, but right now we have no reservations anywhere. When we get back, priority one is to get the Inn back on the market and focus on the sale.

Thanks again for your calls and emails,

Dick

We didn't wait until we got back, for despite the whole purpose of the getaway, most of our break was devoted to discussing the new sales strategy. And we made a few basic and important decisions. Needless to say, we would not even get the least bit excited in the future until we had a signed piece of paper and a healthy deposit in our grubby little hands. Trust would never again play a part in this business.

We had discovered that by changing our tempo and farming out some of the drudgery of being innkeepers that we could hang in as long as necessary until we had a sale. There was no longer any magic associated with being out by the eight-year mark and whatever time it took, we would take it in stride. And the corollary decision to that one was that we would sell the Inn ourselves. We stood to lose too much money because of the code compliance upgrades. And there was no way that we would pay someone else to do the marketing work that we were perfectly capable of doing—even if it were going to take two or three more years to sell the place.

And the most important decision that we made was to do the code upgrades and all the deferred maintenance projects over the following winter, so that they would and could no longer be an issue when we were negotiating the sale. One of the few positive things that had come out of our recent experience was to learn of the loan offering that Tom had received from the same bank in Pittsfield that we dealt with from day one. He had told me the precise terms for which his loan had been approved, so one of the few things that I had done that summer was to sit down and figure out what those same terms could mean to us. Based on the two percent reduction in interest rate below what we had been paying, I discovered that we could refinance our existing loan and borrow the $100,000 needed for the upgrades. And we would still end up paying *$500 less per month* in monthly mortgage payments than we had been paying since we bought the Inn.

Just before the summer season ended, I had sent Bill Davis, our loan officer, a letter requesting him to restructure our loan in accordance with the terms that they had offered Tom, their life-long client. I'm not sure whether we had them over a barrel or whether it was a reward for our good stewardship over the previous seven years—or even a combination of both. But Bill had called me just before we took our break to say that our request was going before their loan board and he fully expected that it would be approved, as requested. And it was.

Most of the leg work with respect to the definition and cost of the upgrades had been completed, so we could get underway almost immediately. The sprinkler system, we decided, would be the top priority but we'd have to close the Inn for about a week so we'd defer all of that until the winter doldrums. But there was plenty more that could be done in the meantime. And it even looked like we'd have some money left over to do one or two of the cosmetic projects that Joan held dear.

The impact of this turn of events—mostly our decisions and the apparent ability to turn those decisions into accomplishments—had a tremendously buoyant impact on both of us. When we returned from the break, we amazed a lot of people with our positive outlook, so much so that they wanted to know where we'd been—they needed a shot of positive optimism as well. And whether or not it had done anything in the first place, we'll never know, but it was time to put the St. John's Wort away. We wouldn't be needing that any more, and of course we didn't.

Within a week after we returned, we had a visitor who very nearly put all of these plans and decisions into the trash can. A man walked into the Inn early one evening—the same chap whom we had seen walking around the grounds three or four times in the previous few days—and he made a brief preliminary announcement. He had been the original developer of the nationally renowned Canyon Ranch of the Berkshires; he had been ill for a few years but was back on his feet again, ready to go back to work; and he wanted to buy the Birchwood Inn.

He was remarkably candid and his illness, it turned out, had been a bi-polar disorder for which he had been in and out of hospitals and therapy for more than five years. He was now on medications that had finally returned him to normal, and unlike a lot of those "nuts" that you hear about (his term, not mine), he was not going to wake up some morning, decide he was cured and discontinue his therapeutic drug regimen. And as if to dispel any doubts that I might have, he had spent the previous evening with Leo Mahoney, his old friend from earlier days (and our Town Moderator) and he encouraged me to call Leo for a reference. Which, of course, I did. But Leo couldn't exactly give him a 100% clean bill of health. He could only comment on who and what he had been a decade before, but "he hadn't seemed quite the same" during their previous evening together.

The man's enthusiasm over the next many days brimmed over and his talents as a developer came fully to the fore as he began to reel off some remarkable ideas of what he was going to do to turn the Birchwood into a smaller version of Canyon Ranch. The ideas, for the most part, were sound and highly creative and he had us wishing that we had borrowed a million dollars so that we might implement the ideas ourselves. Well, we wished that, sort of, but not really.

On the third or fourth day working together, he brought with him a legally correct "Non-Disclosure Agreement" so that we might begin to share detailed financial data with one another. I also told him of the things that needed to be done to the Inn and showed him all the official estimates for the work that I had collected the previous spring. He seemed to be not the least bit fazed by this information and kept saying over and over that our property was a "steal" at a million dollars, even if there was work to be done to bring it up to the new code requirements. He thought he might have to pay maybe a half million more than that, he later confided, before I'd even start talking to him.

Meanwhile he busied himself at shopping to rent a downtown storefront property—offering more than the owner proposed charging for the rental. He intended to set up the joint offices of this new resort he was going to develop as well as the headquarters of a foundation to care for young teenagers that he was about to endow. He was a dynamic ball of fire and stayed directly focused on the issues at hand. Finally, we reached the point where he said that he was going to go to Boston for the weekend, but he would bring me a letter of offer for the Inn, with a $50,000 deposit of earnest money, when he returned on the following Monday.

Perhaps he did what he had said that he would never do—consider himself cured and go off his medication—but that was the last time I saw him, and as far as I could determine, it was the last time that he surfaced in Lenox. He was a charming man, an incessant chatterer whose mind seemed to work at twice the speed of his speech. The financial data that he showed me clearly indicated an ability to "write a check" for a million dollars, if he chose to do so. There was also no doubt that he was who he claimed to be. Yet something hadn't seemed quite right from the beginning.

Joan and I were still "once burned, twice cautious" so we hadn't even thought of counting our chickens yet. It was just another possible sale that didn't turn out, and we lost no sleep over it. We still look back with a sense of regret and a bit of pity, however, that such a brilliant, dynamic man hadn't quite managed to put it all back together again. Wherever he is today, we hope he has recovered his way once more. His energy and talents would be, to paraphrase the slogan of the Negro College Fund, "a terrible thing to waste".

For our part, we were fully recharged and ready to take on anything that might come our way. The ethos under which we had both been raised— honesty, hard work, determination and a positive outlook—had once again prevailed. Whether it was to be another six months or another three years, somehow that didn't matter any more. We would see it through to the end.

*   *   *

November 18, 1998
Dear Chris & Tom,

You'll never guess who called us this morning—and I'm sure you wouldn't because we never expected to hear from him again, either. No, it wasn't Tom Foley. It was the agent from Vermont with whom we "terminated our relationship" about eight months ago. Joan answered the phone but he didn't want to speak to her at all, not even an exchange of pleasantries—he just asked for me. Had I not been here, he would have said nothing and told her that he would call back later. He has a chauvinistic belief that women don't know anything about business and he refuses to talk to them. At least, that has been our impression based upon our dealings with him.

As Joan passed me the phone, my first thought was that he had found out about the collapse of the sale to the Foleys and was calling to gloat about it. No, on second thought I concluded, he's calling on a more positive note and he wants to get us back under contract so that he can collect the $20,000. But in seconds, it was clear that I was wrong on both counts.

His opening remarks were very cordial and he assured me that he was not calling to gloat, rehash the disagreement we had earlier in the year or anything remotely like that. He said that he was sorry that we had parted on such an unpleasant note and he even went so far as to express commiseration over the deal with the Foleys. "It's a shame; you were so close," he commented, as if he really cared. Something strange here, I thought. This is not like him at all.

With the preliminaries out of the way, he asked if we remembered a woman named Ellen Chenaux who had stayed with us in September and then again in October. The lady immediately came to my mind, partially because she was deaf and had to make reservations each time through an operator who spoke to us using special equipment which permits a deaf person to use the phone. The equipment is known as TTY and I suspect it works a lot like a computer chat room. The caller types to the operator; the operator converses with the other party; and then the operator types back to the caller.

It's a good system that works quite smoothly, and we remembered Ms. Chenaux's calls especially because she is the only person to have ever made reservations with us that way. But we also were very impressed with the woman herself. She was probably in her late 40s or early 50s, attractive, exceptionally friendly and vivacious and we liked her instantly. We were also deeply impressed with her spirit. She absolutely refused to let her hearing problems interfere with her quality of life in any way, a determination that was much aided by her uncanny ability to read lips. Yes, indeed, we remembered Ellen Chenaux.

When I confirmed our recollection of the lady, he mentioned that she had enjoyed her stay with us, both times. He confided that she had actually been there to evaluate the Inn for a possible offer to buy it. And indeed, that conjured up the memory that, like many of guests, Ellen had stayed on after she checked out on Sunday so that she could have a tour of all the rooms. "I'm working for her now," he told me, "She likes what she saw and plans to present you with a letter of offer to buy the Inn."

Well I can't remember being so thoroughly bowled over. The last thing that would have entered either of our minds when we rose this morning was that someone was going to make an offer to buy the place today. And coming from such an unexpected source, both in terms of the lady who gave not the slightest indication of her intentions when she stayed with us—and also, coming from the person who had so recently been our nemesis. I wanted to shout something out to Joan but forced myself to be composed. I just gestured for Joan to pay attention to my end of the conversation.

He went on to say that he thought that there would be little problem in completing the transaction. He knew the value of the Inn and I knew that he knew. He was fully aware of the soundness of the business because we had been sending him our monthly sales and expense records for nearly two years. He also knew, he went on, that Ms. Chenaux was completely able to meet the price we were asking because he had personally vetted her net worth. "The only question that needs to be resolved," he concluded, "is the cost of whatever needs to be done to comply with the revised fire and safety code, and how much needs to be deducted from your asking price to take care of that."

He concluded the call by saying that Ms. Chenaux was there in Vermont with him and he would call back the following day with the verbal offer, minus the totals for the upgrades, which I had given him. That's a figure that I was able to give him off the top of my head since I had been dealing with it every day for the previous two months. And as quickly as that, the conversation was over.

I'm tempted to nail my shoes to the floor so I don't float away. And after all of my resolve about playing it cool, not getting too enthused or counting our chickens. But this time, it's not a case of someone walking in off the street to announce his or her intentions. This was an agent calling to announce a firm letter of offer. Could it be as easy as all that? You'll be the first to know. But keep your fingers crossed just in case!

Warmest regards,
Dick

We had actually just begun the active process of marketing the Inn again when the offer from Ellen Chenaux was received. Part of our new approach to selling the Inn was to rely on the same medium that had been serving us so handsomely over the previous two and a half years—the Internet. We were fairly sure that more and more people were looking to the Internet for many things. Why not to buy and inn? And since we had removed the self-imposed pressure of getting out before the eight year point arrived, we decided to use the Internet exclusively for advertising the sale. If that didn't pan out, we could always go in some other direction later on.

The results in just six weeks were astounding. We had inquiries from as far away as Tokyo and Pretoria, South Africa. The first was from a Finnish couple who had been working in Japan but planned to emigrate to the States; and the second from a Boer couple who had run a hotel near Pretoria but were fed up with the social changes in their country and were coming to America. Whether or not they thought that they would find ours a country where apartheid was still in effect, they didn't say.

There were inquiries from all over the States as well, nearly four times the number that had been generated by over a year's worth of print advertising. People came from near and far to look at the place as well, and at the time that we received the offer from Ellen, we suspected that, in time, a few of those inquiries might become more promising. But that was a moot point after the letter offer reached us.

Our best intentions to complete the upgrades to the property also went the way of those best intentions that pave the road to Hell—but not for a lack of trying. We did manage to get the roof redone and four of the five chimneys had been rebuilt before the snows began to fly, but not much else had been done. There was an on-going building boom in the Berkshires and construction companies weren't very interested in penny ante projects.

For example, we needed to run a new four inch water line from the street to the mansion—a distance of about 100 feet—before the sprinkler system could be installed. But few companies would even return my calls requesting an estimate for the job, and the one company who did provide an estimate was "too busy" with higher priority projects to get to it before the frost set in. And like a chain of dominos, the hard-wired fire and smoke alarm system could not be installed before the sprinkler system was completed. So we satisfied ourselves with giving the architect the go-ahead on the design of the exterior fire escape stairway. We'd just have to get our reservations in earlier—next spring.

But now, both the Internet advertising and the upgrade projects had been overtaken by events. Just as promised, Ellen faxed us a letter of offer a day later and we accepted by return fax. It was that quick and that easy. As expected, there were a few stipulations in the offer. The offer was, of course, contingent upon her ability to get financing for the property, a foregone conclusion before she even went to the bank. She wanted the closing to be on the 16th of February. She also wanted an appraiser to look at the property some time up to 30 days prior to the closing, and any major deficiencies could be a cause for renegotiations or cancellation of the agreement. And we would need to agree to provide her (and her yet-to-be-identified assistant) with two weeks of live-in, hands-on training before or after closure.

Joan and I just looked at one another when we saw that last condition. Could this be another situation in which too much of a good thing might serve to our detriment? Probably not, we concluded. Ellen had obviously been looking for "her inn" for quite some time. She had assiduously done her homework. She was doggedly committed to going through with this purchase. And even if she were to make a last minute decision to back out, this time there was a healthy deposit in escrow that she would forfeit if she changed her mind.

Ellen's dogged commitment was clearly apparent the more we got to know her. Some of her life-long friends thought she was crazy to attempt to operate an inn by herself—even if it weren't for the hearing disability. And most of her family, including her former husband who still served as her financial advisor, did their level best to dissuade her from going into such a stressful undertaking—without even considering the one strike against before she got up to bat. But as she told us later, her children "knew better than to argue with Mom" after she had made up her mind. And her mind was clearly made up.

In all candor, we had our reservations as well. In fact, Joan asked me one evening, shortly after we had accepted her offer, if we were doing the correct thing—or were we taking advantage of her. But it took only a short period of time in her company to conclude that no one took advantage of Ellen.

She was a wonderful blend of savvy toughness, bounden determination, disarming charm and unbridled optimism. Ellen never saw the glass half full or half empty. To her, it was always "almost full".

As we expected, there were little glitches that arose as the P&SA was being finalized, but there were no surprises and no problems that couldn't be quickly resolved. Joan became nervous and agitated when the appraiser she had hired spent the better part of the day going over every inch of the property with a fine tooth comb. Joan was particularly frightened when she asked the inspector if he had identified anything wrong and he responded that his report was "a privileged document" and he was not at liberty to divulge its contents to anyone but the person who had commissioned it. Well, la-de-dah.

But in truth, he was exactly correct. So Joan continued to hold her breath, figuratively at least, until Ellen's agent called back two days later to say that "except for a few things that you expect to find in a house that old", the buildings were in excellent shape. I would have been surprised if the determination had been any different than that, but Joan still harbored an intuitive suspicion that the inspection was the straw that broke the back of the deal the last time around.

As expected, financing was not a moment's problem. Ellen also managed to get the same terms from the Berkshire Bank that Tom Foley had been offered and we had later seized upon as "our due". But this time, it was a real competition. Ellen went to all of the major banks in the Berkshires and played one off against the other—best bank wins was the name of her game. And if I recall correctly, she brought one or two out-of-town banks into the mix as well. But still the Berkshire Bank won out. Bill Davis remains the loan officer for the Birchwood Inn—and likely will be for the balance of his career.

So now the only thing left was to repack our personal belongings and officially close on the sale—but only after the training phase was completed. It was another reason for Joan to hold her breath, but by late January we had become confident that there would be nothing to disrupt the orderly transfer of the property.

Ellen's agent had found an assistant innkeeper for her, a woman from Florida who had allegedly been operating her own catering business there for the previous three years. Her duties were to be fairly broad but Ellen would depend on her principally for cooking and answering the reservation phone line. In the latter capacity, she gave all indications of being very gracious and dependable, but she clearly was no cook. The elementary questions that she asked, and her ineptitude at the range, led me to believe that if she had been a caterer, either someone else was doing the cooking or she was the exclusive south Florida agent for Healthy Choice Frozen Dinners. She also proved quickly to be flighty and a whiner. By the fourth day, I drew Ellen aside and told her that this woman would never do. And after close observation and a number of counseling sessions, Ellen let her go about ten days later.

There would be no huge lawn party or massive reception to introduce Ellen to the community this time. But she took her opportunities during those last two weeks to go out on her own and shake hands with all the people she would want or need to know—including the building inspector. She has such a gregarious personality that she quickly accumulated a whole host of new friends in her first days in town—some that we didn't know well ourselves. Her family and friends could rest easily. Ellen Chenaux was not going to have a bit of trouble in her new role.

The night before the closing—the 15th of February 1999—Joan and I hosted our final dinner party in Lenox. We invited all the same friends who had feted us with a farewell party eight months before, plus a few more, and the guest of honor was the soon-to-be owner of the Birchwood Inn. It was such a good time that we almost wanted to stay around for more. And Ellen seemed to enjoy every minute of it, as well. There was too much good food, far too much wine, and while there can never be too much laughter, there was constant laughter late into the evening.

But as the evening wore down, the songs had all been sung, and the stories told, the laughter turned to tears. They were tears of joy, for the most part, but there was also the realization that twenty or so good friends, with whom we had been through good times and bad, were bidding us a final goodbye. The hugs were firm and drawn out, but at last we were alone. Ellen welled up with tears herself and hugging us both, she offered, "I can't thank you enough for the kindness you've shown me and the help you've given me. I know you have looked forward to tomorrow for some time, but I have to say I wish you weren't leaving. Those people will miss you. Lenox will miss you and, though it's only been a brief friendship, I think I'm going to miss you most of all."

And at 11:34 AM the next day, Joan and I became former innkeepers.

*   *   *

Epilogue

The remainder of Friday, the 16th of February, was spent packing another 15' rental truck that was to be our means of travel to Colorado—my third and last crossing by truck, we hoped. Joan had driven me directly to the rental agency after the "closing ceremony" to pick up the truck, and Dan had taken a day off to help me pack, along with our nephew, Brian Vossmer, who had driven up from Boston.

The day was reasonably pleasant, not one of those bitter cold, gray days that are so common in New England in February, and as darkness closed in, the truck was packed and the load tied down. We knew, with the rush of events that blurred the past few days, that we were bound to forget something, but the feelings of elation ran so high that an omission or two didn't seem to matter all that much. And we could have the leftovers sent to storage with our movers, to be added to the shipment that would follow us a few months later.

We left the truck in the Birchwood parking lot over night. Joy and Scotty Farrelly had insisted that we spend our final evening with them at their Cliffwood Inn where they hosted a small dinner that evening for us and Anne and Dan. But first, we still had another farewell reception to go to, hosted by Rebecca Hedgecock at her Candlelight Inn. The *pièce de résistance* was a bottle of '86 Dom Perignon champagne, a wedding gift that Anne and Dan had been saving for the occasion of the sale of the Inn.

We were up before dawn the following day, and after a brief but tearful farewell to the Farrellys, our closest friends in Lenox, we returned to the rental agency for only as long as it took to attach a car trailer and secure the Maxima on it. By 9:00 AM we were on the road. When we reached the New York state border 20 minutes later, we both let out an unrehearsed, spontaneous cheer—not so much in celebration of leaving Massachusetts as it was for starting the journey that would begin the rest of our lives. We had often joked with family and friends that we were headed for our "final resting place" in Colorado, and whether or not it was a euphemism or a reality, at last that journey was underway.

The trip west was routine, for the most part. We hoped that we wouldn't have to contend with snow storms—a highly likely possibility at that time of year. We awoke the second day in Buffalo and the third in Iowa City to about four inches of the white stuff, though neither overnight storm slowed our progress. A broken drive shaft on the truck the third day did, however, and it was to cost us that whole travel day while we waited for repairs. Fortunately, we were only 20 miles south of Des Moines when it happened, and with the kind assistance of an Iowa highway patrolman, we were towed back to Des Moines where Hertz-Penske had a regional repair facility.

We stopped for the night in western Kansas on the fourth day, three hours short of our final destination. But we were tired, having already driven for ten hours, so the stop was wise and timely. Mid-morning on the final day of the trip, from 50 miles east, we saw the sun shining brilliantly on the snow-capped summit of Pikes Peak, towering majestically above Colorado Springs—the first glimpse of our new home. Now a year later, we still feel that same rush of emotion each morning when we look from our front door and behold that glorious crest on which Katherine Lee Bates had been inspired to pen "America the Beautiful" over a century before.

And it's a sight that we now share with Anne and Dan. After driving out to help us get settled—and to return our Big Kitty after four months with them in Lenox—they were completely taken by the beauty of the area and decided to give up their jobs in the Berkshires and join the westward migration. They have lived in the Springs since last November and both are well-settled in new careers. When the four of us get together from time to time, we inevitably think of our previous eight-year adventure as innkeepers. Not surprisingly, the bad times are rapidly fading in our memories, and we talk only of those reminiscences that bring back the humor, the elation, the touching experiences and all the other good times.

We still maintain contact with Ellen Chenaux, unlike the complete severance of contact that was the choice of the people from whom we bought the Inn. At first, Ellen's emails were mostly questions: how do you turn on the outside water taps? or, could we tell her again how to bleed the air out of the radiators on the third floor? She also had a bit of a snit with the Historic District Commission over the fact that we had engraved "1787" on the street sign that identified the Inn. But fortunately she proved to them—using the papers I had left her—that the core of the building had, in fact, been built that year.

Later, however, the emails have basically been newsy items. Ellen has very faithfully kept us informed of the changes she has made to put her personal signature on the Inn, as well as her plans for the future. She always considerately adds in the reports some comment like, "I know you loved that wallpaper in the dining room, Joan, but it just wasn't me. I hope you don't mind." Chances are very good that we will always have a remote tie to the Inn, as long as Ellen is the proprietor, and we appreciate the tender love and care that she is lavishing on the "baby that we gave up for adoption".

We have often been asked, since our retirement, if we have any regrets and, given the chance, we would do it all over again. Our immediate response is an unqualified, yes, to doing all over again, at least. Despite the hard times and the occasional tears, it was the adventure of a lifetime—an opportunity that few ever have the chance to experience. With regard to the regrets, there are, indeed, a few—and with 20/20 hindsight, all are related to what we could or should have done. The only one of these worth mentioning is the sorrow that we had gone into the business, and remained all the time we were the owners, seriously under-funded for the things we wanted to do and the quality with which we wanted to do them.

Our principal regret, if that's the proper term, lies in the lost joy of a family that the Inn brought together. They are regrets that we will not be there at hand as all our grandchildren, grandnephews and nieces continue their inexorable march from adolescence to adulthood. Regrets that we are all growing older and beginning to lose the vibrancy of middle age and the energy and spontaneity that was so infectious in those days. And regrets that we—none of us—will ever again have the splendid opportunity of meeting together under one roof—or as Paula Waterman had described it, "….bumping into someone you've never seen before in your life, yet all the while knowing that person is, at the very least, a first cousin."

The predominant remembrances that we all have—not just Anne and Dan or Joan and me, but all of our wonderful brothers and sisters, nephews and nieces, and others who we left behind in New England—are best summed up in a letter sent to us during our final week at the Inn by our nephew, Gerry Sullivan—the wonderful guy who has been affectionately known as St. Gerard since that first Thanksgiving.

During our final week at the Inn, while all the elders—the brothers, sisters and spouses who were the best supporters we could possibly have hoped for—were there at the Inn for the final time, St. Gerard sent the following email to us. His message was read at dinner that evening, with nary a dry eye in the room, and I can think of no more appropriate way of bring these reflections to a close than to quote it in its entirety.

"Dear Family and Friends,

"This is the last letter I expect to send to the Birchwood Inn because, though the Inn will be there, it is my understanding that the people who gave the Inn life and love will be at a different address. May God, the Angels and the Saints be with you in your new home.

"The Birchwood Inn—once an 'Old Soldiers' Home'—will now be The Toner Family's Old Memory Home. And what great memories there are associated with the Inn on the Hill. The Thanksgiving letter from Paula and Dick Waterman, apologizing for not being there. It seems that a little bundle they named Katherine needed to be picked up in China.

"And how about the second of Anne and Danny's three weddings. Now that was a time if ever there was one. My Catherine on crutches but still dancing. Richard (Waterman) and I being asked to assist with the music (for the vows renewal ceremony). A dangerous proposal, but we resisted. The morning clean-up reminded me of my old college days. But what I remember most incisively on that wonderful occasion were the words (at the ceremony) of the General when he said he appreciated and respected the teacher who instilled a love for classic literature in his soul—and then read a favorite Dostoyevsky passage on marriage that was perfect for the occasion.

"Then there was the first work weekend—supposed to be spring—but it snowed. Seemed that happened a lot. Any way, we didn't go up to Lenox Friday night as planned. Saturday the phone rings—Where are you? It's snowing; we can't do any painting outside. Oh, we have inside work. So off to Lenox, Theresa, Elizabeth and I—in my old truck. We arrive shortly after noon time. NO DRINKING UNTIL FOUR. Per order of the General. And do you believe it, those guys and gals were working away like crazy—obeying the rules. Charlie and Flash were painting the windows in the dining room. I offered to take over but they insisted on doing it themselves. Little did they know nor care that I'm still one of the fastest sash cutters in New England. So I get relegated to woodwork, from the top floor on down. And since a good painter always has a little 'paint thinner' with him—my cooler of 'thinner' was opened immediately. I work on Atlantic Provincial Time.

"That was the same weekend that Elaine asked (after we arrived home) if I was at the same Inn as the kids. Seems they had more interesting tales to tell on homecoming than I did. So much for telling kids to keep their eyes open and their mouths shut.

"And who can forget the yard clean-ups. At first it was a rake and bag operation. But then, thanks to 'Prometheus Navillus' and a book of matches, it became a rake and burn operation. Much more efficient. We'll miss those cold and damp nights around the fire barrel arguing over whose turn it was to make the next beer run. If we had a recording secretary, we could have remembered all the solutions to the world's problems.

"The Peasant Feast—and what a feast it was. I think more conversations, getting to know others and, more importantly, getting to understand others took place that night, more than any other. I hope you don't mind, but Elaine and I plan to use that same dinner format for my Mother's 84th birthday. That way we can have all her children and grandchildren around her at the same time. Thank you for teaching us. We all wish to thank the Lenox Toners for all they have done to enrich our lives.

"The Inn on the Hill will remain in the hearts and minds of many, many people. More importantly, the people who ran the Birchwood Inn will remain in the hearts and minds of many, many people. Years from now, my children will tell their children, and perhaps their grandchildren, about the Birchwood Inn—a magical, mystical place where the whole family gathered, ate and drank, sang songs, burned leaves and danced. There will be stories of this person or that person. There will be stories of this or that happening. But always, there will remain a tremendous sense of family and the great times we had getting to know, understand and love each other.

"May the road rise up to meet you, May the wind be always at your back, And may Almighty God hold you in the Palm of his hand an hour before the devil knows you're dead.

"God bless the Toners of Lenox, Gerard"

There could be no greater tribute or a better way for us to bid our farewell to the "magical, mystical" Birchwood Inn than with St. Gerard's final observations. RJT